CHARTERED INSTITUTE FOR
SECURITIES & INVESTMENT

GW00492906

Securities & Investment
(Schools and Colleges)

• • • • • • • • • • • •

The Official Learning and Reference Manual

2nd Edition, April 2012

This edition will cover examinations from 21 July 2012 to 20 July 2013

PROFESSIONALISM | INTEGRITY | EXCELLENCE

SECURITIES & INVESTMENT (SCHOOLS AND COLLEGES)

Welcome to the Chartered Institute for Securities & Investment's Securities & Investment (Schools and Colleges) study material.

This workbook has been written to prepare you for the Chartered Institute for Securities & Investment's Introduction to Securities & Investment examination.

PUBLISHED BY:
Chartered Institute for Securities & Investment
© Chartered Institute for Securities & Investment 2012
8 Eastcheap
London
EC3M 1AE
Tel: +44 20 7645 0600
Fax: +44 20 7645 0601

Written by Kevin Rothwell and Martin Mitchell
With grateful thanks to IMA

This is an educational manual only and the Chartered Institute for Securities & Investment accepts no responsibility for persons undertaking trading or investments in whatever form.

While every effort has been made to ensure its accuracy, no responsibility for loss occasioned to any person acting or refraining from action as a result of any material in this publication can be accepted by the publisher or authors.

A Learning Map, which contains the full syllabus, appears at the end of this workbook. The syllabus can also be viewed on the Institute's website at cisi.org and is also available by contacting Client Services on +44 20 7645 0680. Please note that the exam is based on the syllabus. Candidates are reminded to check the Candidate Updates area of the Institute's website (cisi.org/updates) on a regular basis for updates that could affect their exam as a result of industry change.

The questions contained in this workbook are designed as an aid to revision of different areas of the syllabus and to help you consolidate your learning chapter by chapter. They should not be seen as a 'mock' exam or necessarily indicative of the level of the questions in the corresponding exam.

Studybook version: 2.1 (April 2012)

FOREWORD

Learning with the CISI

You are now studying for an exam that has already been taken by more than 1,000 students around the world. This workbook and the elearning product is designed to provide you with a basic introduction to the financial services industry, with a focus on investments.

You may not have heard of the CISI, but we have around 40,000 members who are already in work. We hope that this exam will help you to build awareness of career opportunities and personal financial knowledge. If you are wishing to go onto University, then this exam in addition to the extended project attracts up to 60 UCAS points and leads to the full Certificate for Introduction to Securities & Investment.

We work with schools across the UK to make the qualification available to sixth form students. When you register for the exam, you will be able to access a wide range of resources on our website (cisi.org) which will not only help with your studies, but help to broaden awareness of all aspects of the investment banking world.

This workbook and elearning product are updated annually, so please check to ensure you have the correct version for your exam. As well as using industry specialists to update and review the material, we also use students and teachers to ensure that the material is relevant to your needs and level of experience.

For teachers we also offer a host of support for this module, including Train-the-Trainer sessions and accompanying tutor slides, and for the Extended Project, a Teacher-Assessor Guide as well as exemplar projects which are available to download from the CISI website at cisi.org/resources.

We really hope that you enjoy your studies with the CISI and that you find the learning experience a stimulating one.

With best wishes for your studies.

Ruth Martin
Managing Director

CONTENTS

It is estimated that this workbook will require approximately 70 hours of study time.

Putting Financial Services Into Perspective

Putting Financial Services Into Perspective

1. Introduction

The significance of the financial services industry has been made abundantly clear in the past few years – the so-called credit crunch of 2008 was blamed on dubious practices at financial institutions and resulted in governments worldwide 'bailing out' many banks (such as Citigroup in the US and RBS in the UK) as they were 'too big to be allowed to fail'. At the time of writing, the activities of bankers and speculators in the financial services industry are being blamed for all manner of issues, from the high price of oil and gold, to the need for countries to seek assistance to enable them to raise finance at a reasonable price, such as Ireland, Greece and Portugal.

This workbook provides a vital introduction to the world of finance, starting with an outline of just how important it is in a developed economy like the UK.

As with other developed countries, the financial services industry in the UK is a major contributor to the economy. Indeed, financial services firms provide employment opportunities in all of the major cities, especially London.

Traditionally, financial services in London was centred on the City of London, although the reinvigoration of east London's docklands around Canary Wharf is equally important as the hub of the UK's financial services activity today. The firms located in and around the City of London and docklands not only provide considerable employment, but they are also vital in that they generate considerable overseas earnings for the UK economy.

2. The Importance of Financial Services to the UK Economy

As will be developed later in this workbook, economic activity is often measured by gross domestic product (GDP). Over recent years, the UK's economy has seen a significant shift from traditional manufacturing towards services, especially financial services.

Furthermore, the vital importance of financial services to the UK can be underlined by looking at how the financial services share of GDP in the UK has grown, whilst its share of GDP in other developed countries has begun to slowdown.

In terms of employment, over 1 million people work across the UK in financial services – this is nearly 4% of total UK employment. The majority of financial services employment is in banking (around 450,000), insurance (around 325,000) and fund management (around 50,000).

The export of financial services from the UK to other parts of the world has grown strongly in the recent past, making the UK the world's leading exporter of financial services, earning more ten times US exports of financial services in 2008.

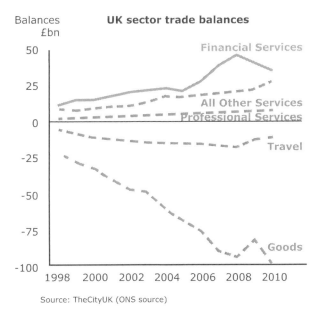

% Shares of GDP

Financial services' share of GDP in major economies

Source: Office for National Statistics (ONS)

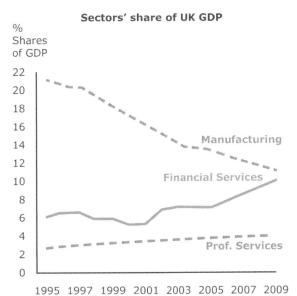

Sectors' share of UK GDP

% Shares of GDP

Source: TheCityUK (ONS National Accounts Blue Book source)

Balances £bn

UK sector trade balances

Source: TheCityUK (ONS source)

The graph above ('UK sector trade balances') further reinforces how the UK has become more services orientated, showing how various sectors of activity performed from 1998 to 2010, with the financial services sector leading the way.

Clearly, all of the activity in financial services in the UK significantly contributes to the UK government's taxes receipts. The total tax taken of UK financial services is estimated to have fallen 13% in 2009/10. However, the total tax take still represents 11% of total UK government receipts (source: TheCityUK).

CISI
CHARTERED INSTITUTE FOR
SECURITIES & INVESTMENT

**Tax contribution of UK
financial services 2010/11**

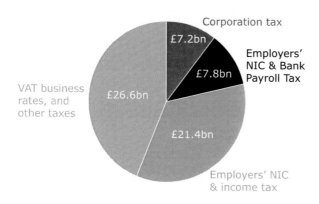

Corporation tax
£7.2bn

Employers'
NIC & Bank
Payroll Tax
£7.8bn

VAT business
rates, and
other taxes
£26.6bn

£21.4bn

Employers' NIC
& income tax

3. Careers in Financial Services

Across the UK as a whole, business services including acting as an intermediary in financial transactions represents almost a third of employment possibilities.

This focus on services is even more pronounced in London and the South East as can be seen from the illustration below.

Of these services roles in London and the South East, 6% are 'City type' financial services roles.

A career in financial services is particularly attractive because financial services salaries are substantially higher than those elsewhere in the economy.

UK financial and associated professional services employment

Totalling: 1,920,658 (September 2010)
FS workforce (% of regional total)

■ FS >7% of regional economy
■ FS 5-7% of regional economy
■ FS <5% of regional economy

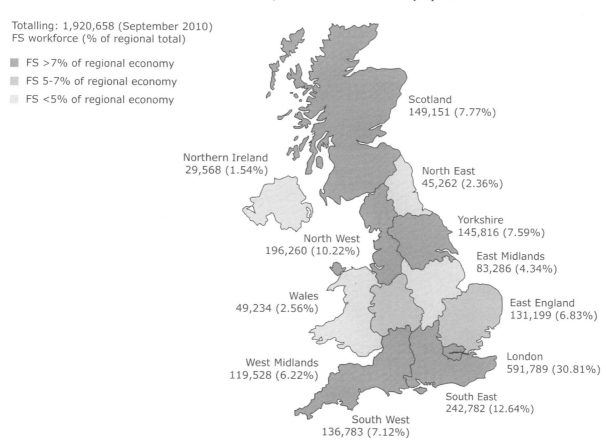

Scotland
149,151 (7.77%)

Northern Ireland
29,568 (1.54%)

North East
45,262 (2.36%)

Yorkshire
145,816 (7.59%)

North West
196,260 (10.22%)

East Midlands
83,286 (4.34%)

Wales
49,234 (2.56%)

East England
131,199 (6.83%)

West Midlands
119,528 (6.22%)

London
591,789 (30.81%)

South East
242,782 (12.64%)

South West
136,783 (7.12%)

Source: TheCityUK Research Centre estimates for 2010 produced by CEBR from Office of National Statistics (ONS) data

The following statistics provide some interesting insights:

- Starting salaries for graduates in investment banks are £32,000 to £40,000 per annum.
- The overall average graduate starting salary in 2008 was £24,000.
- The starting salary of a qualified teacher is £25,000 per annum.
- The average salary across all UK employees in 2008 was only £26,000.

4. Professional and Retail Business

The financial services industry can be divided into two distinct areas:

- The **professional sector** – also known as the wholesale or institutional sector. This involves transactions where both sides are businesses, and are commonly described as **business to business**.
- The **retail sector** – in the retail sector one side of the transaction is an individual 'retail customer' and the transactions are described as **business to customer**.

Certain contrasting assumptions are made about professional and retail business.

In the professional sector it is assumed that the participants know what it is they are getting involved in, so there is little need to explain the trades and the professional clients do not need to be protected from their own ignorance about finance and financial services.

Professional trades also tend to be bigger than those in the retail sector, with the result that prices will be 'wholesale' and cheaper.

In contrast, in the retail sector the customers do not always know what they are getting involved in. So they need to be given as much information as possible and are only allowed to be sold investments which are suitable for their needs. Furthermore, the retail customers are often given the opportunity to pull out of financial transactions for either a particular period after the sale (known as a 'cooling-off' period) or if the products were mis-sold to them, including the provision of insufficient information.

Retail customers also tend to deal in smaller sized transactions than the professionals, so the prices tend to be higher.

4.1 Retail and Professional Business in the Foreign Exchange Market

As detailed above, prices tend to be higher for retail customers when compared to wholesale or professional customers. This can be illustrated by looking at the purchase or sale of one currency for another (the so-called **foreign exchange market**).

Professional sector (B2B)	Retail sector (B2C)
Assumed to know what they are doing.	Assumed to not always know what they are doing – given a 'cooling off' period.
Transactions tend to be larger.	Transactions tend to be smaller.
Cheaper 'wholesale' prices.	More expensive 'retail' prices.

⚙ Exercise 1

A retail customer who is planning a day trip to France has £100 and wants to convert the money into euros. He visits his local bank and sees that the bank is quoting the following:

	Bank buys	**Bank sells**
GBP/EUR	1.32	1.15

Different currencies are described using three letters with GBP being pounds sterling (the Great British pound or £), and EUR being the euro (€). How many euros will the retail customer get for his £100?

Please try to answer the exercise and then check your response against the answer that can be found at the end of the chapter.

Now, in contrast to the foreign exchange quotes provided to retail customers in the 'high street', the foreign currency quotes provided to professional clients will be different. This is illustrated in exercise two.

⚙ Exercise 2

The following are the contrasting quotes from a bank for retail customers and professional clients:

GBP/EUR	Bank buys	Bank sells
Retail customers	1.32	1.15
Professional clients	1.2303	1.2301

1. You have £30,000 which you want to convert into euros. How many euros will you get if you are:

   a) a retail customer
   b) a professional client?

2. You have €75,000 which you want to convert into pounds sterling. How many pounds will you get if you are:

   a) a retail customer
   b) a professional client?

3. In percentage terms, how much less favourable are the buy and sell quotes for the retail customer compared to the professional client?

Please try to answer the exercise and then check your responses against the answer that can be found at the end of the chapter.

As exercise 2 shows, the retail customer pays more to buy another currency than a professional client, and the retail customer gets less than a professional client when he sells one currency for another. As will be developed shortly, the reason is essentially that the professional client will be dealing in larger quantities.

This difference between the prices clients pay to buy a currency and the amount they get from the sale of that same currency can be a major source of profit to the money changing bank. This is best illustrated by developing the earlier example of a retail customer changing money in anticipation of a trip abroad.

⚙ Exercise 3

A retail customer was planning a day trip to France and converted £100 into euros. Unfortunately, due to a family bereavement, he has been forced to stay in the UK. The following exchange rates apply:

	Bank buys	**Bank sells**
GBP/EUR	1.32	1.15

a) How much in pounds sterling will he receive when he sells his euros back to the bank?

b) How much has the bank made on the transaction?

Please try to answer the exercise and then check your response against the answer that can be found at the end of the chapter.

Where professional clients are involved, the percentage profit margin generated by the bank will inevitably be smaller than that generated from retail customers. However, the sums involved tend to be much more substantial.

⚙ Exercise 4

The following are the contrasting quotes from a bank for retail customers and professional clients:

GBP/EUR	Bank buys	Bank sells
Retail customers	1.32	1.15
Professional clients	1.2303	1.2301

A professional client converts £30,000 into euros. The client then reverses the same transaction, exchanging the euros received back into pounds sterling.

a) *How much in pounds sterling will the professional client receive when he sells his euros back to the bank?*
b) *How much has the bank made on the transaction?*

Please try to answer the exercise and then check your responses against the answer that can be found at the end of the chapter.

Professional clients typically have to enter into transactions that meet or exceed a certain minimum quantity. For example, the minimum 'lot' size for a professional (wholesale) currency transaction might be 100,000 units of currency. So despite the bank's profit margin being a modest 0.016%, the minimum gross profit the bank will generate would be: £100,000 X 0.016% = £16 profit.

Furthermore, the typical transaction size will tend to be a lot bigger than the minimum. Indeed, most professional foreign exchange transactions are in lots of 8 to 10 million units of currency. For a £10 million deal the bank's gross profit would be £10m x 0.016 = £1,600.

⚙ Answers to Chapter Exercises

⚙ Exercise 1

A retail customer who is planning a day trip to France has £100 and wants to convert the money into euros. He visits his local bank and sees that the bank is quoting the following:

	Bank buys	**Bank sells**
GBP/EUR	1.32	1.15

How many euros will the retail customer get for his £100?

The bank's quotes are how many euros it requires to give the retail customer £1 (the 'bank buys' quote), and how many euros it will give the customer in exchange for £1 (the 'bank sells' quote). Since this customer wants euros in exchange for £s, the 'bank sells' quote must be used and the retail customer will get £100 x 1.15 = €115.

⚙ Exercise 2

The following are the contrasting quotes from a bank for retail customers and professional clients:

GBP/EUR	**Bank buys**	**Bank sells**
Retail customers	1.32	1.15
Professional clients	1.2303	1.2301

1. *You have £30,000 and you want to convert them into euros. How many euros will you get if you are:*

   a) a retail customer

   b) a professional client?

   You are buying euros and selling pounds, so the bank is selling euros to you and you must use the sell quote.

   a) Retail customer: £30,000 x 1.15 = €34,500

   b) Professional client: £30,000 x 1.2301 = €36,903

2. You have €75,000 which you want to convert into pounds sterling. How many pounds will you get if you are:

    a) a retail customer

    b) a professional client?

    You are selling euros in order to obtain pounds. The bank is buying euros from you, so you must use the buy quote:

    a) Retail customer: €75,000 ÷ 1.32 = £56,818.18

    b) Professional client: €75,000 ÷ 1.2303 = £60,960.74

3. In percentage terms, how much less favourable are the buy and sell quotes for the retail customer compared to the professional client?

    For the buy quotes: 1.32 − 1.2303 = 0.0897

    (0.0897 ÷ 1.2303) x 100 = 7.29% less favourable

    For the sell quotes: 1.2301 − 1.15 = 0.0801

    (0.0801 ÷ 1.2301) x 100 = 6.51% less favourable

⚙️ Exercise 3

A retail customer was planning a day trip to France and converted £100 into euros. Unfortunately, due to a family bereavement, he has been forced to stay in the UK. The following exchange rates apply:

	Bank buys	**Bank sells**
GBP/EUR	1.32	1.15

a) How much in pounds sterling will he receive when he sells his euros back to the bank?

    Remember that the retail customer got £100 x 1.15 = €115 (in exercise 1). When he sells these euros back to the bank he needs to use the bank's buying rate of €1.32 for £1, so he will get €115 ÷ 1.32 = £87.12.

b) How much has the bank made on the transaction?

    The bank received £100 for the €115, and then purchased the same €115 for just £87.12. So the bank has made £100−£87.12 = £12.88. Clearly this is before considering any other costs that the bank has incurred, such as staff salaries and the like, but this is a generous margin of 12.88% (based on £12.88 ÷ £100 expressed as a percentage).

⚙ Exercise 4

The following are the contrasting quotes from a bank for retail customers and professional clients:

GBP/EUR	Bank buys	Bank sells
Retail customers	1.32	1.15
Professional clients	1.2303	1.2301

A professional client converts £30,000 into euros. The client then reverses the same transaction, exchanges the euros received back into pounds sterling.

a) *How much in pounds sterling will the professional client receive when he sells his euros back to the bank?*

Remember that the professional client got £30,000 x 1.2301 = €36,903 (from exercise 2). When the same client sells €36,903 to the bank in exchange for pounds sterling, the client will receive €36,903 ÷ 1.2303 = £29,995.12

b) *How much has the bank made on the transaction?*

The bank has made £4.88 on the transaction (£30,000–£29,995.12), which is only a 0.016% margin (£4.88 ÷ 30,000 expressed as a percentage).

Learning Objectives

Chapter One has covered the following Learning Objectives:

1.0   Introduction

     Lesson 01

Based on what you have learned in Chapter One, try to answer the following end of chapter questions.

📝 End of Chapter Questions

1. In the last 20 to 25 years, how has the share of the UK's gross domestic product developed between the proportion generated by the manufacturing sector and the proportion generated by the services sector?

    Answer Reference: Section 2

    ....

    ....

2. Approximately what proportion of UK jobs is in the financial services sector?

    Answer Reference: Section 3

    ....

    ....

3. How do starting salaries for graduates in investment banks compare to other available options?

    Answer Reference: Section 3

    ....

    ....

4. What is the difference between the professional and retail sectors?

    Answer Reference: Section 4

    ....

    ....

5. What is a 'cooling off' period, and what type of client is a cooling off period most likely to be given to?

    Answer Reference: Section 4

    ....

    ....

6. In the foreign exchange market, how do quotes for retail customers differ from those for professional clients?

    Answer Reference: Section 4.1

    ....

    ....

7. What is the typical size of a professional client transaction in the foreign exchange market?

    Answer Reference: Section 4.1

    ....

    ....

The Financial Services Industry

The Financial Services Industry

1. Introduction

Mention the financial services industry and the first type of business that springs to mind is a bank. This chapter begins by exploring the traditional purpose of banks – gathering money by taking deposits from some of their customers and lending money by granting loans to other customers. It then goes on to explore how some banks specialise in particular activities and highlights whether these activities are typically provided to professional or retail clients. Finally the chapter briefly covers the ways that people can invest surplus money, in particular highlighting the so-called 'distribution channels' that are used to enable potential clients to invest.

2. Cash and Where to Keep It

Cash has to be the most basic form of financial asset, it can be spent easily, but it is also a security risk. Because cash can be spent by whoever may have it, it is important that it is kept somewhere safe and secure, and not simply stuffed under the mattress.

The more appropriate and safer place to keep cash is with some form of '**savings institution**'. In the UK that usually means a bank or a building society. Certain banks are well known because they have branches on the 'high street' and their customers are individuals or, in bank jargon, 'retail clients'. These banks provide services such as enabling their clients to deposit money into bank accounts and perhaps allowing clients to borrow money in the form of loans. Holding money in a bank account allows the client to make payments by writing cheques or transferring money to others by setting up standing orders, perhaps to the providers of electricity or to the television licensing authority. These types of services are known as 'money transmission services'.

In the UK, these high street banks include the likes of HSBC, NatWest and Lloyds TSB. Banks like these attract cash deposits from a wide variety of clients including retail customers, companies, local and national governments and other financial institutions. They are often huge organisations that have grown in size by linking up with other banks as well as with non-bank institutions such as insurance companies. In addition to providing traditional banking services through branches over the internet and by telephone, these larger retail banks also offer products such as investments, pensions and insurance.

Banks differ from building societies in that banks are themselves companies, and just like any other company they are ultimately owned and controlled by shareholders. In contrast, a building society tends to attract just retail clients and is mutually owned by those clients. In other words, building societies do not have a separate group of shareholders and are instead owned by all of their depositors and borrowers. At the time of writing, the biggest and most well known building society in the UK is the Nationwide Building Society, or simply 'the Nationwide'.

Building societies were established in the 19th century when small numbers of people would group together and pool their savings, allowing some members to build or buy houses. As seen, building societies are jointly owned by the individuals that have deposited money with or borrowed money from them – the 'members'. It is for this reason that such savings organisations are often described as mutual societies.

Over the years, many smaller building societies have merged or been taken over by banks. Furthermore, in the late 1980s, legislation was introduced allowing building societies to become companies – a process known as **demutualisation**. However, some large building societies remain as mutuals, continuing to specialise in services for retail customers, especially the provision of deposit accounts and mortgages. Most countries have mutual savings institutions similar to the UK's building societies that started off by specialising in offering savings products to retail customers, but which now tend to offer a similar range of services to banks.

3. Bank Interest

It may not come as a surprise to know that money deposited with banks or building societies does not just sit within the bank's vaults.

The basic model of a bank is to take deposits, paying the depositor interest on their deposited funds and to lend most of the deposited funds on to borrowers, charging interest on the borrowings. Clearly, the interest charged by the bank to the borrowers will be higher than the interest paid to the depositors. The difference between the two should be sufficient to provide the bank with enough surplus to pay its operating costs and generate a profit for its shareholders.

3.1 Characteristics of Cash Deposits

Cash deposits are accounts held with banks or other savings institutions, such as building societies. They are held by a wide variety of depositors – from retail investors, through to companies, governments and financial institutions.

The main characteristics of cash deposits are:

- The return simply comprises interest income.

- The amount invested (the 'capital') is repaid in full either at the end of a set period, or when withdrawn. Other than through the addition of interest, there is no potential for capital growth (for the amount invested to become larger).

Please try the following exercise to illustrate the concepts of capital and income and highlight some of the advantages and disadvantages of cash deposits.

⚙ Exercise 1

Jack Jones has just been left £250,000 by an elderly aunt. He is considering his options and has been told he could buy a one-bedroom flat in a city centre location with the money. Alternatively he could put the money on deposit with a bank.

a) What would make the one-bedroom flat the more attractive option?

b) How much interest could he earn, if instead of buying the flat Jack placed the £250,000 on deposit with a building society paying 3.25% each year, for three years?

Please try to answer the exercise and then check your responses against the answer that can be found at the end of the chapter.

Some accounts are known as **instant access** and the money can be withdrawn at any time; other accounts are for a **fixed term**, of a year or more.

The interest rate paid on deposits will vary with the amount of money deposited and the time for which the money is tied up. Large deposits are more economical for a bank or building society to process and will also earn a better rate. This is illustrated in the diagram on the following page with 'notice' accounts that require a certain period of notice before the money can be withdrawn. In the examples, the notice period is either 30 days (for the 'premier 30' accounts) and 180 days. The right hand column shows that the minimum deposit in all of the 'notice' accounts is £10,000.

The rate will also vary because of competition, and in most developed markets deposit-taking institutions compete intensely with one another to attract new deposits. In the figure overleaf, banks C, D and E are examples of accounts that offer 'easy access' (ie, there is no notice period) and the rates of interest that are available.

3.2 Tax on Bank Interest

Generally, interest received by an individual is subject to income tax. For most deposits, tax

Bank A	Notice Accounts	Premier 30 (Issue 3)	3.25% Variable 1.8% bonus for 12 months Paid Monthly	£10,000 - £50,000

Bank A	Notice Accounts	Premier 30 (Issue 3)	3.25% Variable 1.8% bonus for 12 months Paid Yearly	£10,000 - £50,000

Bank B	Notice Accounts	Premium Gold	3.15% Variable Paid Quarterly	£10,000 min. invest

Bank C	Easy Access	Online Plus	2.80% Variable 2.3% bonus for 12 months Paid Anniversary	£1 min. invest

Bank D	Easy Access	Savings Account	2.75% Variable 2.22% bonus for 12 months Paid Monthly	£1 min. invest

Bank E	Easy Access	Internet Saver	2.75% Variable 1.5% bonus for 12 months Paid Yearly	£1 min. invest

on the interest is deducted 'at source' – that is, by the deposit-taking bank or building society before paying the interest to the depositor. Where this happens, tax is deducted at a flat 20% (regardless of the depositor's tax rate) and paid over to the UK tax authority (Her Majesty's Revenue & Customs, or simply HMRC).

The 'headline' rate of interest quoted by deposit-takers, before deduction of tax, is referred to as **gross interest**, and the rate of interest after tax is deducted is referred to as **net interest**.

⚙ Example

Mrs Jones is entitled to 5% gross interest on £200 deposited in XYZ Bank for a year.

She will earn £200 x 5% = £10 interest on her bank deposit before the deduction of any tax.

She will receive net interest of £8 from XYZ Bank.

XYZ Bank will subsequently pay the £2 of tax on behalf of Mrs Jones to HMRC.

This can be summarised as follows:

- Gross interest earned: £200 x 5% = £10
- Tax deducted by XYZ Bank and paid to HMRC: £10 x 20% (£2)
- Net interest received by Mrs Jones: £10 x 80% = £8

UK individuals earning income below a certain threshold (just short of £44,000 annually at the time of writing) pay income tax at the 'basic rate' and are referred to as basic rate taxpayers. Those earning income above this threshold pay a higher rate of income tax and are known as 'higher rate taxpayers'. For a basic rate taxpayer, the 20% tax deducted at source on interest earned means that no further tax is payable. For a higher rate taxpayer, liable to tax at 40%, a further 20% will have to be paid when she submits her tax return. Those with incomes over £150,000 are liable to the additional rate of tax at 50% (in 2012/13) and will pay a further 30% over the basic rate.

At the end of the tax year, depositors receive a tax certificate from the savings institution which confirms that the basic rate of tax has been paid on their behalf.

Non-taxpayers, such as those on very low incomes, can submit a form known as an 'R85'. This is submitted to HMRC and once approved enables interest to be paid gross, with no deduction of tax at source. This is much easier than having tax deducted at source and filling out and submitting a tax reclaim form.

⚙ Exercise 2

Mr Evans is a basic rate taxpayer. He has had £3,000 on deposit at XYZ Bank for a year, earning 4% gross interest.

How much interest does Mr Evans receive, and how much is deducted at source on his behalf?

⚙ Exercise 3

Alan is 12 years old and his father has submitted an R85 form on his behalf. Alan has had £400 on deposit at XYZ Bank for a year, earning 3% gross interest. How much interest does Alan receive, and how much is deducted at source on his behalf?

Please try to answer the exercises and then check your responses against the answers that can be found at the end of the chapter.

3.3 Risks in Relation to Cash Deposits

Although cash investments are relatively simple products, it does not follow that they are free of risks, as 2008 so clearly demonstrated with the collapse of Northern Rock.

However, deposits are generally protected by some form of compensation scheme. These schemes will typically repay any deposited money lost, up to a set maximum, as a result of the collapse of a deposit taking institution, such as a bank. Depositors based in the UK are covered by the Financial Services Compensation Scheme (FSCS). The FSCS provides protection for the first £85,000 of deposits per person with an authorised institution, like a bank or building society.

As well as the obvious benefit of earning interest, cash deposits are also attractive because of the liquidity they offer. Liquidity is the ease and speed with which an investment can be turned into cash to meet spending needs. Most investors are likely to have a need for cash at short notice and so should plan to hold some cash on deposit to meet possible needs and emergencies before considering other less liquid forms of investment.

The risks inherent when depositing cash include:

- Deposit-taking institutions are of varying creditworthiness and there is a risk of collapse, although the FSCS does mitigate the risk for most modest depositors.
- Inflation reduces returns and could mean the real return after tax is negative. Inflation and real rates will be covered in more detail later in this manual.
- Interest rates change and so the returns from cash deposits will vary.
- If money is deposited overseas in a currency other than £ sterling, there is a risk that exchange rate movements mean it may fall in value in sterling terms, as well as the deposit taking institution being subject to a different regulatory regimes.

As a result, when comparing available deposit options it is important to consider the relevant risks as well as comparing the interest rates available.

4. Borrowing

As seen earlier, the traditional banking model is for the financial institution to take deposits and lend the majority of the deposited funds to borrowers. Individuals can borrow money from banks and building societies in three main ways:

- Overdrafts.
- Credit card borrowing.
- Loans.

4.1 Overdrafts

When an individual attempts to spend more money than he holds in his bank account, for instance by writing a cheque, it is possible that the bank will refuse to honour the cheque. This is referred to as 'bouncing' the cheque, and once upon a time it was quite common as shown by the following example relating to former UK Prime Minister Gordon Brown in his college days.

In 1972, Gordon Brown tried to pay for his university lodgings with a cheque for £3.

The cheque was not honoured by the bank because Mr Brown had insufficient funds in his account. 'Refer to Drawer' is bank-speak for 'this person has insufficient funds in his account to pay the cheque'. The bounced cheque cost Mr Brown an additional 13p in charges.

Today it would be unusual for a bank to bounce a cheque for a relatively small sum, with the bank more likely to honour the cheque whilst charging the account holder a fee and a high rate of interest for going 'overdrawn'. The account is described as being in overdraft when the depositor owes money to the bank.

If the amount overdrawn is within a limit previously agreed with the bank, the overdraft is said to be **authorised**. If it has not been previously agreed, or exceeds the agreed limit, it is **unauthorised**. Unauthorised overdrafts are very expensive, usually incurring both a high rate of interest on the borrowed money and a fee.

Authorised overdrafts agreed with the bank in advance are charged interest at a lower rate. Some banks allow small overdrafts without charging fees to avoid infuriating a customer who might be overdrawn by a relatively low amount.

Overdrafts are a convenient but expensive way of borrowing money and borrowers should try to restrict their use to temporary periods and avoid unauthorised overdrafts as far as possible.

An acceptable and sensible way to use an overdraft is illustrated in the following example.

⚙ Example

XYZ Hot Dog Ltd is due to pay its meat supplier £7,000 on 5 February but does not have enough money in its account to pay the bill. The Finance Director knows he is due to receive £8,500 from a customer on the

19th February but the gap leaves him with a cash-flow problem. He decides to arrange a £10,000 overdraft with a bank to cover that payment and any other expenses over the 14-day period. XYZ Hot Dog Ltd can now pay the bill for £7,000 and not worry about the cheque 'bouncing'. Not only would bounced cheques cost the business money in bank

charges but the company's relationship with its meat supplier would be damaged. The supplier might in future refuse to offer credit to XYZ Hot Dog Ltd and demand cash up front.

XYZ Hot Dog Ltd will be charged interest only on the amount it actually borrows. The overdraft facility is £10,000. If the business only uses say £7,750, it will only pay interest on the £7,750, not the whole £10,000.

4.2 Credit Cards

Customers in the UK are very attached to their 'flexible friends' – a typical pet name for credit cards from savings institutions like banks and building societies and other cards from retail stores known as store cards. In other countries, including much of Europe, the use is much less widespread.

A wide variety of retail goods such as food, electrical goods, petrol and cinema tickets can be paid for using a credit card. The retailer is paid by the credit card company for the goods sold; the credit card company charges the retailer a small fee, but this enables the store to sell goods to customers using their credit cards.

Customers are typically sent a monthly statement by the credit card company. Customers can then choose to pay all the money owed to the credit card company, or just a percentage of the total sum owed. Interest is charged on the balance owed by the customer.

0% 18 months 2.89% fee	0% 3 months	16.8% APR
* Instant online decision is available * 18.9% APR on transferred balances * 10% off ABC Holidays		

XYZ Credit Card

Generally, the interest rate charged on credit cards is relatively high compared to other forms of borrowing, including overdrafts. However, if a credit card customer pays the full balance each month, he is borrowing interest-free. It is also common for credit card companies to offer 0% interest to new customers for balances transferred from other cards and for new purchases for a set period, often six months. However, these offers are often only available if a fee is paid, as illustrated below.

Credit card interest is so profitable to banks that they entice people to switch their outstanding balance over to a new card.

The bait is 0% interest charged on transferred balances for an extended period. The catch is there's a fee that has to be paid on the balance transferred – in this case 2.89%.

4.3 Loans

Loans can be subdivided into two groups:

- secured loans; and
- unsecured loans.

Unsecured loans are typically used to purchase consumer goods, although another example is a student loan to be repaid after university. The lender will check the creditworthiness of the borrower – assessing whether he or she can afford to repay the loan and interest over the agreed term of, say, 48 months from income given existing outgoings.

The unsecured loan is not linked to the item that is purchased with the loan (in contrast to mortgages which are covered below), so if

the borrower fails to meet the repayments it can be difficult for the lender to enforce the loan agreement. The usual mechanism for the unsecured lender to enforce repayment is to start legal proceedings to get the money back.

In contrast, if **secured** loans are not repaid, the lender can repossess the specific property which was the security for the loan.

⚙ Example

Jenny borrows £500,000 to buy a house.

The loan is secured on the property. Jenny loses her job and is unable to continue to meet the repayments and interest.

Because the loan is secured, the lender is able to take the house to recoup the money. If the lender takes this route, the house will be sold and the lender will take the amount owed and give the rest, if any, to Jenny.

As seen in the above example, it is common for loans made to buy property to be secured. Such loans are referred to as **mortgages** and the security provided to the lender means that the rate of interest is likely to be lower than on other forms of borrowing, like overdrafts and unsecured loans.

⚙ Exercise 4

This exercise returns to the earlier example of XYZ Hot Dog Ltd utilising a £10,000 overdraft facility. XYZ Hot Dog Ltd is worried that its

CISI
CHARTERED INSTITUTE FOR
SECURITIES & INVESTMENT

bank might withdraw the overdraft facility without any warning. It is considering taking out a loan at 13% for £10,000 for a fixed, three-year period. What are the advantages and disadvantages of using a loan instead of an overdraft?

Please try to answer the exercise and then check your response against the answer that can be found at the end of the chapter.

4.4 Interest Rates

The costs of borrowing (mainly interest) vary depending on the form of borrowing, how long the money is required for, the security offered and the amount borrowed.

Mortgages, secured on a house, are much cheaper than credit cards and authorised overdrafts. Unauthorised overdrafts will incur even higher rates of interest plus charges.

Borrowers also have to grapple with the different rates quoted by lenders – loan companies traditionally quote flat rates that are lower than the true rate or **effective annual rate**.

⚙ Example

The Moneybags Credit Card Company quotes its interest rate at 12% per annum, charged on a quarterly basis.

The effective annual rate can be determined by taking the quoted rate and dividing by four (to represent the quarterly charge). It is this rate that is applied to the amount borrowed on a quarterly basis; 12% ÷ by 4 = 3%.

Imagine an individual borrows £100 on his/her Moneybags credit card. Assuming he or she makes no repayments for a year, how much will be owed?

At the end of the first quarter, £100 x 3% = £3 will be added to the balance outstanding, to make it £103.

At the end of the second quarter, interest will be due on both the original borrowing and the interest. In other words there will be interest charged on the first quarter's interest of £3, as well as the £100 original borrowing. £103 x 3% = £3.09 will be added to make the outstanding balance £106.09.

At the end of the third quarter, interest will be charged at 3% on the amount outstanding (including the first and second quarters' interest). £106.09 x 3% = £3.18 will be added to make the outstanding balance £109.27.

At the end of the fourth quarter, interest will be charged at 3% on the amount outstanding (including the first, second and third quarters' interest). £109.27 x 3% = £3.28 will be added to make the outstanding balance £112.55.

In total the interest incurred on the £100 was £12.55 over the year. This is an effective annual rate of 12.55 ÷ 100 x 100 = 12.55%.

There is a shortcut method to arrive at the effective annual rate seen above. It is simply to take the quoted rate, divide by the appropriate frequency (four for quarterly, two for half-yearly, 12 for monthly) and express the result as a decimal – in other words 3% will be expressed as 0.03, 6% as 0.06, etc.

The decimal is then added to 1, and multiplied by itself by the appropriate frequency. The result minus 1, and multiplied by 100 is the effective annual rate.

From the above example:

12% ÷ by 4 = 3%, expressed as 0.03.

1 + 0.03 = 1.03.

1.03^4 = 1.03 x 1.03 x 1.03 x 1.03 = 1.1255.

1.1255 − 1 = 0.1255 x 100 = 12.55%.

This formula can also be applied to deposits to determine the effective rate of a deposit paying interest at regular intervals.

To make comparisons easier, lenders must quote the true cost of borrowing, embracing the effective annual rate and including certain fees that are required to be paid by the borrower. This is known as the **Annual Percentage Rate (APR)**. The additional fees that the lender adds to the cost of borrowing might be loan arrangement fees. Under UK law, all lenders have to disclose what their APR before the loan is agreed. However, even the APR doesn't include all the costs associated with a credit agreement – such as:

- charges for late or missed payments;
- balance transfer fees on a credit card;
- charges for optional payment protection insurance.

⚙ Exercise 5

Company A is offering:

- *Minimum agreement period of two years.*
- *0% introductory rate for 14 months on all balance transfers.*
- *2.98% fee payable upon transfer of balance.*
- *16.6% APR on the balance from month 15 onwards.*

Company B is offering:

- *Minimum agreement period of two years.*
- *3.5% introductory rate for first 12 months on all balance transfers.*
- *No fee payable upon transfer of balance.*
- *12% on the balance from month 13 onwards.*

You have a credit card balance of £1,800. You want to switch to a new credit card company. You are determined not to put any more spending on your new card at all. You just want the cheapest cost over the life of the two year deal. Which offer do you choose?

Please try to answer the exercise and then check your response against the answer that can be found at the end of the chapter.

5. Other Types of Financial Institution

Banks have evolved beyond the 'high street bank' and the building society's traditional purpose of deposit taking and lending. They have specialised, sometimes as a result of regulatory developments, and today there is a wide range of both types of bank and other financial institutions. The services they provide generally revolve around investments such as shares issued by companies, bonds issued by companies and governments and derivatives. All of these investments will be looked at in more detail later in this manual. In this section, these financial institutions are explored in a little more detail.

5.1 Investment Banks

Confusingly, investment banks do not take deposits and grant loans. Instead, they provide advice and arrange finance for companies that want to make their shares available to the investing public (known as 'floating' on the stock market), that want to raise additional finance by issuing further shares or bonds, or carry out mergers and acquisitions. Many investment banks also provide services for those who might want to invest in shares and bonds, for example, pension funds and asset managers. All of this will be considered in greater detail later in this workbook.

The financial crisis of 2008 saw the disappearance of many of the larger independent investment banks. They were either taken over by other banks or converted into bank holding companies. For example, Merrill Lynch was taken over by Bank of America.

Typically, an investment banking group provides some or all of the following services, either in divisions of the bank or in associated companies within the group:

- **Corporate finance and advisory work**, normally in connection with new issues of securities for raising finance, takeovers, mergers and acquisitions.

- **Treasury dealing** for corporate clients in foreign currencies, with financial engineering services to protect them from interest rate and exchange rate fluctuations.
- **Investment management** for sizeable investors such as corporate pension funds, charities and private clients. They may do this either via direct investment for the wealthier, private clients or by way of collective investment schemes. In larger firms, the value of funds under management runs into many billions of pounds.
- **Securities trading** in equities, bonds and derivatives and the provision of broking and distribution facilities.

Only the largest few investment banks provide services in all these areas. Most others tend to specialise to some degree and concentrate on only a few product lines. A number of banks have diversified their range of activities by developing businesses such as proprietary trading, servicing hedge funds, or making private equity investments.

5.2 International Banks

International banking refers to banking activities that involve cross-border transactions, and its growth reflects the increasingly global nature of trade and the associated banking activities.

Typical activities involved in this sector relate to the financing of trade between parties in different countries. Trade finance involves the bank acting as an intermediary between an exporter who prefers an importer to pay in advance for goods before they are shipped, whilst the importer wants documentary evidence from the exporter that the goods have been shipped before payment is made. Traditionally, this involved the importer's bank providing a letter of credit to the exporter that guaranteed payment upon presentation of documentation which proved the goods had been shipped. More recently, this has developed to utilise the international payment systems provided by the Society of Worldwide Interbank Financial Telecommunication (SWIFT) to facilitate the payment for goods and speed up the flow of trade.

5.3 Pension Funds

Most individuals hope that, in later life, they will be able to stop working and retire. However, in order to save enough money to enjoy this period of retirement, the individuals will inevitably need income. This is where pension schemes come in. They are the key planning method by which individuals can make provision for retirement. There is a variety of pension schemes available, ranging from those provided by employers to those that are run by the individual, known as self-directed schemes.

Pension funds are often large, long-term investors in shares, bonds and cash. Some also invest in physical assets, like property. To meet their aim of providing a pension on retirement, the sums of money invested in pensions are substantial.

5.4 Insurance Companies

One of the key functions of the financial services industry is to provide protection and enable risks to be managed effectively. This includes the obvious insurance services such as car insurance, household contents insurance and life assurance. Car insurance will pay out in the event of a car accident, household contents will enable the replacement of possessions in the event of a burglary or flood and life assurance will pay out in the event that the insured person dies. However, the insurance industry provides solutions for much more than these standard areas of life and general insurance cover.

Protection planning is a key area of financial advice, and the insurance industry offers a wide range of products to meet many potential scenarios. These products range from payment protection policies designed to pay out in the event that an individual is unable to meet repayments on loans and mortgages, to fleet insurance against the risk of an airline's planes crashing.

Insurance companies also market a wide range of investment products, and have recently become large players in what is known as the 'structured products' market by offering guaranteed stock market related bonds.

Generally, insurance companies collect **premiums** in exchange for the cover provided, and this premium income is used to buy investments such as shares and bonds. As a result, the insurance industry is a major player in the London stock market.

Insurance companies will subsequently realise these investments to pay any claims that may arise on the various policies.

The UK insurance industry is the largest in Europe and the second largest in the world.

5.5 Fund Management

In essence, fund management is selecting the investments that make up the portfolios for pension funds, insurance companies and collective investment schemes and is also known as '**asset management**' or '**investment management**'.

Other areas of fund management include private wealth management and the provision of investment management services to institutional entities, such as companies, charities and local government authorities. This area also includes hedge funds.

Individual fund managers, also known as investment or asset managers, run these portfolios of investments for others. They invest money held by institutions, such as pension funds and insurance companies, as well as for collective investment schemes, such as unit trusts and open-ended investment companies (OEICs), and for wealthier individuals. Some fund management organisations focus solely on this activity; others are divisions of larger entities, such as insurance companies or banks.

Investment managers who buy and sell shares, bonds and other assets in order to increase the value of their clients' portfolios can conveniently be subdivided into '**institutional**' and '**private client**' fund managers. Institutional fund managers work on behalf of institutions, for example, investing money for a company's pension fund or an insurance company's fund, or managing the investments in a unit trust. Private client fund managers invest the money of relatively wealthy individuals. Generally, institutional portfolios are larger than those of private clients.

Investment management firms charge their clients for managing their money, with their charges often based on a small percentage of the value of the fund being managed.

5.6 Stockbrokers

Stockbrokers arrange stock market trades on behalf of their clients, who are mainly 'private clients' but also include investment institutions and fund managers. They may advise investors about which individual shares, bonds or funds they should buy or, alternatively, they may offer execution-only services. Execution-only services involve simply arranging the trade ('executing the trade') that the client requests and providing no advice.

Like fund managers, firms of stockbrokers can be independent companies, but usually they are divisions of larger entities, such as investment banks. They earn their profits by charging fees for their advice and commissions on transactions. Additionally, like fund managers, stockbrokers also look after client assets and charge custody and portfolio management fees.

5.7 Custodian Banks

Custodians are banks that specialise in keeping assets safe for others. These safe custody services typically involve looking after portfolios of shares and bonds on behalf of others, such as fund managers, pension funds and insurance companies.

The core activities they undertake include:

- holding assets in safekeeping, such as equities and bonds;
- arranging settlement – making the appropriate payment for any purchases and collecting the proceeds of any sales of securities;
- collecting income from assets, namely dividends in the case of equities and interest in the case of bonds;
- providing information on the underlying companies in which shares are held, such as their annual general meetings;
- generally managing the cash held within the portfolios;
- performing foreign exchange transactions where required; and
- providing regular reporting on all of their activities to their clients.

Competition has driven down the charges that a custodian can make for its traditional custody services and has resulted in consolidation within the industry. The custody business is now dominated by a small number of global custodians which are often divisions of large banks.

5.8 Trade and Professional Bodies

The investment industry is a dynamic, rapidly changing business, and one that requires co-operation between firms to ensure that the views of various industry sections are represented, especially to government and regulators. The industry also facilitates and enables cross-firm developments to take place to create an efficient market in which the firms can operate.

This is essentially the role of the numerous professional and trade bodies that exist across the world's financial markets. Examples of such bodies include:

- In the **bonds** market – International Capital Markets Association (ICMA).

- In the **derivatives** market – Futures and Options Association (FOA); International Swaps and Derivatives Association (ISDA).
- For **fund managers** – Investment Management Association (IMA).
- For **insurance companies** – Association of British Insurers (ABI).
- For stockbrokers and investment managers providing **private client investment management** – Association of Private Client Investment Managers and Stockbrokers (APCIMS).
- For **banks** – British Bankers' Association (BBA).

5.9 Third Party Administrations

Third party administrators (TPAs) undertake investment administration on behalf of other firms, and specialise in this area of the investment industry.

The number of firms involved and the scale of their operations have grown with the increasing use of outsourcing. The rationale behind outsourcing is that it enables a firm to focus on the core areas of its business (for example, in investment management the selection of the right investments, or for financial advisers the provision of appropriate financial planning) and leaves another firm to carry on the administrative functions, which it can process more efficiently and cost-effectively.

5.10 Professional and Retail Business

As already seen in the first chapter of this manual, there are two distinct areas within the financial services industry, namely the wholesale or professional sector (also known as the institutional sector) and the retail sector.

The financial activities that make up the **wholesale/professional** sector include:

- **Equity markets** – the trading of quoted shares.

- **Bond markets** – the trading of government, supranational or corporate debt.
- **Foreign exchange** – the trading of currencies.
- **Derivatives** – the trading of options, swaps, futures and forwards.
- **Fund management** – managing the investment portfolios of collective investment schemes, pension funds and insurance funds.
- **Insurance** – re-insurance, major corporate insurance (including professional indemnity), captive insurance and risk-sharing insurance.
- **Investment banking** – services tailored to organisations, such as undertaking mergers and acquisitions, raising finance by issuing equity or bonds and private equity.
- **Custodian banking** – provision of services to asset managers involving the safekeeping of assets; the administration of the underlying investments; settlement; corporate action and other specialised activities.
- **International banking** – cross-border banking transactions.

By contrast, the retail sector focuses on services provided to personal customers including:

- **Retail banking** – the traditional range of current accounts, deposit accounts, lending and credit cards.
- **Insurance** – the provision of a range of life assurance and protection solutions for areas such as medical insurance, critical illness cover, motor insurance, property insurance, income protection and mortgage protection.
- **Pensions** – the provision of investment accounts specifically designed to capture savings during a person's working life and provide benefits on retirement.
- **Investment services** – a range of investment products and vehicles ranging from execution-only stockbroking to full wealth management services and private banking.
- **Financial planning and financial advice**.

6. Investment Distribution Channels

6.1 Financial Advisers

Financial advisers are professionals who offer advice on financial matters to their clients. Some recommend suitable financial products provided by anyone – known as 'whole of market' advisors – whilst others can only recommend from a narrower range of products.

Typically a financial adviser will conduct a detailed survey of a client's financial position, preferences and objectives; this is sometimes known as a 'fact-find'. The adviser will then suggest appropriate action to meet the client's objectives and, if necessary, recommend a suitable financial product to match the client's needs.

In the UK, there are four main classes of adviser:

- **Tied advisers**, who advise on the products of one financial institution.
- **Multi-tied advisers**, who advise on the products of more than one financial institution.
- **Whole of market advisers**, who advise on the products of all the UK companies active in that area and who are paid by way of commission on the products they sell.
- **Independent financial advisers**, who also advise on the whole range of products on offer in the market – but who must also offer their clients the option to pay for advice by fee rather than by commission.

This classification is, however, changing significantly. Over the last few years, the Financial Services Authority (FSA) has been consulting on changes as to how investment products and services are distributed to retail clients. The Retail Distribution Review (RDR) contains proposals to change the classes of adviser referred to above. Investment firms will have to clearly describe their services as either 'independent advice' or 'restricted advice'. Firms that describe their advice as independent will have to ensure that they genuinely do make their recommendations based on comprehensive and fair analysis, and provide unbiased, unrestricted advice. Where a firm chooses to only give advice on its own range of products, this will have to be made clear.

The FSA is due to implement the proposals from the end of 2012.

6.2 Platforms

Platforms are online services used by intermediaries to view and administer their clients' investment portfolios. Platform providers also make their services available direct to investors.

They offer a range of tools which allow advisers to see and analyse a client's overall portfolio and to choose products for them. As well as providing facilities for investments to be bought and sold, platforms generally arrange custody for clients' assets.

The term 'platform' refers to both **wraps** and **fund supermarkets**. These are similar, but, while fund supermarkets tend to offer wide ranges of funds such as unit trusts and OEICs, wraps often offer greater access to other products too, such as the tax efficiency offered by Individual Savings Accounts (ISAs), pension plans and insurance bonds. Wrap accounts enable advisers to take a holistic view of the various assets that a client has in a variety of accounts. Advisers also benefit from using wrap accounts to simplify and bring some level of automation to their back-office using internet technology.

The advantage for fund management groups is the ability of the platform to distribute their products to financial advisers.

Platforms earn their income by either charging for their services or by taking commission from the product provider rather than the agent or client.

6.3 Execution-only

As already mentioned, a firm carries out transactions on an execution-only basis if the customer asks it to buy or sell a specific named investment product without having been prompted or advised by the firm. In such instances, customers are responsible for their own decision about a product's suitability.

The practice of execution-only sales is long-established. To ensure that firms operate within regulatory guidelines they need to record and retain evidence in writing that the firm:

- gave no advice; and
- made it clear, at the time of the sale, that it was not responsible for the product's suitability.

⚙ Exercise 6

All of the following financial institutions have been mentioned in the manual so far – who do they serve? Are their clients predominantly retail or professional, or a mix of both?

Please try to answer the exercise and then check your responses against the answer that can be found at the end of the chapter.

Financial Institution	Retail	Professional	Both
High street bank			
Pension fund			
Fund manager			
Building society			
Retail bank			
Insurance company			
Investment bank			
Stockbroker			
Institutional fund manager			
Custodian bank			
Private wealth manager			
Third party administrator			

⚙ Answers to Chapter Exercises

⚙ Exercise 1

Jack Jones has just been left £250,000 by an elderly aunt. He is considering his options and has been told he could use the money to buy and then let a one-bedroom flat in a city centre location. Alternatively he could put the money on deposit with a bank.

a) *What would make the one-bedroom flat the more attractive option?*

b) *How much interest could he earn, if instead of buying the flat Jack placed the £250,000 on deposit with a building society paying 3.25% each year, for three years?*

a) For Jack to invest his £250,000 of capital in a buy-to-let flat, he is hoping for two things:

- For the value of that flat to rise, ie, for Jack's capital to grow.
- To earn a competitive rent from letting out the flat to tenants.

Obviously there is a risk of capital loss, if the value of the flat falls rather than increases and there is also a risk to the income, the rent. The rent may not be competitive due to oversupply, or the flat may be without a tenant for a time.

In contrast, if Jack put the money on deposit in the bank, his capital will not grow – when he withdraws his deposit, he will receive back his original sum. He will only earn interest income.

b) If Jack had placed the £250,000 of capital on deposit with a building society at 3.25% for three years:

- In the first year he would earn interest of £8,125 (£250,000 x 3.25%).
- Assuming he does not leave the interest in the account, he could earn the same in each of the other two years.
- In total the interest would be £24,375 (£8,125 x 3).

⚙ Exercise 2

Mr Evans is a basic rate taxpayer. He has had £3,000 on deposit at XYZ Bank for a year, earning 4% gross interest. How much interest does Mr Evans receive, and how much is deducted at source on his behalf?

Interest earned = £3,000 x 4% = £120

Deducted at source = £120 x 20% = £24

Received by Mr Evans = £120 x 80% = £96

⚙ Exercise 3

Alan is 12 years old and his father has submitted an R85 form on his behalf. Alan has had £400 on deposit at XYZ Bank for a year, earning 3% gross interest. How much interest does Alan receive, and how much is deducted at source on his behalf?

Interest earned and received by Alan = £400 x 3% = £12. No tax is deducted at source since an R85 form has been submitted.

⚙ Exercise 4

This exercise returns to the earlier example of XYZ Hot Dog Ltd utilising a £10,000 overdraft facility. XYZ Hot Dog Ltd is worried that its bank might withdraw the overdraft facility without any warning. It is considering taking out a loan at 13% for £10,000 for a fixed, three-year period. What are the advantages and disadvantages of using a loan instead of an overdraft?

Advantages of the loan over an overdraft	Disadvantages of the loan over an overdraft
As long as XYZ Hot Dog Ltd complies with the conditions of the loan agreement, the bank cannot demand repayment of the loan before the term expires.	XYZ Hot Dog Ltd has to borrow the full amount of the loan, despite it perhaps being more than it needs for most of the time.
The interest rate on the loan at 13.0% is likely to be substantially cheaper than the rate applied to the overdraft.	It pays interest on the full amount of the loan.
	It may have to offer security to prove it can repay the loan.

⚙ Exercise 5

Company A is offering:

- *Minimum agreement period of two years.*
- *0% introductory rate for 14 months on all balance transfers.*
- *2.98% fee payable upon transfer of balance.*
- *16.6% APR on the balance from month 15 onwards.*

Company B is offering:

- *Minimum agreement period of two years.*
- *3.5% introductory rate for first 12 months on all balance transfers.*
- *No fee payable upon transfer of balance.*
- *12% on the balance from month 13 onwards.*

You have a credit card balance of £1,800. You want to switch to a new credit card company. You are determined not to put any more spending on your new card at all. You just want the cheapest cost over the life of the two year deal. Which offer do you choose?

Company A – 24-month deal	
Balance transferred	£1,800.00
Fee of 2.98% on balance transferred	£53.64
New balance after the addition of the 2.98% transfer fee	£1,853.64
Introductory interest rate quoted on the new balance for the first 14 months	0.00%
16.6% APR interest charge on the new balance for the remaining 10 months	£256.42
Total cost of the Virgin deal (53.64 + 256.42)	£310.06

Company B – 24-month deal	
Balance transferred	£1,800
Introductory rate (APR) charged for first 12 months (3.56% x 1,800)	£64.08
New balance after first 12 months	£1,864.08
Rate (APR) charged for the remaining 12 months (12.68% x 1,864.08)	£236.41
Total cost of Magic Bank deal	£300.49

The Company B deal is the cheaper option

⚙ Exercise 6

All of the following financial institutions have been mentioned in the manual so far – who do they serve? Are their clients predominantly retail or professional, or a mix of both?

Financial Institution	Retail	Professional	Both
High street bank			✔
Pension fund	✔		
Fund manager			✔
Building society	✔		
Retail bank	✔		
Insurance company			✔
Investment bank		✔	
Stockbroker			✔
Institutional fund manager		✔	
Custodian bank		✔	
Private wealth manager	✔		
Third party administrator		✔	

⭐ Learning Objectives

Chapter Two has covered the following Learning Objectives:

1.1.1 Know the role of the following within the financial services industry: retail banks; building societies; investment banks; pension funds; insurance companies; fund managers; stockbrokers; custodians; third party administrators (TPAs); industry trade and professional bodies

Lesson 02, Lesson 10 (retail banks; building societies), Lesson 14 (pension funds; insurance companies), Lesson 15 (investment banks), Lesson 23 (fund managers, custodians, stockbrokers), Lesson 44 (TPAs), and Lesson 45 (industry trade and professional bodies)

1.1.2 Know the function of and differences between retail and professional business and who the main customers are in each case: retail clients and professional clients

Lesson 02

1.1.3 Know the role of the following investment distribution channels: independent financial adviser; tied adviser; platforms; execution-only

Lesson 44

3.1 Cash deposits

Lesson 03

3.1.1 Know the characteristics of fixed term and instant access deposit accounts

Lesson 03 and Lesson 16

3.1.2 Understand the distinction between gross and net interest payments

Lesson 40

3.1.3 Be able to calculate the net interest due given the gross interest rate, the deposited sum, the period and tax rate

Lesson 03 and Lesson 40

3.1.4 Know the advantages and disadvantages of investing in cash

Lesson 03

10.1.1 Know the differences between bank loans, overdrafts and credit card borrowing

Lesson 04

10.1.2 Know the difference between the quoted interest rate on borrowing and the effective annual rate of borrowing

Lesson 04

10.1.3 Be able to calculate the effective annual rate of borrowing, given the quoted interest rate and frequency of payment

 Lesson 04

10.1.4 Know the difference between secured and unsecured borrowing

 Lesson 05

Based on what you have learned in Chapter Two, try to answer the following end of chapter questions.

End of Chapter Questions

Think of an answer for each question and refer to the appropriate section for confirmation.

1. What are the two major types of saving institution in the UK?

    Answer Reference: Section 2

    ....

    ....

2. What makes a building society different?

    Answer Reference: Section 2

    ....

    ....

3. How do traditional banks make money?

    Answer Reference: Section 3

    ....

    ....

4. What two factors typically determine the amount of interest received from a savings institution?

    Answer Reference: Section 3.1

    ....

    ....

5. How much tax is typically deducted at source from bank interest?

    Answer Reference: Section 3.2

    ....

    ....

6. What is the FSCS?

   Answer Reference: Section 3.3

   ....

   ....

7. What are the three main ways that individuals use to borrow from financial institutions?

   Answer Reference: Section 4

   ....

   ....

8. What are the two forms of overdraft and which form is the most expensive?

   Answer Reference: Section 4.1

   ....

   ....

9. What are the two forms of loan?

   Answer Reference: Section 4.3

   ....

   ....

10. How does the flat rate differ from the effective annual rate?

    Answer Reference: Section 4.4

    ....

    ....

11. How does the annual percentage rate differ from the effective annual rate?

    Answer Reference: Section 4.4

    ....

    ....

12. What does an investment bank do?

    Answer Reference: Section 5.1

    ....

    ....

13. What are the two types of client that investment managers serve?

    Answer Reference: Section 5.5

    ....

    ....

14. Who do custodian banks serve?

    Answer Reference: Section 5.7

    ....

    ....

15. What are the four main classes of investment adviser?

    Answer Reference: Section 6.1

    ....

    ....

3

Equities

Equities

1. Introduction

The workbook has already mentioned both equities and bonds as investment possibilities. This chapter looks in detail at the features of equities. The next chapter (Chapter 4) provides further detail about how equities are traded on stock markets. Bonds will be covered in detail in Chapter 5.

So, what is equity? Well, in the stock market, it refers to shares in a company. Shares and equities are alternative terms for the same thing, and it is the shareholders that own and control companies. Shareholders generally hope that the value of their shares will increase (they will make a 'capital gain') and that the company will pay regular and increasing amounts of income to them each year in the form of 'dividends'.

In contrast a bond is basically a certificate that represents a loan. It is the equivalent of an IOU (I owe you) and could be issued by a company or another issuer, such as a government. Bondholders are rewarded for lending money to the bond issuer, by receiving regular income in the form of interest or '**coupons**'.

This chapter considers equities, which are shares in companies – initially outlining how a company is formed, before moving on to the requirements for the company to become listed on a stock exchange. It then considers the features of equities – the benefits and risks of owning them.

2. Company Formation and Administration

2.1 Forming a Company

Many businesses, large and small, are set up as companies. It is important to appreciate that companies are owned by shareholders and run by directors. In many smaller companies the shareholders and the directors are the same people, but in larger companies the majority of the shareholders are not directors. Because of this potential separation between the running of the company (by the directors) and the ownership of the company (by shareholders), the law includes the requirement for the company to hold regular meetings at which the directors consult with their shareholders, and report on company progress. This concept can be illustrated by the following example.

⚙ Example

Local Veg Ltd

Jake Onions is a recent school leaver and he and his friends Johnny and Jenny Plant have come up with an idea for a business – buying locally grown vegetables from within the community (either grown in allotments or gardens), and selling them from a market stall. As the business begins to generate income Jake and his friends may decide to formalise things by setting it up as a company 'Local Veg Ltd'. At this stage it is Jake and his friends that both own the shares and are also directors running the company.

To form a simple company (like Local Veg Ltd) is inexpensive and requires the founders of the company to complete a series of documents and lodge these with the appropriate authority. In the UK these documents are required to be lodged with the Registrar of Companies at Companies House.

To form a company, two constitutional documents are required:

- Memorandum of Association;
- Articles of Association.

The **Memorandum of Association** is a document that gives details of the company to the external world. It simply states the name of the company, the location of its registered office, its authorised share capital, its business objectives and whether it is a private or public (plc) company. Below is a simplified example of a memorandum of association for Local Veg Ltd.

In contrast to the memorandum, the **Articles of Association** detail the relationship between the company and its shareholders. The articles include details such as the rights of the shareholders to appoint and remove directors and the frequency of company meetings.

2.2 Private and Public Companies

Companies are established either as:

- **private companies**, such as Local Veg Ltd, where Ltd stands for Limited. Such companies can have just a single shareholder; or
- **public companies**, such as International Veg plc, where plc stands for public limited company. Plcs are required to have a minimum of two shareholders.

It is only plcs that are permitted to issue shares to the public. As a result, Local Veg Ltd would need to become a plc before it could issue shares to the general public (termed an initial public offering, or just an IPO).

PRIVATE COMPANY LIMITED BY SHARES
MEMORANDUM OF ASSOCIATION
OF
LOCAL VEG LTD

1. The company's name is Local Veg Limited.

2. The Company's registered office is:

   Under the Arches, 6 High Street, Newtown, Newtownshire, NE61 5SW.

3. The Company's objects are to carry on the business of a general commercial company, principally this will involve buying vegetables from producers and selling those vegetables on to consumers.

4. The liability of the shareholders/members is limited.

5. The Company's authorised and issued share capital is £1,000 divided into 1,000 Ordinary £1 Shares of £1 each.

   We, the subscribers to this Memorandum of Association, wish to be formed into a Company pursuant to this Memorandum and to take the number of shares shown beneath our respective names.

   Jake Onions, 42A High Street, Newtown, Newtownshire, NE61 5SW.

   Number of shares taken: 400

   Johnny Plant, 36 High Street, Newtown, Newtownshire, NE61 5SW.

   Number of shares taken: 300

   Jenny Plant, 36 High Street, Newtown, Newtownshire, NE61 5SW.

   Number of shares taken: 300

⚙ Example

Local Veg Ltd becomes a plc

Local Veg Ltd is doing so well that it is becoming difficult for Jake, Johnny and Jenny to keep control and grow the business further. They find a more experienced person (Vicky Mature) to join as a director, Vicky has got plans for the company including spreading the concept internationally and raising the money to do so by selling shares to the public in an IPO. Jake, Johnny and Jenny are all in agreement and the first step is for Local Veg has to become a plc, so Vicky organises the amendment of the constitutional documents to rename the business 'International Veg plc'.

It is a requirement for companies that are listed on stock exchanges to be plcs, because listed companies have all gone through an IPO stage selling shares to the public. However not all plcs are listed. It is perfectly possible for a company to like International Veg to 'just be' a plc, and not be listed on a stock exchange. Virgin Holdings, the business empire of Richard Branson, is a public limited company but is not listed on any stock exchanges. In contrast, the global bank HSBC Holdings is a public limited company and is listed on a number of stock exchanges including: the London Stock Exchange (LSE), the New York Stock Exchange (NYSE), the Tokyo Stock Exchange (TSE) and the Hong Kong Stock Exchange (HKSE).

'Limited', whether as in 'Ltd' for a private company or within 'plc' for a public company, means that the liability of shareholders for the debts of the company is limited to the amount they agreed to pay to the company on initial subscription. This is explained in the following example:

⚙ Example

Slip Up Ltd is a UK company that is created with a share capital of £100 which is made up of 100 ordinary £1 shares.

Assuming that each share is fully paid, an initial shareholder who subscribes for 20 shares will pay £20.

In the event that Slip Up is unsuccessful and goes into liquidation, the liability of that shareholder for the company's debts is limited to the amount they subscribed, that is £20.

The position would be different if the shares were only partly paid. For example, the shares might be ordinary £1 shares but only require 80p per share to be paid at the outset, the remainder being payable at some future date. In the event of liquidation, the shareholder may be required to subscribe the balance of 20p per share to help meet the company's debts.

2.3 Company Meetings

As mentioned earlier, companies have meetings between the directors that are running the business and the shareholders. Companies must hold **annual general meetings (AGMs)** at which the shareholders are given the opportunity to question the directors about the company's strategy and operations.

The shareholders are also given the opportunity to vote on matters such as the appointment and removal of directors and the payment of the dividend recommended by the directors. Most matters put to the shareholders are

'**ordinary resolutions**', requiring a simple majority of those shareholders voting to be passed. Matters of major importance, such as a proposed change to the company's constitution, require a '**special resolution**' and at least 75% to vote in favour.

⚙ Example

The appointment of Vicky Mature as a director at Local Veg Ltd would have only required a majority of the shareholders to vote in favour. Given that Jake Onions held 40% of the votes (with 400 of the 1,000 shares) and Johnny and Jenny Plant each held 30% (with 300 shares each), a combination of Jake and either of the Plants would be sufficient (at 70%), or alternatively the two Plants voting in favour (at 60%).

In contrast, changing Local Veg Ltd into International Veg plc would require a special resolution and at least 75% to vote in favour. Presuming Jake, Johnny and Jenny all voted, they would all have to vote in favour for the change in name to take effect.

The shareholders can either attend the meeting and vote in person, or if they prefer, they might not attend but they can still have their vote counted at the meeting by appointing someone else to vote on their behalf, known as **proxy voting**. This involves the completion of a proxy voting form, enabling someone else to register their vote on their behalf.

The other main type of company meeting is an **extraordinary general meeting (EGM)**. An EGM can be called at any time and is usually used where there is a major decision to be made by shareholders that cannot wait for the next annual general meeting.

Some of the reasons why an EGM may be called include:

- approving a major transaction, such as the company acquiring another company (an acquisition);

- approving major changes to the company's financial structure that require an increase or reduction in share capital;
- allowing shareholders to remove directors with whom they have a major disagreement;
- changing the name of the company.

3. Listing

3.1 Primary and Secondary Markets

When a company like International Veg plc decides to seek a listing for its shares, the process is known by a number of terms:

- making an 'Initial Public Offer' (IPO);
- becoming 'listed' or 'quoted';
- 'floating' on the stock market; or
- 'going public'.

Typically, the company making the IPO will have been in existence for many years, and will have grown to a point where it wishes to expand further. The IPO will enable the company to raise money by selling shares to the public, which will help finance the expansion of the company.

Other relevant terminology is 'primary market' and 'secondary market'. The term **primary market** refers to the marketing of new shares in a company to investors for the first time. So clearly, an IPO is a primary market transaction. Once they have acquired shares, investors will at some point wish to dispose of some or all of their shares and will generally do this through the stock exchange trading system. This latter process is referred to as 'dealing on the **secondary market**'.

Primary markets exist to facilitate the raising of capital and enable surplus funds to be matched with investment opportunities. The secondary market is necessary because investors would not be willing to invest in shares unless there was some sort of mechanism to sell them.

So the secondary market allows the primary market to function efficiently by providing trading in issued securities.

3.2 Advantages and Disadvantages of Listing

There are a number of advantages and disadvantages to gaining a listing, and these would need to be considered carefully before deciding to float the company. It is helpful to reconsider International Veg plc – what would a listing do for the company? Well, the advantages and disadvantages include the following:

Advantages

- **Capital** – the IPO provides the possibility of raising capital and, once listed, further offers of shares are much easier to make. If the shares being offered to the public are those of the company's original founders – Jake, Johnny and Jenny – then the IPO offers them an exit route and a means to convert their shareholdings and hard work into cash.
- **Takeovers** – a listed company like International Veg plc could use its shares as payment to acquire the shares of other companies as part of an acquisition.
- **Status** – being International Veg plc, being listed on the LSE should help the business in marketing itself to customers, suppliers and potential employees.
- **Employees** – providing key employees with options to buy shares (often term stock or share options) are a way of providing incentives and retaining employees for both unlisted and listed companies. However options to buy listed.

Disadvantages

- **Regulations** – as a listed company, International Veg plc would have to govern itself in a more open way than as an unlisted, private company. This includes a requirement to provide detailed and timely information on the company's financial situation and progress.
- **Takeovers** – as a listed company, International Veg plc is at risk of being taken over if another company can convince the public shareholders of International Veg to sell to them.
- **Short-termism** – shareholders of listed companies tend to exert pressure on the company to reach short-term goals, such as increasing profits every year, rather than being more patient and looking for longer-term investment and growth.

3.3 Requirements for Listing on the LSE

The London Stock Exchange (LSE) is the most well known stock exchange in the UK and lists some very large companies like the mobile telecommunications company Vodafone, banks like Barclays and HSBC and the oil giant BP. However, it is not necessary to be quite as large as these companies to be listed on the LSE.

The requirements to be met before a company is allowed to be listed on the LSE are laid down by a division of the UK's financial services regulator, the Financial Services Authority (FSA). The particular division is known as the United Kingdom Listing Authority (UKLA).

The UKLA's requirements for companies seeking a listing for their shares are mainly aimed at making sure the company is sizeable and well established, and that it discloses sufficient information to potential investors so that they can decide whether or not they want to invest. The main requirements are as follows:

- The company must be a public limited company (plc).
- The company's expected market capitalisation (the share price multiplied by the number of shares in issue) must be at least £700,000.
- The company should have been trading for at least three years and at least 75% of its business must be supported by a historic revenue earning record for that period.
- At least 25% of the company's shares should be in public hands or available for purchase by the public. The term 'public' excludes directors of the company and their associates, and significant shareholders who hold 5% or more of the company's shares.
- A trading company must demonstrate that it has sufficient working capital for the next 12 months.

Please try the following exercise in relation to the eligibility of companies seeking a listing.

⚙ Exercise 1

Based solely on the information provided below, which of the following three companies would NOT be eligible to list on the LSE?

1) *Langley Property Rentals plc*
   - *Established five years ago.*
   - *First rental properties acquired two years ago.*
   - *100% of revenues from property rentals.*
   - *Directors, associates and significant share-holders own 70% of the shares.*
   - *Expected market cap £2 million.*

2) *Kelsey Market Research Ltd*
   - *Established 10 years ago.*
   - *Company has been trading profitably since 2nd year of operation.*
   - *85% of revenues from market research.*
   - *Has sufficient working capital for 14 months of operations.*

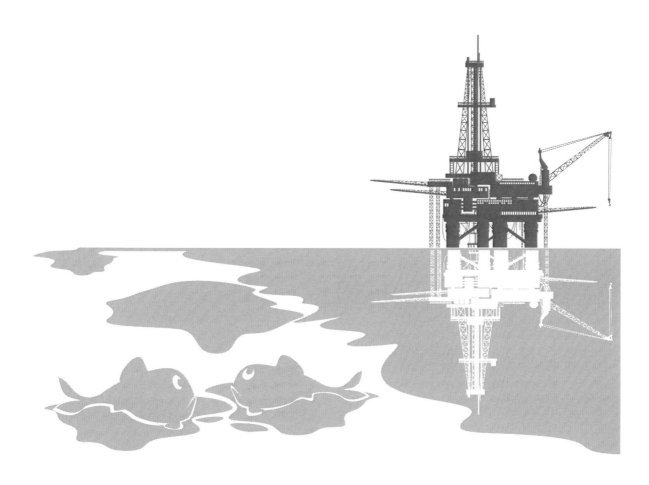

3) *Eden Park IT Services plc*

- *Established four years ago.*
- *75% of revenues from IT services.*
- *Been trading profitably from company's inception.*
- *Directors, associates and significant share-holders own 25% of the shares.*
- *Expected market cap £1 million.*

The answer and explanation can be found at the end of this chapter.

Once listed, companies are expected to fulfil rules known as the '**continuing obligations**'. For example, they are obliged to issue a half-yearly report that includes financial information, such as trading performance, and listed companies are required to notify the market of any new 'price-sensitive' information. An example would be when the oil giant BP had a major oil spill in the Gulf of Mexico in 2010.

A listing on the LSE is often referred to as a 'full listing'. This distinguishes it from cases where a company's shares are admitted to the **Alternative Investment Market (AIM)**, a market also run by the LSE where the requirements are less demanding, as explained below.

3.4 The Alternative Investment Market (AIM)

The Alternative Investment Market (AIM) was established by the LSE as a 'junior' market targeted at younger, smaller companies than those eligible for a full listing. Such companies apply to the LSE to join AIM, whereas full

---

AIM	Full Listing
No trading history required; the company could be newly established.	Three years' trading history is needed.
No minimum market capitalisation required.	£700,000 is the minimum market cap.
No requirement for a minimum proportion of the shares to be held by the 'public'.	At least 25% of the shares must be held by outside investors.

listing requires application to the UKLA. The requirements for a listing on AIM, in comparison to the requirements for a full listing, are as shown in the table on the opposite page.

Amongst the companies traded on the AIM are the wine retailer Majestic, the fashion label Mulberry, and the football clubs Celtic and Tottenham Hotspur.

A company wanting to gain admission to AIM is required to appoint a **nominated adviser (NOMAD)** and a **nominated broker**. The role of the NOMAD is to advise the directors of the company of their responsibilities in complying with AIM rules, including the information required to accompany the company's application for admission to AIM. The role of the nominated broker is to make a market and facilitate trading in the company's shares, as well as to provide ongoing information about the company to interested parties such as company presentations.

Certain rules are common to both AIM and fully listed companies. They must both release price-sensitive information promptly (such as legal cases lodged against them and the resignation of a director) and produce financial information at both the half-yearly (interim) stage and the full year (final) stage.

4. Types of Equities

Remember that the capital of a company is made up of a combination of borrowing and the money invested by its owners. The long-term borrowings, or debt, of a company are often a combination of bonds and long term bank loans, and the money invested by its owners are referred to as shares, stock or equity. Shares are the equity capital of a company, hence the reason they are referred to as equities; they may comprise ordinary shares and preference shares.

4.1 Ordinary Shares

The share capital of a company always includes ordinary shares and the owners of the ordinary shares own the company. If an individual were fortunate enough to own 20% of the telecom giant Vodafone's ordinary shares, he would own one-fifth of Vodafone.

Ordinary shares carry the full risk and reward of investing in a company. If a company does well, its ordinary shareholders will do well. As the ultimate owners of the company, it is the ordinary shareholders who vote 'yes' or 'no' to each resolution put forward by the company directors at company meetings. For example, an offer to take over a company may be made and the directors may propose that it is accepted but this will be subject to a vote by shareholders. If the shareholders vote 'no', then the directors will have to think again.

Ordinary shareholders share in the profits of the company by receiving dividends declared by the company, which tend to be paid half-yearly or even quarterly. For example, the company directors will propose a dividend which will need to be ratified by the ordinary shareholders before it is formally declared as payable. The amount of dividend paid will depend on how well the company is doing. However, some companies pay large dividends and others none as they plough all profits made back into the future growth.

⚙ Example

Company XYZ plc has been very profitable for many years but has never paid a dividend. Only now that its meteoric expansion is showing signs of slowing down will the company start to return cash to its shareholders.

If the company does badly, it is the ordinary shareholders that will suffer. If the company closes down, often described as the company being 'wound up', the ordinary shareholders are paid last, after everybody else. If there is nothing left, then the ordinary shareholders get nothing. If there is money left after all creditors and preference shareholders have been paid, it all belongs to the ordinary shareholders.

Some ordinary shares may be referred to as partly paid or contributing shares. This means that only part of their nominal value has been paid up. For example, if a new company was established with an initial capital of £100, this capital may be made up of 100 ordinary £1 shares.

If the shareholders to whom these shares are allocated have paid £1 per share in full, then the shares are termed **fully paid**.

Alternatively, the shareholders may contribute only half of the initial capital, say £50 in total, which would require a payment of 50p per share, ie, one-half of the amount due. The shares would then be termed **partly paid**, but the shareholder has an obligation to pay the

remaining amount when called upon to do so by the company.

4.2 Preference Shares

Some companies have preference shares as well as ordinary shares. The company's internal rules (their Articles of Association) will set out precisely how the preference shares differ from the ordinary shares.

Preference shares have elements of both bonds and equities, so they are often referred to as 'hybrid' securities. Although they are technically a form of equity investment, they also have characteristics that are more like debt, particularly in that most preference shares pay a fixed income.

Preference shares have legal priority (known as seniority) over ordinary shareholders in respect of their dividends and, if the issuing company collapsed, they would get their money back ahead of the ordinary shareholders.

Normally, preference shares:

- are non-voting, so preference shareholders cannot vote at the General Meetings of the company. This may change in certain special circumstances, such as when their dividends have not been paid;
- pay a fixed dividend each year, the amount being set when they are first issued;
- rank ahead of ordinary shares in terms of being paid back if the company is wound up, up to a limited amount to be repaid.

Preference shares may be non-cumulative, cumulative and/or participating.

If dividends cannot be paid in a particular year, perhaps because the company has insufficient profits, preference shares would get no dividend. However, if they were cumulative preference shares then the dividend entitlement accumulates. Assuming sufficient profits, the **cumulative** preference shares will have the arrears of dividend paid in the subsequent year. If the shares were **non-cumulative**, the dividend from the first year would be lost.

Participating preference shares entitle the holder to a basic dividend of, say, 3p a year, but the directors can award a bigger dividend in a year where the profits exceed a certain level. In other words, the preference shareholder can participate in bumper profits.

Preference shares may also be convertible or redeemable. **Convertible** preference shares carry an option to convert into the ordinary shares of the company at set intervals and on pre-set terms. **Redeemable** shares, as the name implies, have a date at which they may be redeemed; that is, the nominal value of the shares will be paid back to the preference shareholder and the shares cancelled.

5. Benefits of Owning Shares

Holding shares in a company is having an ownership stake in that company. Ownership carries certain benefits and rights, and ordinary shareholders expect to be the major beneficiaries of a company's success.

As we will see in Section 6 below, shares carry risks. As a reward for taking this risk, shareholders hope to benefit from the success of the company. This reward or return can take one of the following forms.

5.1 Dividends

A dividend is part of the return that an investor gets for providing the risk capital for a business. Dividends are typically an annual (or semi-annual) payment to equity investors. Dividends are paid out of the company's profits, which form part of their **distributable reserves**. Distributable reserves are the profits after tax, and after payment of dividends which have been accumulated over the life of the company. This is exhibited in the following example.

⚙ Example

XYZ plc was formed some years ago. Over the company's life it has made £20 million in profits and paid dividends of £13 million. Distributable reserves at the beginning of the year are, therefore, £7 million.

This year XYZ plc makes post-tax profits of £3 million and decides to pay a dividend of £1 million.

At the end of the year distributable reserves are:

Opening balance	*£7m*
Profits after tax for the year	*£3m*
	£10m

XYZ plc share price compare to FTSE 100

Less, dividend to be paid	*(£1m)*
Closing balance	*£9m*

*Note, despite only making £3 million in the current year, it would be perfectly legal for XYZ plc to pay dividends of more than £3 million, because it can use the undistributed profits from previous years. This would be described as a '**naked**' or '**uncovered**' dividend, because the current year's profits were insufficient to fully cover the dividend. Companies occasionally do this, but it is obviously not possible to maintain this long-term.*

UK companies generally seek, where possible, to pay steadily growing dividends. A fall in dividend payments can lead to a negative reaction amongst shareholders and a general reduction in the willingness to hold the company's shares.

Potential shareholders will compare the dividend paid on a company's shares with alternative investments. These would include other shares, bonds and bank deposits. This involves calculating the **dividend yield**.

⚙ Example

ABC plc has 20 million ordinary shares, each trading at £2.50. It pays out a total of £1 million in dividends.

Its dividend yield is calculated by expressing the dividend as a percentage of the total value of the company's shares (the market capitalisation):

Dividend (£1m) ÷ Market capitalisation (20m x £2.50) x 100

So the dividend yield is:

[1m ÷ (20m x £2.50)] x 100 = 2%

Since ABC plc paid £1 million to shareholders of 20 million shares, the dividend yield can also be calculated on a per share basis by dividing the dividend per share by the share price.

The dividend per share is £1 million ÷ 20 million shares, ie, £0.05. So £0.05 ÷ £2.50 (the share price) is again 2%.

Some companies have a higher than average dividend yield, which may be for one of the following reasons:

- The company is mature and continues to generate healthy levels of cash, but has limited growth potential. For example, water and electricity supply companies ('utilities') have their prices regulated by the government and demand for water and electricity tends to grow at a steady but low rate.
- The company has a low share price for some other reason, perhaps because it is, or is expected to be, relatively unsuccessful; its comparatively high current dividend is, therefore, not expected to be sustained and its share price is not expected to rise.

In contrast, some companies might have dividend yields that are relatively low. This is generally because:

- the share price is high, because the company is viewed by investors as having strong growth prospects; or
- a large proportion of the profit being generated by the company is being ploughed back into the business, rather than being paid out as dividends (as shown with the Company XYZ example earlier).

5.2 Capital Gains

Capital gains can be made on shares if their prices increase over time.

If an investor purchases a share for £3.00, and two years later that share price has risen to £5.00, then the investor has made a £2.00 capital gain. However, the shares need to be sold to realise any capital gains. If he does not sell the share, then the gain is described as being 'unrealised'; and he runs the risk of the share price falling before he does realise the shares and 'bank' his profits. This is illustrated in the following example based on Company XYZ plc.

Example

Investors who bought the stock in 2005 had made a capital gain of 100% on their investment in 1½ years. Company XYZ plc was a 'growth' stock – expanding its operations across Europe and as its profits increased, investors bought the stock in anticipation of more capital gains and future dividends.

If a shareholder had bought XYZ plc in mid-2005 and sold the stock at the end of quarter 1 in 2007, a capital gain of 100% would have been realised. However, if the shareholder held onto the shares for another year until 2008, all that profit would have been wiped out. The lesson is that capital gains have to be 'banked' to be realised.

5.3 Shareholder Benefits

Some companies provide perks to shareholders, such as a telecoms company offering its shareholders a discounted price on their mobile phones or a shipping company offering cheap ferry tickets. Such trade benefits can be a pleasant bonus for small investors, but are not normally a major factor in investment decisions.

5.4 Shareholder Rights

5.4.1 Right to Subscribe for New Shares

If a company were able to issue new shares to anyone, then existing shareholders could lose control of the company, or at least see their share of ownership diluted. As a result, under UK legislation, existing shareholders in UK companies are given '**pre-emptive**' rights to subscribe for new shares. What this means is that, unless the shareholders agree to permit the company to issue shares to others, they must be given the option to subscribe for the new share offering, before it is offered to the wider public.

Pre-emptive rights are illustrated in the following example.

Example

An investor, Mr B, currently holds 20,000 ordinary shares of the 100,000 issued ordinary shares in ABC plc. He therefore owns 20% of ABC plc.

If ABC plc planned to increase the number of issued ordinary shares, by allowing investors to subscribe for another 100,000 new ordinary shares, Mr B would be offered 20% of the new shares, ie, 20,000 shares. This would enable Mr B to retain his 20% ownership of the enlarged company. In summary:

	Before the issue (000's)	%	New issue (000's)	After the issue (000's)	%
Mr B	20	20%	20	40	20%
Other share-holders	80	80%	80	160	80%
Total	100	100%	100	200	100

If this were not the case, Mr B's stake in ABC plc could be diluted, as shown below:

	Before the issue (000's)	%	New issue (000's)	After the issue (000's)	%
Mr B	20	20%	nil	20	10%
Other share-holders	80	80%	100	180	90%
Total	100	100%	100	200	100%

A rights issue is one method by which a company can raise additional capital, complying with pre-emptive rights, with existing shareholders having the right to subscribe for new shares. The mechanics of a rights issue will be looked at in Section 7.2.

5.4.2 Right to Vote

As seen earlier in this chapter, ordinary shareholders have the right to vote on matters presented to them at company meetings. This would include the right to vote on proposed dividends and other matters, such as the appointment, or reappointment, of directors.

The votes are normally allocated on the basis of **one share = one vote**. The votes are cast in one of two ways:

- The individual shareholder can attend the company meeting and vote.
- The individual shareholder can appoint someone else to vote on his behalf – this is commonly referred to as '**voting by proxy**'.

6. Risks of Owning Shares

Shares are generally considered to be relatively high-risk, but have the potential for high returns when a company is successful.

The main risks associated with holding shares can be classified under the following three headings.

6.1 Price Risk

Price risk is the risk that share prices in general might fall. Even though the company involved might maintain dividend payments, investors could face a loss of capital. Price risk can be illustrated by looking at the behaviour of the equity market over the past 25 years or so.

On 19 October 1987 worldwide equities once fell by nearly 20% in a single day, with some shares falling by even more than this. That is generally referred to as 'Black Monday' and the Dow Jones Industrial Average (DJIA)

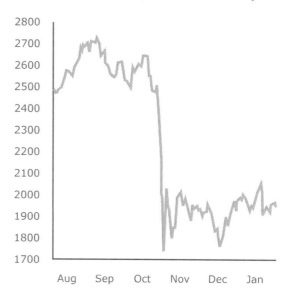

Dow Jones (Jul 1987–Jan 1988)

index of large US company shares fell by 22.3% on that day, wiping US$500 billion off share prices. Markets in every country around the world followed suit and collapsed in the similar fashion. Central banks intervened to prevent a depression and a banking crisis and, remarkably, the markets recovered much of their losses quite quickly from the worst-ever, one-day crash.

After the 1987 crash, global equity markets resumed an upward trend driven by computer technology. The arrival of the internet age sparked suggestions that a new economy was in development and led to a surge in internet stocks. Many of these stocks were quoted on the NASDAQ exchange, where share prices rapidly increased in the period leading up to the year 2000. This led the Chairman of the Federal Reserve to describe investor behaviour as 'irrational exuberance'.

By early 2000, reality started to settle in and the 'dot.com' bubble was firmly popped, with prices of NASDAQ company shares crashing. Economies went into recession and heralded the decline in world stock markets, which continued in many of them until 2003.

The markets then had a period of growth, until the sub-prime crisis and credit crunch brought about another fall in stock markets.

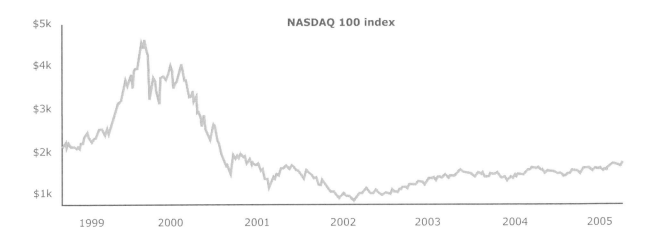

In 2008, indices of share prices in the US and the UK exhibited the size of the collapse as the NASDAQ composite index of NASDAQ listed shares had its worst-ever fall, declining by 40.54% over the year, the Dow Jones Industrial Average index of the largest US companies fell 33.84%, and the FTSE 100 index of the biggest UK listed companies tumbled 31% in the largest annual drop seen since its launch in 1984. At the time of writing, more recent falls have been attributed to the crisis in the eurozone that has seen Ireland, Portugal, Greece and Italy requiring international assistance.

As well as general collapses in prices, any single company can experience dramatic falls in its share price when it discloses bad news, such as the loss of a major contract. Again, the recent oil spill problems for BP provide a good example, where in the month or so following the announcement of the spill, BP's shares had fallen by more than 50% of their value before the problems were announced.

However, price risk does vary between companies: certain so-called 'defensive' shares, such as utility companies and general retailers tend to exhibit less price risk than many other companies. It takes something pretty major to stop households using gas and electricity or doing their weekly shop at the supermarket, so the shares in such companies do not tend to move in price as much as others.

6.2 Liquidity Risk

Liquidity risk is the risk that shares may be difficult to sell at a reasonable price or traded quickly enough in the market to prevent a loss. It essentially occurs when it is difficult to find a buyer willing to purchase the shares.

This typically occurs in respect of shares in 'thinly traded' companies – private companies that are not often bought and sold, or those public companies that may be listed, but in which there is not much trading activity.

Liquidity risk can also feature, to a lesser degree, when share prices in general are falling. In such circumstances the spread between the bid price (the price at which dealers will buy shares) and the offer price (the price at which dealers will sell shares) may become larger.

⚙ Example

Prices for ABC plc shares might be 720–722p on a normal day. This means investors can buy the shares for 722p each (at the dealer's offer price), and they can sell the shares to the dealer for 720p each (the dealer's bid price).

To begin to see a capital gain, an investor who buys shares (at 722p) needs the price to rise so that the bid (the price at which he could sell) has risen by more than 2p (eg, from 720 to 723p).

If there was a general market downturn, the dealer will reduce his prices and he might also widen the price spread to, say, 700–720p to deter sellers. An investor wanting to sell would be forced to accept the much lower price of 700p.

Unsurprisingly, shares in smaller companies tend to have a greater liquidity risk than shares in larger companies – with these smaller companies also tending to have a wider price spread between bid and offer prices than larger, more actively traded companies.

6.3 Issuer Risk

This is the risk that the issuing company collapses and the ordinary shares become worthless.

In general, it is very unlikely that larger, well-established companies will collapse, so the risk could be viewed as very small and insignificant. However, recent events such as the collapse of household names like Northern Rock, HBOS, Bradford & Bingley and Woolworths show that the risk is a real and present one and cannot be ignored.

Furthermore, shares in newer companies, especially those that have not yet managed to report profits, may have a substantial issuer risk.

6.4 Foreign Exchange Risk

This is the risk that currency price movements will have a negative effect on the value of an investment.

⚙ Example

A UK investor may buy 1,000 US shares today at, say, $1 per share when the exchange rate is $1:£0.65. This would give a total cost of $1,000 or £650 ignoring dealing costs. Let's say that the shares rise to $1.2 per share and the investor sells their holding for $1,200 and so has made a gain of 20% in dollar terms. if

the exchange rate changes, however, the full amount of this gain might not be realised. if the dollar has weakened to, say, $1:£0.60, then the proceeds of sale when they are converted back into sterling would only be worth £720, a gain of only 10.8%.

Currency movements can therefore wipe out or reduce a gain, but equally can enhance a gain if the currency movement is in the opposite direction.

7. Corporate Actions

In simple terms, a corporate action is where a company (a corporate entity) does something that affects its investors, such as its shareholders. An obvious example is the payment of a dividend and many companies pay dividends to their shareholders twice a year.

Corporate actions can be classified into three types:

1. A **mandatory corporate action** gives the investors no choice. It is obligatory and mandated by the company, and does not require any intervention from the investors. The most obvious example of a mandatory corporate action is the payment of a dividend, since all shareholders automatically receive the dividend. Shareholders do not have to apply for the dividend.

2. A **mandatory corporate action with options** has an element of choice. It is an action that has some sort of default option that will occur if the shareholder does not intervene by selecting another option. Until the date at which the mandatory default option occurs, the individual shareholders are given the choice to select another option. Two examples of mandatory with options corporate actions are the rights issue (detailed below) and a dividend in the form of cash or additional shares. In the latter situation, the shareholder can choose whether he would prefer more shares or cash by a set deadline. If he does not express a preference by the deadline, he will typically receive his dividend in cash.

3. A **voluntary corporate action** gives the investor a choice. It is an action that requires the shareholder to make a decision. An example is where another company is bidding to takeover the company (a takeover bid). To achieve the takeover the bidding company needs the shareholders of the company being bid for, to agree to sell their shares – each individual shareholder needs to choose whether to accept the offer or not.

This classification is the one that is used throughout Europe and by the international central securities depositories Euroclear and Clearstream. It should be noted that, in the US, corporate actions are simply divided into two classifications: voluntary and mandatory. The major difference between the two is therefore the existence of the category of mandatory events with options. In the US these types of events are split into two or more different events that have to be processed.

7.1 Securities Ratios

Before we look at various types of corporate action, it is necessary to know how the terms of a corporate action, such as a rights issue or bonus issue are expressed – a securities ratio. When a corporate action is announced, the terms of the event will specify what is to happen. This could be as simple as the amount of dividend that is to be paid per share. For

other events, the terms will announce how many new shares the holder is entitled to receive for each existing share that they hold.

So, for example, a company might announce a bonus issue whereby it gives new shares to its investors in proportion to the shares it already holds. The terms of the bonus issue may be expressed as 1:4, which means that the investor will receive one new share for each existing four shares held. This is the standard approach used in European and Asian markets and can be simply remembered by always expressing the terms as the investor will receive 'X new shares for each Y existing shares'.

The approach differs in the US. The first number in the securities ratio indicates the final holding after the event; the second number is the original number of shares held. The above example expressed in US terms would be 5:4. so, for example, if a US company announced a 5:4 bonus issue and the investor held 10,000 shares, then the investor would end up with 12,500 shares.

7.2 Rights Issues

A company may wish to raise additional finance by issuing shares. This might be to provide funds to grow the company, Ryanair buying a new fleet of aircraft for example. In such circumstances, it is common for a company to approach its existing shareholders with an offer to buy some more shares. This is often termed a 'cash call' – they have already bought some shares in the company, so would they like to buy some more?

The announcement of a rights issue is not always greeted positively.

The initial response to the announcement of a planned rights issue will reflect the market's view of the scheme. If it is to finance expansion, and the strategy makes sense to the investors, the share price could well rise. If investors have a negative view of why a rights issue is being made (eg, to hastily find the cash to solve an issue that the directors perhaps should have anticipated), the share price could fall.

UK company law gives a series of protections to existing shareholders. As already stated, shareholders have pre-emptive rights – the right to buy shares so that their proportionate holding is not diluted. A rights issue is an offer of new shares to existing shareholders, in proportion to their initial holdings. It is an offer and each shareholder has a choice, but if they fail to make a choice the company can sell the right to buy the shares to someone else, paying the proceeds to the shareholder. So the rights issue is an example of a 'mandatory with options' type of corporate action.

As an example of a rights issue, the company might offer shareholders the right that for every four shares owned, they can buy one more at a specified price that is at a discount to the current market price, as shown below.

⚙ Example

ABC plc has 100 million shares in issue, currently trading at £4.00 each.

To raise finance for expansion, it decides to offer its existing shareholders the right to buy one new share for every four previously held. This would be described as a 1 for 4 rights issue.

The price of the rights would be set at a discount to the prevailing market price, at say £2.00.

Each shareholder is given choices as to how to proceed following a rights issue. For an individual holding four shares in ABC plc, he could:

- *Take up the rights, by paying the £2.00 and increasing his holding in ABC plc to five shares.*
- *Sell the rights on to another investor. The rights entitlement is transferable (often described as 'renounceable') and will have a value because it enables the purchase of a share at the discounted price of £2.00.*

- *Do nothing. If the investor chooses this option, the company's advisers will sell the rights at the best available price and pass on the proceeds (after charges) to the shareholder.*

The share price of the investor's existing shares will also adjust to reflect the additional shares that are being issued. So, in the example above, the investor originally had four shares priced at £4 each, worth £16, and can acquire one new share at £2.00. Assuming the rights are taken up by the investor, he will have five shares worth £18 or £3.60 each. So, logic suggests that the share price after the rights issue will be £3.60.

This adjusted share price of £3.60 is known as the 'theoretical ex-rights price' – it is theoretical as the actual price will depend upon the interaction of buyers and sellers in the market at the time and 'ex-rights' simply means after the rights issue has happened.

As mentioned above, the rights can be sold and the price is known as the premium. If the theoretical ex-rights price is £3.60 and a new share can be acquired for £2.00, then the right to acquire that share has a value. That value is the premium and should be approximately £1.60 (the difference between the £3.60 the shares will be worth and the £2.00 required to buy them).

The initial response to the announcement of a planned rights issue will reflect the market's view of the scheme. if it is to finance expansion, and the strategy makes sense to the investors, the share price could well rise. if investors have a very negative view of why a rights issue is being made (eg, to fund activities that investors view negatively) and what it says for the future of the company, the share price can fall substantially.

This was seen with HBOS and RBS where the price of shares on the open market fell below the discounted rights issue price. The rights issues were flops and the underwriters ended up having to take up the new shares.

Underwriters of a share issue agree, for a fee, to buy any portion of the issue not taken up in the market at the issue price. The underwriters then sell the shares they have bought when market conditions seem opportune to them, and may make a gain or a loss on this sale. The underwriters agree to buy the shares if no one else will, and the company's investment bank will probably underwrite some of the issue itself.

The company and their investment banking advisers will have to consider the numbers carefully. If the price at which new shares are offered is too high, the cash call might flop. This would be embarrassing – and potentially costly for any institution that has underwritten the issue.

7.3 Bonus Issues

A bonus issue (also known as a '**scrip**' or '**capitalisation**' issue) is a corporate action where the company gives existing shareholders extra shares without their having to pay anything.

The company is simply increasing the number of shares held by each shareholder, and it is an example of a mandatory corporate action. Again, it is useful to look at an example.

⚙ Example

XYZ plc's shares currently trade at £12.00 each.

The company decided to make a 1 for 1 bonus issue, giving the shareholders an additional share for each share they currently hold.

The result is that a single shareholder who held one share worth £12.00 now has two shares worth the same amount in total. As the number of shares has doubled, the share price halves to £6.00.

Why do companies have bonus issues? The reason generally cited is that the bonus issue will increase the liquidity of the company's shares in the market because it brings about a lower share price. This is based on the view that psychologically a company's share price can become too high, making the shares less attractive to investors. Traditionally, most large UK companies have tried to keep their share prices below £10 for this reason. For example, several years ago HSBC shares were trading at about £21 and were subject to a 2:1 scrip issue (two new shares for every one previously held), that saw the share price fall to £7.

7.4 Dividends

The payment of a dividend is an example of a mandatory corporate action. The dividend represents the part of a company's profit that is passed to its shareholders.

Dividends for many large UK companies are paid twice a year, with the first dividend being declared by the directors and paid approximately halfway through the year (commonly referred to as the 'interim dividend'). The second dividend is paid after approval by shareholders at the company's AGM, held after the end of the company's financial year and is referred to as the 'final dividend' for the year. The amount paid per share may vary, as it depends on on factors such as the overall profitability of the company and any plans it might have for future expansion.

The individual shareholders will receive the dividends either by cheque, or by the money being transferred straight into their bank accounts.

A practical difficulty, especially in a large company where shares change hands frequently, is determining the correct person to receive dividends. So, procedures have been established to minimise the extent that people receive dividends they are not entitled to, or fail to receive the dividend to which they are entitled.

Shares are bought and sold with the right to receive the next declared dividend up to the date shortly before the dividend payment is made. Up to that point the shares are described as '**cum-dividend**' ('cum' is the Latin word for 'with'). If the shares are purchased cum-dividend, the purchaser will receive the declared dividend. At a certain point between the declaration date and the dividend payment date, the shares go '**ex-dividend**' ('ex' is the Latin word for 'without'). Buyers of shares when they are ex-dividend are not entitled to the declared dividend. The following example illustrates a typical sequence of events leading up to the payment of a dividend.

⚙ Example

The sequence of events might be as follows:

Holding plc is listed on the London Stock Exchange. Holding plc calculates its interim profits (for the six months to 30 June) and decides to pay a dividend of 8p per share. It announces ('declares') the dividend on 16 August and states that it will be paid to those shareholders who are entered on the shareholders' register on Friday 12 October.

This latter date (always on a Friday) is variously known as the:

- *record date;*
- *register date; or*
- *books closed date.*

Given the record date of Friday 12 October, the LSE sets the ex-dividend date as Wednesday 10 October.

The ex-dividend date is invariably a Wednesday, and on this day the shares will go ex-dividend and should fall in price by 8p. This is because any new buyers of Holding plc's shares will not be entitled to the dividend.

The actual payment of the dividend will then be made to those shareholders on the register at the record date at a later specified date, say Wednesday 24 October.

Why is the ex-dividend date a Wednesday? Well, the settlement timetable for equity trades in London is that the shares are transferred to the buyer, and the money is paid to the seller three business days after day of the trade ('T+3'). So if an investor (Jack Jones) purchased shares in Holding plc on Tuesday 9 October, he would be purchasing cum-dividend and his name would be entered into the shareholders' register three business days later on Friday 12 October. It is the register at the end of this date that is used as basis for payment of the dividend, so Jack will get the dividend he is entitled to.

In contrast, if another investor (Cassie Smith) purchased shares in Holding plc on Tuesday 9 October, she would be purchasing ex-dividend and her name would be entered into the shareholders' register three business days later on Monday 15 October. This is after the record date, so Cassie will not get the dividend.

7.5 Takeovers and Mergers

Companies seeking to expand can grow organically or by buying other companies. In a takeover, one company (the predator) seeks to acquire another company (the target). A relatively recent example was the purchase of Cadbury plc by the US food giant Kraft Foods.

The two parties to a takeover are the company bidding to buy the other, usually referred to as the 'predator' company, and the company that is being bid for, usually described as the 'target' company. In the above example Kraft Foods is the predator and Cadbury is the target.

Takeovers can be friendly or hostile. A friendly takeover is where the directors of the target company consider the terms of the takeover bid to be acceptable, and recommend acceptance to their shareholders. The Kraft Cadbury bid was a friendly takeover as the directors recommended that Cadbury's shareholders accepted, and ultimately the bid was successful. Success is generally where the predator company manages to buy more than 50% of the shares of the target company – where the predator holds more than half of the shares of the target company, the predator is described as having 'gained control' of the target company. However, the predator company will usually look to buy all of the shares in the target company, perhaps for cash, perhaps in exchange for some of its own shares, or a mixture of cash and shares (as in the Kraft bid for Cadbury).

In contrast, a hostile takeover is one where the directors of the target company consider the terms of the offer are not attractive, perhaps undervaluing the target. As a result, the directors will recommend that their shareholders reject the offer. However, given that the shareholders can choose whether to accept or reject the bid (it is a voluntary corporate action), a hostile takeover bid can still be successful.

A **merger** is a similar transaction to a takeover. However the term 'merger' is reserved for situations where two companies of similar size come together to form a single, larger entity. The two companies agree to merge their interests. In a merger it is usual for one company to exchange new shares for the shares of the other entity. A recent example is the merger between British Airways and the Spanish airline Iberia to create the International Airline Group.

⚙ Answers to Chapter Exercises

⚙ Exercise 1

Which of the following three companies would NOT be eligible to list on the LSE?

1) Langley Property Rentals plc – Ineligible for listing because it has only been revenue generating for two years. Companies need a revenue earning period of at least three years.

   - *Established five years ago.*
   - *First rental properties acquired two years ago.*
   - *100% of revenues from property rentals.*
   - *Directors, associates and significant share-holders own 70% of the shares.*
   - *Expected market cap £2 million.*

2) Kelsey Market Research Ltd – Ineligible because it is a private (Ltd) company rather than a public (plc) company.

   - *Established ten years ago.*
   - *Company has been trading profitably since second year of operation.*
   - *85% of revenues from market research.*
   - *Has sufficient working capital for 14 months of operations.*

3) Eden Park IT Services Plc – Eligible for listing

   - *Established four years ago.*
   - *75% of revenues from IT services.*
   - *Been trading profitably from company's inception.*
   - *Directors, associates and significant share-holders own 25% of the shares.*
   - *Expected market cap £1 million.*

Learning Objectives

Chapter Three has covered the following Learning Objectives.

4.1 Equities

 Lesson 06

4.1.1 Know how a company is formed and the differences between private and public companies

 Lesson 06 and Lesson 18

4.1.2 Know the features and benefits of ordinary and preference shares: dividend; capital gain; share benefits; right to subscribe for new shares; right to vote

Lesson 06, Lesson 19 (dividend; capital gain, share benefits), Lesson 20 (right to vote), Lesson 22 (right to subscribe for new shares)

4.1.3 Understand the advantages, disadvantages and risks associated with owning shares: price risk; liquidity risk; issuer risk

Lesson 06 and Lesson 21

4.1.4 Know the definition of a corporate action and the difference between mandatory, voluntary and mandatory with options

Lesson 22

4.1.5 Understand the following terms: bonus/scrip/capitalisation issues; rights issues; dividend payments; takeover/merger

Lesson 19 (bonus/scrip/capitalisation issues; dividend payments), Lesson 22 (rights issues; takeover/merger)

4.1.6 Know the purpose and format of annual general meetings and extraordinary general meetings

Lesson 20

4.1.7 Know the difference between the primary market and secondary market

Lesson 24

4.1.10 Know the advantages and disadvantages of a company obtaining a listing of its shares

Lesson 24

Based on what you have learned in Chapter Three, try to answer the following end of chapter questions.

End of Chapter Questions

Think of an answer for each question and refer to the appropriate section for confirmation.

1. What are the two constitutional documents required in order to set up a UK company? And with whom must they be lodged?

    Answer Reference: Section 2.1

    ....

    ....

2. What are the two types of company?

    Answer Reference: Section 2.2

    ....

    ....

3. What are the two types of meeting called by companies and what are the two types of resolution that can be considered at these meetings?

    Answer Reference: Section 2.3

    ....

    ....

4. How does the primary market differ from the secondary market?

    Answer Reference: Section 3.1

    ....

    ....

5. What are the key advantages and disadvantages of becoming a listed company?

    Answer Reference: Section 3.2

    ....

    ....

6. How long does a company need to have been established to qualify for a listing in the UK?

   Answer Reference: Section 3.3

   ....

   ....

7. What is AIM? And what two appointments are required of AIM companies?

   Answer Reference: Section 3.4

   ....

   ....

8. What are the two possible types of shares?

   Answer Reference: Section 4.1

   ....

   ....

9. What are the key benefits of owning shares?

   Answer Reference: Section 5

   ....

   ....

10. What is a 'naked' dividend?

    Answer Reference: Section 5

    ....

    ....

11. What is a pre-emptive right?

    Answer Reference: Section 5.4.1

    ....

    ....

12. What are the three main types of risk faced by equity investors?

    Answer Reference: Section 6

    ....

    ....

13. What are the three types of corporate action?

    Answer Reference: Section 7

    ....

    ....

14. What is a rights issue?

    Answer Reference: Section 7.2

    ....

    ....

15. What is a bonus issue?

    Answer Reference: Section 7.3

    ....

    ....

16. What is most likely to happen to the price when a share goes ex-dividend?

    Answer Reference: Section 7.4

    ....

    ....

17. How does a merger differ from a takeover?

    Answer Reference: Section 7.5

    ....

    ....

Securities & Investment (Schools and Colleges)

4

Equities Trading and Settlement

Equities Trading and Settlement

1. Introduction

This chapter follows on from Chapter 3 by considering how equities are bought and sold. This is primarily done through stock exchanges and this chapter begins by looking at some of the world's most important stock exchanges and the use of share indices. This is followed by focusing in greater detail on how shares are traded on the London Stock Exchange, including the way deals are settled.

2. World Stock Markets

Stock exchanges, alternatively referred to as stock markets, have been around for hundreds of years. They began simply as meeting places where investors gathered to discuss companies and their shares, and to trade shares. As they became more formal, these meeting places became the trading floors of exchanges, where traders made deals face to face. At certain times, these floors became very noisy and busy and the trading was therefore described as '**open outcry**'. Today, many of these exchange floors have been replaced by sophisticated electronic dealing systems run on computer systems that now operate in major cities throughout the world.

As already seen, companies with shares traded on an exchange are said to be '**listed**'. Before they are admitted as listed companies, they must meet specific criteria. The requirements for the London Stock Exchange have already been encountered, and similar criteria exist across the various exchanges of the world.

Below is a brief review of some of the world's most important stock exchanges.

2.1 United States

Almost half of all stock exchange activity takes place in the US, particularly through two major exchanges – The New York Stock Exchange (NYSE) and NASDAQ. These exchanges do not just list and trade the shares of US companies, they are also involved in trading the shares of many major international companies. An example is the Japanese motor manufacturer Honda.

2.1.1 New York Stock Exchange (NYSE) – NYSE Euronext

The NYSE, operated by NYSE Euronext, is the largest stock exchange in the world, as measured by its market capitalisation. It is located in Wall Street in Manhattan, New York City. Market capitalisation is the total value of all the shares listed on the exchange and below is a recent league table of the world's biggest exchanges by market capitalisation.

The NYSE is significantly larger than any other exchange worldwide based on market capitalisation. However, it trails NASDAQ for the number of companies listed on it, but because many of the NASDAQ companies relatively small, the NYSE is comfortably larger in terms of the value of shares traded.

The NYSE is one of the few major stock exchanges that continues to use a trading floor and 'open outcry' trading. The NYSE trading involves member firms acting as auctioneers to bring buyers and sellers together, a process known as the **continuous auction format**. However since more than 50% of its order flow is now delivered to the floor electronically, it is effectively a hybrid structure combining elements of open outcry and electronic markets.

NYSE merged with Euronext in 2007 to create the world's largest and most liquid exchange group, called NYSE Euronext.

2.1.2 NASDAQ

NASDAQ, once an acronym for the National Association of Securities Dealers Automated Quotation system, is an electronic stock exchange with around 3,200 companies listed on it. It is the third-largest stock exchange in the world by market capitalisation and has the second-largest trading volume.

There is a variety of companies traded on the NASDAQ exchange, but it is particularly well

Source: © Copyright 2011, The NASDAQ OMX Group, Inc.
Reprinted with permission.

Securities & Investment (Schools and Colleges)

known for being a high-tech exchange – that is, many of the companies listed on it are telecoms, media or technology companies such as the software giant Microsoft as well as companies like Cisco Systems and Logitech. It remains a popular exchange for many new, high-growth and volatile stocks.

It is an electronic exchange, with trades undertaken through **market makers**. These market makers provide prices at which brokers can purchase shares from them, or sell shares to them. These are the market maker's buy and sell prices, alternatively known as bid and ask prices. Below is a NASDAQ trading screen for Cisco Systems where Prudential Securities (PRUS) is one of the market makers. It is willing to buy shares for $110 and five sixteenths of a dollar, and sell shares for $110 and seven sixteenths of a dollar. Clearly every time it does buy and sell at these prices, Prudential will make two sixteenths of a dollar for each share.

2.2 Europe

Europe accounts for a number of the top world exchanges, particularly the London Stock Exchange, Euronext and the Deutsche Börse.

2.2.1 London Stock Exchange (LSE)

The LSE is the most important exchange in Europe and one of the largest in the world. It has over 3,000 companies listed on it and is the most international of all exchanges, with 350 of the companies coming from 50 different countries.

Its main trading system is **SETS** (the Stock Exchange Trading Service), an automated trading system that operates on an **order-driven basis**. This means that when a buy and sell price match, an order is automatically executed.

For securities that trade less regularly, the LSE uses the **SETSqx** (the Stock Exchange Trading Service – quotes and crosses) and **SEAQ** (the Stock Exchange Automated Quotation)

systems, where **market makers** keep the shares liquid.

The LSE is also the majority shareholder in MTS, the electronic exchange that dominates trading in the European government bond market. The MTS market model uses a common trading platform, while corporate governance and market supervision are based on the respective national regulatory regimes.

Each of these systems will be covered in more detail later in this Chapter.

2.2.2 NYSE Euronext (NYX)

As mentioned above, the New York Stock Exchange (NYSE) and Euronext merged in 2007.

NYSE Euronext is a cross-border exchange that operates equity, bond and derivatives markets (NYSE Liffe) in Belgium, France, the UK (derivatives only), the Netherlands and Portugal.

NYSE Euronext provides listing and trading facilities for a range of instruments including equities and bonds and for other products such as investment funds. It is an order-driven market and equities and bonds are traded via a harmonised order book so that all listed stocks from the five NYSE Euronext European countries are included on a single trading platform that operates in the same way in each country.

2.2.3 Deutsche Börse

Deutsche Börse is the main German exchange operator and provides services that include securities and derivatives trading, transaction settlement and the provision of market information, as well as the development and operation of electronic trading systems.

Xetra is Deutsche Börse's electronic trading system for the cash market, and matches buy and sell orders from licensed traders in a central, fully electronic order book.

In May 2011, floor trading at the Frankfurt Stock Exchange migrated to Xetra technology. The new Xetra Specialist trading model combines the advantages of fully electronic trading – especially in the speed of order execution – with the benefits of trading through Specialists who ensure that equities remain liquid and continually tradable. The machine fixes the price, the Specialists supervise it; investors benefit from faster order processing.

Deutsche Börse also owns Clearstream, an international central securities depositary. Clearstream offers integrated banking, custody and settlement services for the trading of shares and bonds.

2.3 Asia

2.3.1 Tokyo Stock Exchange (TSE)

The Tokyo Stock Exchange (TSE) is one of five exchanges in Japan, and is undoubtedly one of the more important world exchanges.

The TSE uses an electronic, continuous auction system of trading. This means that brokers place orders online and, when a buy and sell price match, the trade is automatically executed. Deals are made directly between buyer and seller, rather than through a market maker. The TSE uses price controls so that the price of a stock cannot rise above or fall below a certain point throughout the day. These 'circuit breaker' controls are used to prevent dramatic swings in prices that may lead to market uncertainty or stock crashes. If a major swing in price occurs, the exchange will stop trading in that stock for a specified period of time.

3. Stock Market Indices

The media constantly provides details of stock indices like the FTSE 100 (the 'Footsie' 100) and the Dow Jones Industrial Average. These stock indices provide a snapshot of how share prices are performing in a particular stock market, or across several markets. They can measure price movements across the following:

- A selection of shares from several different stock markets around the world.
- All shares listed on a single stock market.
- A selection of shares from a single stock market, perhaps:
  - shares classified according to the size of the company (its market capitalisation).
- Large cap.
- Mid cap.
- Small cap:
  - shares classified according to business type.
- Industrials.
- Utilities.
- Pharmaceuticals, etc:
  - shares classified according to business philosophy.
- 'Green' stocks (following sustainable, environmental friendly policies).
- Sin free' stocks (avoiding earnings from alcohol, tobacco, gambling and weapons).

A stock index calculates the aggregate price movement of its targeted stocks on a daily basis, providing a single figure for ease of comparison.

These stock indices are useful because it is very difficult for investors to gauge the overall performance of the market by looking at individual share price movements. On a given day some shares may have moved up sharply, others may have moved down sharply and some sector specific news may have had a strong influence on particular shares that are active in that sector. A stock index will smooth out these anomalies and provide a consistent picture of the mood across the market.

This is illustrated in the charts opposite.

In addition to providing a snapshot of how share prices are progressing across the whole group of constituent companies, stock indices also provide a benchmark for investors, allowing them to assess whether their portfolios of

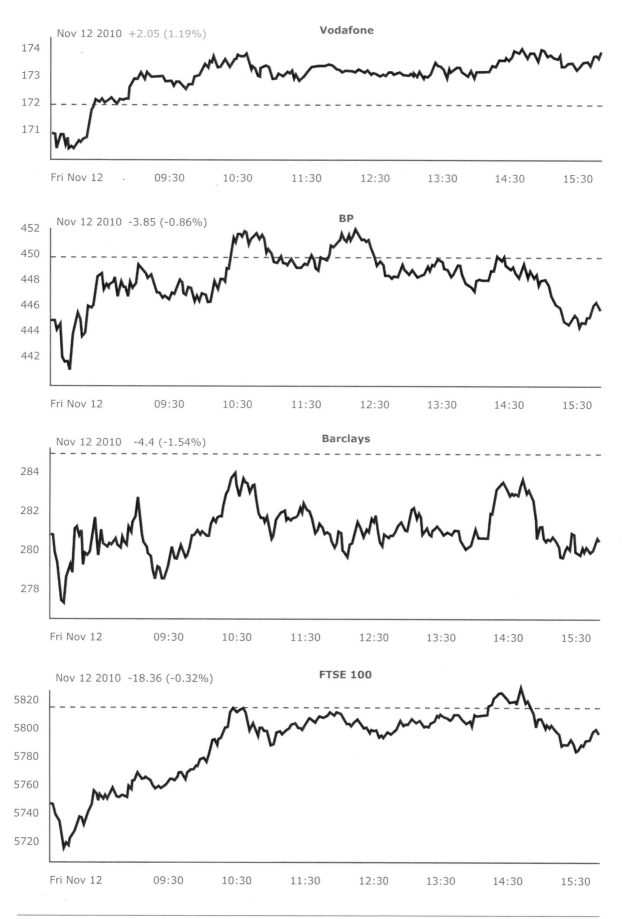

Country	Name	Number of stocks
US	Dow Jones Industrial Average (DJIA or 'The Dow'): Providing a narrow view of the US stock market	30
US	Standard & Poor's 500 (S&P 500): Providing a wider view of the US stock market	500
US	NASDAQ Composite: Focusing on the shares traded on NASDAQ, including many technology companies	3,000+
Japan	Nikkei 225	225
France	CAC 40	40
Germany	Xetra DAX	30
Hong Kong/ China	Hang Seng	58

shares are doing better (outperforming) or worse (underperforming) than the market in general.

3.1 UK Indices

In the UK, the indices are provided by FTSE International, originally a joint venture between the Financial Times and the London Stock Exchange. The relevant indices in the UK are:

- **FTSE 100** – this is an index of the largest 100 UK companies, commonly referred to as the 'Footsie'. The Footsie covers about 70% of the UK market by value.
- **FTSE 250** – an index of the next 250 medium- or middle-sized (mid cap) companies below the 100.
- **FTSE 350** – a combination of the 100 and the 250 indices. The 350 is broken down into industry sectors, for example, retailing and transport.
- **FTSE All Share** – this index covers over 800 companies (including the FTSE 350) and accounts for about 98% of the UK market by value. It is often used as the benchmark against which diversified share portfolios are assessed.

Reviews of the 100, 250 and, therefore, the 350 are carried out every three months. Companies whose share price has grown strongly, and whose market capitalisation has increased significantly, will replace those whose price and, hence, market capitalisation is static or falling. The FTSE All Share Index is reviewed quarterly.

3.2 World Indices

Some of the other main indices that are regularly quoted in the financial press are shown in the table above.

4. Trading on the LSE

As already discussed, stock markets (alternatively referred to as stock exchanges) began as informal meeting places where investors congregated to swap information and to trade shares face-to-face. The LSE has been operating for over 300 years with its origins being gathering of investors in the coffee houses in the City of London in the 17th century. Throughout its history, the LSE's trading methods have evolved and face-to-face trading stopped around 25 years ago.

Example of a SETS screen

Last traded price including time and volume

Normal market size

Company Name

Trade Type Indicator of last published trade

Company Code

Volume Weighted Average price of today's trading

Previous days closing price

Currency
GBX = pence
GBP = pounds
EUR = euros

International Security Number (ISIN)

Last five traded prices

Highest and lowest prices of the day on and off the order book

Total volume traded

Number of buy orders at the best price

Total volumes of buy orders

Buy market order volume

Volume at best bid price

Cumulative order book price & volume information

Buy order

The auction match price; if no auction match price the next automatic trade

Order price per share

Best bid/offer (the spread)

Sell order

Sell market order volume

Total of shares traded yesterday

Total of today's shares traded

Total of today's shares traded (order book only)

Number of sell orders at the best price

Total volume of sell orders

Volume at best offer price

ABC Holdings	ABC			P Close	517½	GBX
NMS 200,000		Segment SET1	Sector FT10	ISIN GB012345678		
				TVol		8.50m
Last	524½ AT	at 11:06	Vol 3,952			
Prev	524 525AT	524¼AT 524	524			
Trade Hi 530		Open	520	Total Vol	4.61m	
Trade Lo 517		VWAP	527	SETS Vol	2.58m	

	TVol 543,906		Base 520		TVol 707,746	
BUY	MOVol				MOVol	SELL
1	20,000		524 – 525		10,000	2
524.00	20,000	20,000	524 525	10,000	10,000	525.00
523.62	77,780	57,780	523½ 525½	21,900	31,900	525.34
523.38	138,785	61,005	523 526	50,000	81,900	525.74
522.88	188,785	50,000	521 526½	20,000	101,900	525.80
521.49	189,185	400	519 529	50,000	151,900	526.25

Source: London Stock Exchange

Today, the LSE is one of the most important stock exchanges in Europe and one of the largest in the world. It is also the most international of all exchanges with more than 3,000 companies listed, of which around 350 companies are incorporated outside the UK from 50 different countries.

4.1 SETS

The main trading system of the LSE is referred to as SETS – the Stock Exchange Trading Service. It is an automated trading system that operates on an order-driven basis. In other words, orders from investors wishing to buy particular shares and orders from investors wishing to sell particular shares are posted onto the system. As soon as a buy price and a sell price match, the order is automatically executed.

The diagram above is an example of a SETS screen. In this system, LSE member firms (investment banks and brokers) input orders via computer terminals. These orders may be for the member firms themselves, or for their clients.

Very simply, the way the system operates is that these orders will be added to the 'buy queue' or the 'sell queue', or executed immediately. Investors who add their order to the relevant queue are prepared to hold out for the price they want. Those seeking immediate execution will trade against the queue of buyers (if they are selling) or against the sellers' queue (if they are buying).

For large actively traded shares like those of the telecoms company Vodafone, there will be a 'deep' order book – the term 'deep' implies that there are lots of orders waiting to be dealt on either side. The top of the queues might look like the table overleaf.

Queue priority is given on the basis of price and then time.

So, for the equally priced orders noted (note 1), the order to buy 19,250 shares must have been placed before the 44,000 order – hence

Buy Queue		Sell Queue	
We will buy the following number of shares for a maximum price of:		We will buy the following number of shares for a minimum price of:	
7,000 shares	£1.24	3,500 shares	£1.25
5,150 shares	£1.23	1,984 shares (2)	£1.26
19,250 shares (1)	£1.22	75,397 shares (2)	£1.26
44,000 shares (1)	£1.22	17,300 shares	£1.27

its position higher up the queue. Similarly, for the orders noted (2), the order to sell 1,984 shares must have been input before the order to sell 75,397 shares.

4.2 SETSqx

Not all shares have sufficient liquidity for SETS, which clearly requires plenty of buy and sell orders to work effectively. So, the London Stock Exchange has an alternative system for shares where the volume of shares traded is low. Less liquid securities that are not traded on the SETS order book are traded on SETSqx, which stands for Stock Exchange Electronic

Trading Service – quotes and crosses. This combines periodic auctions with quotes from market makers so that trading can take place throughout the trading day. The periodic auctions happen at set times during the day. They give interested investors the chance to post orders with prices at which they will buy or sell and the system 'uncrosses' the orders to maximise the number of shares that can be traded at a single price. The market-maker is required to ensure that trading in the shares is reasonably liquid by providing buy (bid) and sell (ask or offer) prices.

An example of a SETSqx screen is shown below.

Example of a SETSqx screen

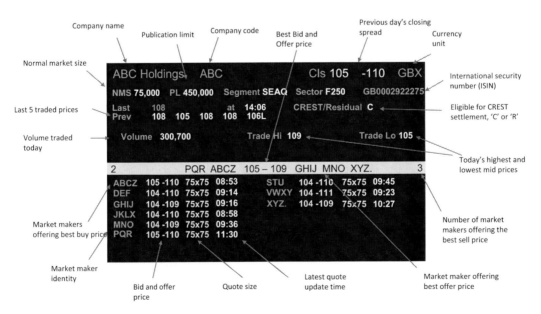

Source: London Stock Exchange

An investor wanting to buy shares in 'ABC Holdings' would be able to buy them from the market maker at the offer price of 109p. An investor wanting to sell ABC Holdings' shares would be able to sell them at 105p each, the market maker's bid price. Evidently, every time the market maker does a deal buying shares at 105p each and selling them at 109p each, he will make 4p per share. This is commonly referred to as the 'bid-offer spread'.

Alternatively investors wanting to buy and sell could post their orders in the hope that they will be matched in the next auction.

4.3 SEAQ

Securities that are not traded on either of the above platforms are traded using another LSE trading platform – SEAQ.

SEAQ is an acronym for Stock Exchange Automated Quotation. Each security has a page on which LSE member firms can choose to be market makers displaying their 'quoted prices', the prices at which they are willing to buy (the 'bid prices'), the prices at which they are willing to sell (the 'offer prices') and the sizes of transaction in which they are willing to deal.

In the same way as the market maker quotes on SETSqx, the SEAQ screens can be thought of as advertisements of prices and quantities. Deals are done when a member firm reacts to the advertised prices and contacts the market maker by telephone. The market maker has to honour the prices and quantities that it is displaying on SEAQ.

5. Clearing and Central Counterparties

Clearing is the process through which the obligations of the buyer and seller to a trade are defined and legally formalised. In simple terms, this procedure establishes what each of the counterparties expects to receive when the trade is settled. It also defines the obligations

each must fulfil, in terms of delivering securities or funds, for the trade to settle successfully.

Specifically, the clearing process includes:

- Recording key trade information so that counterparties can agree on its terms.
- Formalising the legal obligation between counterparties.
- Matching and confirming trade details.
- Agreeing procedures for settling the transaction.
- Calculating settlement obligations and sending out settlement instructions to the brokers, custodians and central securities depository (CSD).
- Managing margin and making margin calls.

Margin relates to collateral paid to the clearing agent by counterparties to guarantee their positions against default up to settlement.

Trades may be cleared and settled directly between the trading counterparties – known as **bilateral settlement**. When trades are cleared bilaterally, each trading party bears a direct credit risk against the counterparty that it trades with. Hence, it will typically bear direct liability for any losses incurred through counterparty default.

The alternative is to clear trades using a central **counterparty or CCP**. A CCP interposes itself between the counterparties to a trade, becoming the buyer to every seller and the seller to every buyer. As a result, buyer and seller interact with the CCP and remain anonymous to each other. This process is known as **novation**.

Regulators are increasingly keen to promote the use of CCPs across a wide range of financial products. While this does not eliminate the risk of institutions going into default, it does spread this risk across all participants, and makes these risks progressively easier to monitor and regulate. The risk controls extended by a CCP effectively provide an early warning system to financial regulators of impending risks and are an important tool in efforts to contain these risks within manageable limits.

6. Settlement

Settlement is the process through which legal title (ie, ownership) of a security is transferred from seller to buyer in exchange for the equivalent value in cash. Ideally, these two transfers should occur simultaneously.

6.1 Methods of Holding Title

Before exploring how purchases and sales of shares are settled – ie, how the seller gets his money and the buyer gets her shares, it is important to consider how ownership of a share is evidenced. Shares can be issued in either registered or bearer form, with the former (registered) being a lot more common than the latter (bearer).

Holding shares in registered form involves the investor's name being recorded on the share register and, often, the investor being issued with a share certificate to reflect their ownership. Below is a simplified summary of a share register and a share certificate.

It is relatively obvious from the above that for listed companies, substantial quantities of the shares are held on behalf of investors by fund managers.

The above example of a share certificate shows that is was customary for the name of the owner of the shares to be written on the share certificate. However, many companies have today 'dematerialised' their shares. In other words, they do not use physical share certificates and instead use electronic records of ownership. This is often described as issuing shares on a **non-certificated basis**.

The alternative to holding shares in registered form is to hold **bearer** shares. As the name suggests, the person who holds, or is the 'bearer' of, the shares is the owner. Ownership passes by transfer of the share certificate to the new owner. This adds a degree of risk to holding shares – loss of the certificate might equal loss of the person's investment. As a result, holding bearer shares is relatively rare, especially in the UK.

As well as being a security risk, regulatory authorities are regarded unfavourably by the regulatory authorities due to the opportunities they offer for money laundering, and evading tax. As will be developed later in this workbook, money laundering is an attempt to make criminally derived money appear legitimate.

6.2 Share Settlement

With very few exceptions, UK companies are required to maintain a **share register**. As seen, this is simply a record of all current shareholders in that company, and how many shares they each hold. The share register is kept and maintained by the company registrar, who might be an employee of the company itself or a specialist firm of registrars. Specialists in maintaining registers on behalf of companies include firms like Capita Registrars, Equiniti and Computershare.

In contrast, bearer shares which have no register are usually kept safe in authorised depositories. These can be international organisations like Euroclear, or country based depositories like Singapore's central depository.

Bearer shares kept in this way are said to be 'immobilised' in depositories.

Returning to the more common situation of shares being registered, when a shareholder sells some, or all, of his shareholding, there must be a mechanism for updating the register to reflect the new buyer and for transferring the money to the seller. This is required in order to settle the transaction – accordingly, it is described as '**settlement**'.

Historically, when each shareholder held a **share certificate** as evidence of the shares they owned, the seller sent their share certificate and a stock transfer form, providing details of the new owner, to the company registrar. Acting on these documents, the registrar would delete the seller's name and insert the name of the buyer into the register. The registrar then issued a new certificate to the buyer. This was commonly referred to as 'certificated settlement' because the completion of a transaction required the issue of a new share certificate.

Certificated settlement is cumbersome and inefficient; over the past decade most UK settlement has moved to a paperless, dematerialised (or uncertificated) form of settlement through a system called CREST.

6.3 CREST Settlement

6.3.1 Introduction

CREST is the computer-based system operated by Euroclear UK & Ireland, the central securities depository for UK and Irish equities.

Some of its key features are:

- Holdings are uncertificated, that is, share certificates are not required as evidence of transfer of ownership.
- There is real-time matching of trades, in other words, buyers and sellers are matched instantaneously.
- Settlement of transactions takes place in multiple currencies.
- Electronic transfer of title takes place on settlement.
- Settlement generates guaranteed obligations to pay cash outside CREST.
- Coverage includes shares, corporate and government bonds and other securities held in registered form.
- CREST can also handle a range of corporate actions, including dividend distributions and rights issues.

Each of these key features will be put into context as the settlement process via CREST is explored in more detail below.

6.3.2 CREST Structure

CREST offers membership and each CREST member is given a unique participant ID and at least one member account ID. The shares of different companies are held within the member's account.

Users of CREST input their instructions and receive information via one of the two electronic networks operated by BT SettleNET and SWIFT.

Shares in CREST are held in an uncertificated form in one of the following three ways:

- **Direct member** – the direct member's name will appear in the issuing company's register. Each direct member has a stock account containing records of its securities and each appoints a CREST payment bank to pay out and receive money in respect of CREST transactions. Direct members are permitted to hold more than one account, which will be useful if the direct member has several underlying clients.
- **Sponsored members** – these are generally private investors and their name will appear on the issuing company's register. A direct member will need to sponsor the membership and provide the link to CREST. The sponsor is typically a broker, fund manager or custodian who charges a fee for the service. Like a direct member, a sponsored member is also required to appoint a CREST payment bank.
- **Custodian** – where the beneficial shareholder appoints a nominee who is a direct member of CREST. The nominee holds the securities on behalf of the shareholder, through a specially designated stock account. The nominee company's name appears on the issuing company's share register, as opposed to the shareholder's name. The nominee company is typically operated by a broker, fund manager or custodian.

6.3.3 Payment Banks and Cash Memorandum Accounts

As mentioned above, CREST members are required to appoint a CREST payment bank to receive and pay out money in respect of settlements in CREST.

CREST maintains one or more **Cash Memorandum Accounts (CMAs)** for each member. The CMA can be denominated in sterling, euros or US dollars. The CMA is basically an electronic transaction ledger which shows the net balance of payments made and received at any time during the course of the settlement day.

Settlement is instantaneous and payments are made between the 'payment' banks across their accounts at the Bank of England as settlement occurs.

6.3.4 Transfers and Registers of Title

The Companies Act confers powers on the Treasury to make regulations to enable title to securities to be evidenced and transferred without the need for a written instrument.

The legal framework for the CREST settlement system was implemented by the Uncertificated Securities Regulations 1995. In 2001 further regulations eliminated the interval between settlement in CREST and transfer of legal title by entry on the share register, by introducing transfer of legal title at the point of electronic settlement, known as 'Electronic Transfer of Title' (ETT).

Under the CREST system, the 'register' of securities comprises two parts:

* CREST maintains the uncertificated part of the register – the so-called 'Operator Register of Securities'.
* The relevant issuer maintains the certificated part of the register – the Issuer Register of Securities.

When any transfer of title occurs in CREST, the CREST system will generate a Register Update Request (RUR) requiring the issuer to amend the relevant record of uncertificated shares. The issuer's Register of Uncertificated Securities is simply a duplicate of the CREST register but the combination of this and the issuer's Register of Certificated Securities means that the issuer is aware of, and can communicate with, all the holders of its securities.

6.3.5 Settlement in CREST

The diagram opposite illustrates the four stages that occur to settle a typical transaction between two counterparties in CREST.

Stage 1 – Trade Matching

The buying and selling members input instructions to CREST detailing the terms of the agreed trade.

CREST authenticates these instructions to check that they match. As long as the input data from both members is identical, CREST creates a matching transaction.

Stage 2 – Stock Settlement

On the intended settlement date, CREST checks that the buying member has the funds, the selling member has sufficient stock in its stock account and the buyer's CREST settlement bank has sufficient liquidity at the Bank of England to proceed to settlement of the transaction.

If so, CREST moves the stock from the selling member's account to the buying member's account.

Stage 3 – Cash Settlement

CREST also credits the CMA of the selling member and debits the CMA of the buying member which simultaneously generates a settlement bank payment obligation of the buying member's settlement bank in favour of the Bank of England.

The selling member's settlement bank receives that payment in Bank of England funds immediately upon the debit of the purchase price from the buying member's CMA.

Stage 4 – Register Update

CREST then automatically updates its Operator Register of Securities to effect the transfer of shares to the buying member.

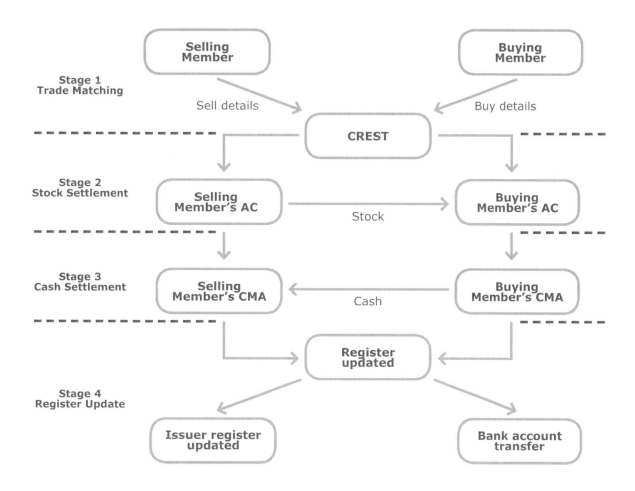

Legal title to the shares passes at this point – this is an Electronic Transfer of Title (ETT).

This prompts the simultaneous generation by the CREST system of a RUR requiring the issuer to amend its record of uncertificated shares.

In practice, stages 2, 3 and 4 occur simultaneously.

6.3.6 Holding of Securities in Certificated Form

If a member of CREST sells securities that are in certificated form, in order to use CREST for settlement the first stage is to 'dematerialise' the shares and reflect the ownership electronically. To do this, the member or his broker will deposit a CREST transfer form and the relevant share certificate at one of

four regional CREST counters and input an electronic CREST record.

The transfer form and certificate are processed and transferred to the appropriate registrar. The registrar will check the documents and delete securities registered in the name of the transferor from the register and ensure that the securities are credited to the CREST membership of the buyer as specified in the transfer form. The buyer thereby obtains title to the securities in electronic form.

Similarly, if a member purchases and receives securities in electronic form but wishes to hold them in certificated form, when the seller receives the purchase funds he will instruct CREST to remove the securities from his register and instruct the registrar, through CREST, to register the securities in the name of the purchaser. The registrar will then produce a certificate in the purchaser's name.

Learning Objectives

Chapter Four has covered the following Learning Objectives:

4.1.8 Know the characteristics of the following exchanges: London Stock Exchange; New York Stock Exchange; NASDAQ; Euronext; Tokyo Stock Exchange; Deutsche Börse

Lesson 26

4.1.9 Know the types and uses of a stock exchange index

Lesson 29

4.1.11 Know how shares are traded on the London Stock Exchange – electronic trading platforms; quote-driven; order-driven; SETS/SEAQ/SETSqx

Lesson 29

4.1.12 Know to which markets the following indices relate: FTSE, Dow Jones Industrial Average, S&P 500, Nikkei 225 CAC 40, Xetra DAX, NASDAQ Composite

Lesson 29

4.1.13 Know the method of holding title – registered/bearer/immobilised/dematerialised

Lesson 28

4.1.14 Understand the role of the central counterparty in clearing and settlement

Lesson 28

4.1.15 Understand the role played by Euroclear in the clearing and settlement of equity trades: uncertificated transfers, participants (members, payment banks, registrars)

Lesson 28

Based on what you have learned in Chapter Four, try to answer the following end of chapter questions.

📑 End of Chapter Questions

Think of an answer for each question and refer to the appropriate section for confirmation.

1. How does an open outcry method of trading work?

   Answer Reference: Section 2

   ....

   ....

2. What are the two major US stock exchanges and how do they differ?

   Answer Reference: Section 2

   ....

   ....

3. In Europe the London Stock Exchange is rivalled by which two exchanges?

   Answer Reference: Section 2.2

   ....

   ....

4. What are Xetra and Clearstream?

   Answer Reference: Section 2.2

   ....

   ....

5. What are the circuit breakers used on the Tokyo Stock Exchange?

   Answer Reference: Sections 2.3.1

   ....

   ....

6. What is the key use of a stock market index?

   Answer Reference: Section 3

   ....

   ....

7. What are the four main indices of the UK market and how often are the constituents reviewed?

   Answer Reference: Section 3.1

   ....

   ....

8. What are the three major indices in the US market and how many constituent companies do they have?

   Answer Reference: Section 3.2

   ....

   ....

9. What is SETS and is it order-driven or quote-driven?

   Answer Reference: Section 4.1

   ....

   ....

10. What are the SETSqx and SEAQ systems and how do they differ?

    Answer Reference: Section 4.2

   ....

   ....

11. What are the two methods of holding title to shares?

    Answer Reference: Section 6.1

    ....

    ....

12. What is 'immobilisation'?

    Answer Reference: Section 6.2

    ....

    ....

13. Who owns and operates CREST?

    Answer Reference: Section 6.3.1

    ....

    ....

14. What are the three ways uncertificated shares can be held in CREST?

    Answer Reference: Section 6.3.2

    ....

    ....

15. What is a CMA and what is it used for?

    Answer Reference: Section 6.3.3

    ....

    ....

16. How does the 'Operator Register of Securities' differ from the 'Issuer Register of Securities'?

    Answer Reference: Section 6.3.4

    ....

    ....

17. What is an RUR?

    Answer Reference: Section 6.3.4

    ....

    ....

18. What is required before settling a certificated shareholding via CREST?

    Answer Reference: Section 6.3.6

    ....

    ....

5

Bonds

Bonds

1. Introduction

Almost every newspaper and news bulletin mentions the shares market by giving the latest level of the FTSE 100 or the Dow Jones Industrial Average. In contrast, bonds generate little media attention despite the global investment value of bonds actually being greater than shares.

Bonds are roughly equally split between 'government' and 'corporate' bonds. Unsurprisingly, government bonds are issued by national governments such as the UK and the US, whilst corporate bonds are issued by companies. Most of the corporate bonds are issued by listed companies, such as the large banks and other large corporate like McDonald's.

In this chapter, we will firstly look at the common characteristics of bonds and then consider the key features of both government and corporate bonds.

2. Characteristics of Bonds

A bond is, very simply, a loan that is represented by an IOU (I owe you). So, if a company wants to borrow some money to enable it to expand, it could borrow it from a bank, or alternatively the company could issue bonds instead. With bonds, investors typically lend money to the company in return for the promise to have the loan repaid on a fixed future date and to receive a series of interest payments.

For example, Company A could decide to issue bonds in units of £10,000, promising to repay the £10,000 in 2019 and agreeing to pay 7% interest each year (or £700 per annum) to the holder of the bond until it is repaid. In the jargon of the bond market, Company A is the 'issuer' of the bond, the £10,000 is known as the 'face' value, the 'nominal' value, the 'par' value or the 'principal'. The date at which the £10,000 is scheduled to be repaid is the 'maturity' or 'redemption' date and the 7% interest paid each year is referred to as the 'coupon' on the bond.

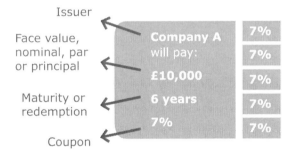

Bonds are also known by other names, such as loan stock, debt instruments and, because they tend to pay a fixed amount of interest each year, fixed interest securities. The key feature that distinguishes a bond from most loans is that a bond is tradeable – the investor in a bond could sell that bond onto another investor without the need to refer to the original borrower (Company A in the above example).

It is vital to appreciate that a bond will not always trade at its nominal value. For example, the above bond might have been issued for £10,000 to the original investor, but the original investor may choose to sell the bond after, say, two years. If the interest rate in the wider market has risen over those two years, the 7% available on the bond may not be competitive anymore, so the new buyer will only be willing to pay perhaps £9,950 for the bond. If he holds the bond until its maturity date, the new buyer will get £10,000 back. The difference between the two (£10,000-£9,950) of £50 will be the new buyer's compensation for accepting the uncompetitive 7% coupon.

Although there are a wide variety of fixed interest securities in issue, they all share similar characteristics and some more of these characteristics will be described by looking at an example of a bond issued by the UK government.

Let us assume that an investor has purchased a holding of £10,000 nominal of 5% Treasury stock 2016. This is ultimately a loan to the UK Treasury that will pay 5% each year until it reaches its maturity date in 2016. The convention in the bond markets is to quote the prices of bonds per £100 nominal, so, if the stock is currently priced at £101.25, then the holding has a market value of £10,125.00 – that is, the nominal value of £10,000, divided by £100 and multiplied by the price of £101.25.

Nominal[1]	=	£10,125.00
Stock[2]	=	5%[3] Treasury stock 2016[4]
Price[5]	=	£101.25
Value[6]	=	£10,125.00

Each of the terms annotated above is explained below:

1. **Nominal** – as seen, this is the amount of stock purchased and is not necessarily the same as the amount invested or the cost of purchase. This is the amount on which interest will be paid and the amount that will eventually be repaid. It is also known as the 'par' or 'face' value of the bond.
2. **Stock** – 5% Treasury stock 2016 is the name given to identify the stock.
3. **5%** – this is the nominal interest rate payable on the stock, also known as the coupon. The rate is quoted gross (before the deduction of any tax that might be payable) and for UK government bonds it is normally paid in two separate and equal half-yearly interest payments. The annual amount of interest paid is calculated by multiplying the nominal amount of stock held by the coupon; that is, in this case, £10,000 times 5% (ie, £500).

4. **2016** – this is the year in which the stock will be repaid, known as the redemption date or maturity date. Repayment will take place at the same time as the final interest payment is made. The amount repaid will be the nominal amount of stock held; that is, £10,000.
5. **Price** – the convention in the bond markets is to quote prices per £100 nominal of stock. So, in this example, the price is £101.25 for each £100 nominal of stock.
6. **Value** – the value of the stock is calculated by multiplying the nominal amount of stock by the current price.

⚙ Example

Government bonds are named by their coupon rate and their redemption date, for example, 6% Treasury stock 2028. These particular bonds pay coupons on 7 June and 7 December each year until the redemption date of 7 December 2028.

The coupon indicates the percentage of the nominal value that the holder will receive each year (assuming no tax is deducted at source). This interest payment is usually made in two equal semi-annual payments on fixed dates, six months apart.

An investor holding £1,000 nominal of 6% Treasury stock 2028 will receive two coupon payments of £30 each, on 7 June and 7 December each year, until the repayment of £1,000 on 7 December 2028.

3. Government Bonds

Governments issue bonds to finance their spending and investment and to bridge the gap between their actual spending and the tax and other forms of income that they receive. Clearly, issuance of government bonds will be high when tax revenues are significantly less than government spending.

Western governments like the UK, the US, Germany and France are major borrowers of money, so the volume of government bonds in issue is very large and forms a major part of the investment portfolio of many institutional investors (such as pension funds and insurance companies).

UK government bonds are known as gilts. This dates back to the days when the physical certificates were issued with a real gold or 'gilt' edge to them, so they became known as 'gilts' or 'gilt-edged stock'. The bonds are issued on behalf of the government by the Debt Management Office (DMO). The chart on the following page gives some detail of the UK government's sales of new gilts and redemptions of old gilts. The total amount of new gilts issued is called the 'gross' amount and the total amount less redemptions is the 'net' amount. The chart also shows the percentage of GDP represented by the total of gilts in issue.

3.1 Types of Government Bonds

The main types of government bonds, such as gilts can be classified as follows:

- conventional;
- dual-dated;
- index-linked; and
- irredeemable.

3.1.1 Conventional Bonds

Conventional government bonds are instruments that carry a fixed coupon and a single repayment date, such as in the example used above of 6% Treasury stock 2028. It is conventional bonds that represent the majority of government bonds in issue.

3.1.2 Dual-Dated Bonds

These types of bonds will carry a fixed coupon but show two dates, between which they can be repaid. The decision as to when to repay will be made by the government and will depend on the prevailing rates of interest at that time.

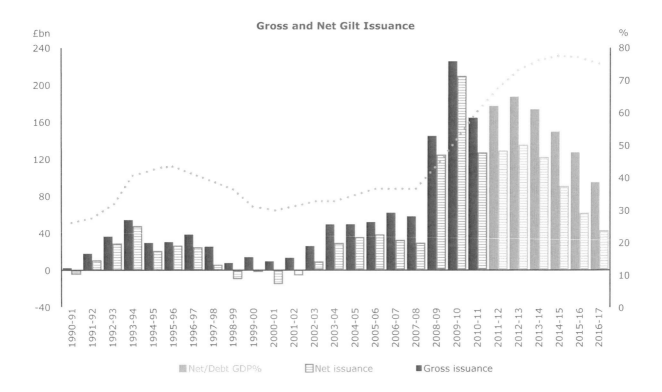

Gross and Net Gilt Issuance

Net/Debt GDP%   Net issuance   Gross issuance

An example of this is 7¾% Treasury loan 2012–15. In this case, the government must repay the stock in full by 2015 but has the option to do so earlier, starting in 2012. If the government can issue new bonds carrying a coupon of less than 7¾% then it can save money by repaying the bond earlier and refinancing it with another bond at a lower rate of interest. If interest rates are higher, it will not have any incentive to repay the bond early and will wait until the final redemption date.

Bonds such as these can be attractive to governments as they give them a little more flexibility than conventional bonds, enabling them to better manage the country's finances. By contrast, they are not as attractive to investors because they are likely to be repaid when interest rates are low, and the investor will only be able to reinvest the proceeds at the lower rate of interest.

3.1.3 Index-Linked Bonds

Index-linked bonds are linked to an index of inflation, such as the consumer price index. They are like conventional bonds in that they specify a coupon and a redemption date, however both the coupon and the redemption amount are increased by the amount of inflation. Below is an example of a real UK gilt that is index-linked.

An example is 2½% Treasury index-linked stock 2020. So this stock carries a coupon rate of 2½% but this is uplifted by the amount of inflation between the interest payment date and the bond issue date. Simplistically if inflation had been 10% between the issue date and the coupon payment date, the cash coupon *will be 10% higher. Similarly, the principal amount that will be repaid in 2020 is adjusted upwards to reflect inflation between the bond's issue date and redemption date. The result is that the investor's purchasing power (what the investor can buy with the cash received) keeps pace with inflation throughout the bond's life.*

Clearly, index-linked bonds are particularly attractive to investors worried about inflation, because in periods where a government's control of inflation is uncertain these bonds provide extra protection to the investor.

Furthermore, these bonds tend to be attractive to long-term investors such as pension funds. Such investors like to know that the returns on their investments will maintain their real value after inflation so that they can meet their obligations to pay pensions.

3.1.4 Irredeemable Bonds

There are a limited number of government stocks which are irredeemable; that is, they have no fixed repayment date. They are also called **perpetual** stocks or **undated** stocks, because they have no set date for the nominal value to be repaid.

⚙ Example

An example is 3½% War Loan, these bonds pay 3½% interest on the nominal value each year and have not set date at which the nominal value will be repaid. They are called 'War Loan' because the bonds were issued to help fund government expenditure during the Second World War.

Needless to say, the lack of a certain repayment date is unattractive to investors. However, the government does repay a small amount of its undated stock each year using a mechanism called a sinking fund. If an investor is lucky enough to be selected by ballot, their undated stock will be repaid at nominal value.

3.2 Classifications

Given that the majority of government bonds tend to be conventional, fixed coupon bonds with a single date of redemption, it is usual to classify these bonds by the amount of time that still remains before redemption. This is usually done by classifying the bonds as short-term, medium-term and long-term.

Generally, short-term debt is considered to be one year or less and long-term is more than ten years. Medium-term debt falls somewhere in the middle. However, the actual classifications vary by market. As an example, UK government stocks are classified in terms of the number of years that remain until the nominal value is repaid:

- 0–7 years remaining: short-dated;
- 7–15 years remaining: medium-dated;
- 15 years and over remaining: long-dated.

In 2005, new gilts were issued in the UK with redemption dates of over 50 years for the first time. Although these are classified within the banding of 15 years and over, they are often referred to as 'ultra-long' gilts.

3.3 Primary Market Issuance

Government bonds are usually issued through agencies that are part of that country's Treasury department. In the UK, for example, when a new gilt is issued, the process is handled by the **Debt Management Office (DMO)**, which is an agency acting on behalf of the Treasury.

Issues are typically made in the form of an auction, where large investors (such as banks, pension funds and insurance companies) submit competitive bids. Often they will each bid for several million pounds' worth of an issue. Issue amounts are normally between £0.5 billion and £2 billion. The DMO accepts bids from those prepared to pay the highest price.

Smaller investors are able to submit non-competitive bids. Advertisements in the *Financial Times* and other newspapers will include details of the offer and an application form. Non-competitive bids can be submitted for up to £500,000, and the successful applicant will pay the average of the prices paid by the competitive bidders.

4. Corporate Bonds

As the name suggests, a corporate bond is a bond that is issued by a corporate entity – in other words a company, such as *McDonalds* as seen earlier in the chapter.

The term **corporate bond** is usually restricted to longer-term debt instruments, with a redemption date that is more than one year away at the point of issue. The term **commercial paper** is used for instruments with a shorter maturity. Furthermore, it only tends to be well established and relatively stable companies that can issue bonds with a maturity greater than ten years at an acceptable cost.

Most corporate bonds are listed on stock exchanges, however the majority of trading does not take place on the stock exchange systems. Instead, most bonds dealing is done in the 'over-the-counter' (OTC) market, between professionals.

4.1 Features of Corporate Bonds

There is a wide variety of corporate bonds and they can be differentiated by looking at some of their key features, such as security; and redemption provisions.

4.1.1 Bond Security

When an individual borrows money in the form of a mortgage, the lending bank or building society makes sure that it has the ability to repossess the property if the scheduled mortgage payments are not made. In a similar way, when a company is seeking to raise new funds by way of a bond issue, it will often offer 'security' to provide the investor with some guarantee for the repayment of the bond.

In this context, security usually means a legal charge over some or all of the bond issuer's assets. These might include properties, like offices and factories, and other items such as the company's unsold goods or uncollected debts. If the issuer fails to pay the required coupons or the principal on the bonds, the bondholders can claim those assets in order to recoup the money that is owed to them. This enables the bondholders to regard their borrowings as safer than if there were no security. Logically, the greater the value of the security offered relative to the amount borrowed, the lower the cost of borrowing should be.

The security offered may be fixed or floating. Fixed security is where a specific asset, such as the head office of the company, or a particular factory, provides the security for the loan. Because there is a fixed legal charge over a particular asset, or a number of particular assets, this is commonly referred to as a 'fixed charge'. In contrast, a floating charge is where the general assets of the company are offered as security for the loan, which might include the company's cash at the bank, trade debtors and unsold stock.

In some cases, rather than being provided by something the company owns, the security takes the form of a third party guarantee – for example, a guarantee by a bank that, if the issuer defaults, the bank will repay the bondholders.

4.1.2 Redemption Provisions

Sometimes, corporate issuers want to have the right to redeem the bonds early. This gives them the ability to repay a bond that may be paying higher coupons, perhaps replacing it with a new bond issue paying lower coupons because the general level of interest rates has fallen. Technically, bonds where the issuer has the right to redeem early are referred to as bonds with a **call provision**. This is because the issuer has the right to 'call' the bonds back early.

Although attractive to the issuer because of the flexibility of early repayment, bonds with call provisions are relatively unattractive to investors because they can lose out on hoped for coupon payments. This disadvantage to the investors, means that they will demand a greater return from bonds with a call provision than an equivalent bond without the call provision.

Call provisions can take various forms. For example, there may be a schedule of dates at which the issuer could redeem all of the bond issue, or there might be a requirement for the issuer to redeem a specified amount at regular intervals using a **sinking fund**, as seen above when considering undated gilts.

Some bonds are also issued with **put provisions**, and are known as 'puttable' bonds. These give the bondholder the right to require the issuer to redeem early, on a set date or between specific dates – they can 'put' the bond back with the issuer in return for a redemption payment. This makes the bond attractive to investors because they can get their money back and reinvest if interest rates have risen. So a put provision may increase the chances of selling a bond issue in the first instance. However, put provisions increase the issuer's risk that it will have to refinance the bond at an inconvenient time when the costs of finance (general interest rates) have risen. An example of a bond with a put provision is shown below in the section on medium-term notes.

4.2 Types of Corporate Bonds

Over and above the considerations of security and redemption, there is a wide variety of corporate bonds that are traded around the world. The variety is largely due to innovative structures devised by banks to assist their client companies in raising finance – this is referred to as 'financial engineering'. Some of the main types are described below.

4.2.1 Medium-Term Notes (MTNs)

Medium-term notes are standard corporate bonds with maturities ranging usually from just nine months to five years, though the term is also applied to instruments with maturities as long as 30 years. The key difference with other types of bond is the way they are sold to investors. Rather than marketing and selling the bonds at a single point, medium-term notes are offered to investors continually over a period of time by an agent acting for the issuer, typically an investment bank.

⚙ Example

The supermarket giant Tesco has a number of medium-term notes in issue. As part of a larger financing programme it issued a £200 million tranche of 6% sterling-denominated notes in 1999 which are repayable in 2029. The issue price was £98.59 and at the end of 2010 the notes were trading at £107.98.

This bond contains an example of an investor put provision. It provides that, if there is a restructuring event (which for this bond is essentially a takeover of Tesco, when anyone party becomes entitled to more than 50% of the voting rights in the company) and this results in a credit rating downgrade, then holders of the bonds can give notice to Tesco requiring it to redeem the bond at par together with any accrued interest.

4.2.2 Fixed Rate Bonds

The key features of fixed rate bonds have already been described in Section 2. Essentially, they have fixed coupons which are paid either half-yearly or annually and predetermined redemption dates.

4.2.3 Floating Rate Notes (FRNs)

Floating rate notes are often referred to as FRNs – they are bonds that have variable rates, rather than a fixed rate of coupon.

The coupon rate will be linked to a published rate of interest, such as, the London InterBank Offered Rates (LIBOR) that are published daily by a trade body called the British Bankers' Association. LIBOR is the rate of interest at which banks will lend to one another in London in a particular currency (eg, pounds sterling) for a particular period (eg, six months), and LIBOR rates are often used as a basis for cash flows on financial instruments.

An FRN will usually pay interest at LIBOR plus a quoted margin or spread.

⚙ Example

The European Investment Bank exists to further the interests of the European Union by making long-term investment finance available. As part of this, it raised finance by issuing a floating rate bond in the UK. The issue was launched in March 2010 and is repayable in 2015. Interest is payable quarterly at a rate of 0.10% above three-month LIBOR. After each quarterly payment, the interest due for the next quarter is fixed so, for example, in November 2010 the interest rate for the period from 19 November to 21 February 2011 was fixed at 0.84% per annum, meaning that £0.22 interest will be payable per £100 nominal of stock held.

4.2.4 Permanent Interest Bearing Shares (PIBS)

Permanent Interest Bearing Shares (PIBS) are peculiar to the UK. They are issued by building societies, carry fixed coupons and typically have with no set date for redemption. The term 'shares' is a misnomer. PIBS are bonds paying regular coupons.

⚙ Example

PIBS have been issued by the Coventry Building Society. In 2006, it issued a bond titled 6.092% Permanent Interest Bearing Shares. Unusually these PIBS have a redemption date, but it is not until 31 December 2099. At the end of 2010, the PIBS were trading at £90 per £100 nominal.

4.2.5 Convertible Bonds

Convertible bonds are issued by companies. They give the investor holding the bond two possible choices:

- to simply collect the interest payments and then the repayment of the bond on maturity; or
- to convert the bond into a predefined number of ordinary shares in the issuing company, on a set date or dates, or between a range of set dates, prior to the bond's maturity.

Convertibles are relatively attractive to investors because, if the company prospers, its share price will rise this may make converting into shares profitable. In contrast, if the company hits problems, the investor can simply retain the bond – as long as the company survives, the coupons will be collected and, if the company goes bust the bondholder will possibly get some or all of his money back before the shareholders will get anything.

For the company issuing the convertible bonds, finance might be raised relatively cheaply. This is because investors will pay a higher price for a bond that is convertible since there is a possibility of a capital gain.

4.2.6 Zero Coupon Bonds (ZCB)

A zero coupon bond (ZCB) is a bond that pays no coupons at all. This is best explained by looking at an example.

⚙ Example

Imagine that the issuer of a bond (Example plc) offered you the opportunity to purchase a bond with the following features:

- *£100 nominal value.*
- *Issued today.*
- *Redeems at its par value (that is £100 nominal value) in five years.*
- *Pays no coupons.*

Would you be interested in purchasing the bond?

It is tempting to say no – who would want to buy a bond that pays no interest?

However, there is no requirement to pay the par value – a logical investor would presumably happily pay something less than the par value, for example £60. The difference between the price paid of £60 and the par value of £100 recouped after five years would provide the investor with his return of £40 over five years.

As the example illustrates, these zero coupon bonds are issued at a **discount to their par value** and they repay, or redeem, at par value. All of the return is provided in the form of capital growth rather than regular coupon income.

4.3 Domestic and Foreign Bonds

Bonds can be categorised geographically. A **domestic bond** is issued by a domestic issuer into the domestic market, for example, a UK company issuing bonds, denominated in sterling, to UK investors.

In contrast, a **foreign bond** is issued by an overseas entity into a domestic market and is denominated in the domestic currency. Examples of foreign bonds include a German company issuing a sterling bond to UK investors, or a US dollar bond issued in the US by a non-US company.

4.4 Eurobonds

Despite what the name suggests, Eurobonds are not necessarily denominated in the euro currency and may have little to do with Europe. Eurobonds are basically large international bond issues that are often made by governments and multinational companies.

Despite the first eurobond being issued on behalf of the Italian motorway operator, Autostrade, in 1963, the eurobond market really developed in the early 1970s when oil sales from the Middle East were generating substantial quantities of US dollars (because oil is priced in US dollars) and US financial institutions were subject to ceiling on the rate of interest that could be paid on dollar deposits. Bonds were issued from financial centres like London, denominated in US dollars to attract these international investors with dollars to invest. Since then, the eurobond market has grown rapidly to become the world's largest market for longer-term capital.

The defining characteristic of eurobonds is that they are denominated in a currency different from that of the financial centre or centres in which they are issued. So, a dollar denominated bond issued out of London is a eurobond, as is a Yen denominated bond issued out of Hong Kong. In fact, eurobond issues are often issued in a number of financial centres simultaneously.

Eurobonds issued by companies generally do not provide any underlying fixed or floating security to the bondholders, but instead tend to be assessed by one of the credit ratings agencies (see Section 5.3 below). To provide some measure of safety to the bondholders, the issuing company typically includes a 'negative pledge' clause in the bond's documentation. This prevents the company from subsequently making any secured bond issues, or bond issues that would confer a greater seniority or entitlement to the company's assets in the event of its liquidation, unless an equivalent level of security is provided to existing eurobond investors.

The eurobond market offers a number of advantages over a domestic bond market, making it attractive for companies as a way to raise capital, including:

- the ability to reach potential lenders internationally rather than just domestically;
- anonymity to investors as issues are made in bearer form (there is no register of bondholders maintained by the issuer);
- gross interest payments made to investors;
- lower funding costs due to the competitive nature and greater liquidity of the market;
- the ability to make bond issues at short notice; and
- less regulation and disclosure.

Most eurobonds are issued as conventional bonds (or 'straights'), with a fixed nominal value, fixed coupon and known redemption date. Other common types include floating rate notes, zero coupon bonds, convertible bonds and dual-currency bonds – paying coupons in one currency and the redemption amount in another currency, but they can also assume a wide range of other innovative features.

4.5 Asset-Backed Securities (ABSs)

Asset-backed securities is the term given to bonds which bundle together financial assets which – on their own – would be too small or too illiquid to be traded in the market. Typical examples are mortgage loans or loans made on credit cards.

Asset-backed securities are best understood by looking at an example. Imagine that a bank (ABC Bank) has made lots of loans to individuals to buy their own homes. The bank can expect money to flow in over the forthcoming years from the interest and the repayment of these mortgage loans. However, ABC Bank needs cash now, perhaps to make further mortgage loans or perhaps to buy new premises or another bank. ABC Bank can use the mortgage loans as assets to back the issue of bonds.

- **Step 1**: ABC Bank selects a suitable group of mortgages to use as assets for the bonds. Creating a bond in this way is known as securitisation, and it began in the US in 1970 when the government first issued mortgage certificates, a security representing ownership of a pool of mortgages.

- **Step 2**: These bonds are grouped together to form a 'pool' of mortgages. This pool is typical constructed within a particular organisation that has been set up by the bank for the purpose of issuing bonds. This is known as a 'special purpose vehicle' or simply an 'SPV'.

- **Step 3**: The SPV issues bonds to investors. Some of these bonds will be safer, and therefore attract a credit rating (detailed later in this chapter) that is better than others, because they will have a higher priority of entitlement to the interest and repayments flowing from the mortgages. Indeed, some might be considered so safe that they attract the best 'triple A' credit rating and others so risky that they cannot attract a rating at all and are 'unrated'.

- **Step 4**: As interest is received from the mortgages and the mortgages are repaid, the money will be funnelled through to the appropriate bondholders. Clearly, in line with the credit ratings the bonds have been able to attract, some bonds will get a greater yield (return) than others. Furthermore, if there are any problems

with the mortgages, it will be the most risky bonds that suffer first. They are described as suffering the first loss.

It is important to appreciate that the mortgage holders themselves are probably unaware that their mortgages are being used as assets to back a bond issue. ABC Bank that originally provided the mortgages to the home-buyers will continue to be responsible for collecting the monthly payments on the mortgages.

Recently, asset-backed securities and particularly mortgage backed securities have become a controversial asset class. This is because one of the principal causes of the 2007–2009 credit crunch was the collapse of the US 'sub-prime' housing loan market.

Sub-prime loans are loans made to borrowers with poor credit histories or with insufficient income to meet the monthly payments comfortably and, by the beginning of 2007, the values of most US properties were falling. A large number of sub-prime borrowers found it impossible to meet the monthly payments on their loans, triggering defaults on the mortgages, many of which had been pooled together and sold on to investors as asset-backed securities. Because many mortgage-backed securities were found to contain sub-prime housing loans, there was a general collapse in confidence in the whole asset-backed securities market as a result.

Despite the negative connotations in relation to the credit crunch, it is important to appreciate that asset-backed securities can be useful. They bring together a pool of financial assets, as seen these might be mortgage loans or credit card loans, that otherwise could not easily be traded in their existing form. By pooling together a large portfolio of these illiquid assets, they can be converted into instruments that can be offered and sold freely in the capital markets. As seen with the earlier example of ABC Bank, this can be an important source of finance.

In Conclusion

The advantages to the bank are:

- Total funding available to the bank is increased by accessing capital markets rather than being dependent solely on its deposits.
- The mortgages are removed from the bank's balance sheet and the risk exposure of the mortgages is passed to another lender.
- The bank's liquidity position is helped, as the term to maturity of a mortgage may be 25 years and the securitisation issue replaces the financing that may have come from deposits that can be withdrawn at short notice.

From the investor's point of view, mortgage-backed bonds offer the following benefits:

- They provide a marketable asset-backed instrument to invest in.
- The mortgages will provide good security if well diversified and equivalent in terms of quality, terms and conditions.
- Credit enhancements make the securitised bonds less of a credit risk.

4.5.1 Covered Bonds

A variation on asset-backed bonds are covered bonds which are widely used in Europe.

These are issued by financial institutions and are corporate bonds that are backed by cash flows from a pool of mortgages or public sector loans. The pool of assets provides cover for the loan hence the term covered bond.

They are similar in many ways to asset-backed securities but the regulatory framework for covered bonds is designed so that the bonds that comply with those requirements are considered as particularly safe investments.

The main differences are:

- They remain on the issuer's balance sheet.
- The asset pool must provide sufficient collateral to cover bondholder claims throughout the whole term of the covered bond.
- Bondholders must have a priority claim on the cover (the asset pool) in case of default of the issuer.

Covered bonds are an important part of the financing of the mortgage and public sector markets in Europe and represent an important source of term funding for banks. A thriving covered bond market is seen as essential for the future of the European banking sector and the ability of individuals to finance house loans at a reasonable rate.

5. Investing in Bonds

5.1 Advantages, Disadvantages and Risks

As one of the main asset classes, bonds clearly have a role to play in most portfolios.

The main **advantages** of bonds are:

- For fixed-coupon bonds, a regular and certain flow of income;
- For most bonds, a fixed maturity date (however, there are bonds which have no

redemption date, and others which may be repaid on either of two dates or between two dates – sometimes at the investor's option and sometimes at the issuer's option);

- A range of income yields to suit different investment and tax situations.

The main **disadvantages** of bonds are:

- The 'real' value of the income flow is eroded by the effects of inflation (except in the case of index-linked bonds);
- Default risk, namely the risk that the issuer will not be able to make the coupon payments as they fall due or repay the capital at the maturity date.

As has been seen, there are a number of **risks** attached to holding bonds.

Firstly, bonds generally have **default risk**, the possibility of the issuer defaulting on the payment of coupons and/or capital, for example a corporate issuer of a bond could go bust. Bonds also have **price risk or market risk**, which is the effect of **movements** in interest rates, which can have a significant impact on the value of bonds.

Most government bonds have only price risk, as there is little or no risk that the government will fail to pay the coupons or repay the capital on the bonds. However, recent turmoil in government bond markets has resulted from fears that certain European governments (such as Greece, Ireland and Portugal) may be unable to meet their obligations on these loans, and the prices of their bonds have fallen significantly as a result.

Price or market risk is best explained by two simple examples.

⚙ Example

Price Risk (Example 1)

Interest rates are approximately 5%, and the government issues a bond with a coupon rate of 5%. Three months later, interest rates have

doubled to 10%. What will happen to the value of the bond?

The value of the bond will fall substantially. Its 5% coupon is no longer attractive, so its resale price will fall to compensate and make the return the bond offers more competitive.

⚙ Example

Price Risk (Example 2)

Interest rates are approximately 5%, and the government issues a bond with a coupon rate of 5%. Subsequently interest rates generally fall to 2.5%. What will happen to the value of the bond?

The value of the bond will rise substantially. Its 5% coupon is very attractive, so its resale price will rise to compensate and make the return it offers fall to more realistic levels.

With both of the above examples, remember that it is the current value of the bond that is changing. Changes in interest rates do not affect the coupon or the amount payable at maturity, which will remain as the nominal amount of the stock.

As the above examples illustrate, there is an inverse relationship between interest rates and bond prices:

- If interest rates increase, bond prices will decrease.
- If interest rates decrease, bond prices will increase.

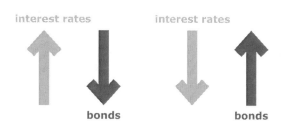

Some of the other main risks associated with holding bonds are:

- **Early redemption** – the risk that the issuer may invoke a call provision (if the bond is callable). A call provision is the right to 'call in' or redeem the bonds early, if, for instance, the issuer has been able to refinance the borrowing at a cheaper interest rate.
- **Seniority risk** – the seniority with which corporate debt is ranked in the event of the issuer's liquidation. The issuer might issue new, additional bonds, which rank higher in seniority. These bonds will then be repaid first in the event of liquidation; so debt with the highest seniority has a greater chance of being repaid than debt with lower seniority. If the company raises more borrowing and it is entitled to be repaid before the existing bonds, then the bonds have suffered from seniority risk.
- **Inflation risk** – the risk of inflation rising unexpectedly and eroding the real value of the bond's coupon and redemption payment.
- **Liquidity risk** – liquidity is the ease with which a security can be converted into cash. Some bonds are more easily sold at a fair market price than others.
- **Exchange rate risk** – bonds denominated in a currency different from that of the investor's home currency are potentially subject to adverse exchange rate movements. The value of the issuer's currency might have declined relative to the investor's currency.

5.2 Flat Yields

Yields are measures of the return that can be earned on bonds.

⚙ Example

1888 US railway company 30-year bond certificate '4.4% Pennsylvania Railroad Company 1931' (as shown on Lesson 30) required an initial investment of US$1,000 and paid an annual coupon of US$44. So the bond's yield at issue (par) was 4.4%.

However, remember that the coupon reflects the interest rate payable on the nominal or principal amount. An investor may have paid a different amount to purchase the bond, so a method of calculating the true return to him or her is needed. The return, as a percentage of the cost price, which a bond offers is often referred to as the bond's yield. The most straightforward yield is to look at the coupon paid on a bond as a percentage of its market price – this is referred to as the flat or **running yield**.

The flat yield is calculated by taking the annual coupon and dividing by the bond's price and then multiplying by 100 to obtain a percentage. The bond's price is typically stated as the price payable to purchase £100 nominal value. This is best illustrated by looking at the following examples.

⚙ Example

Flat Yields

1. *A bond with a coupon of 5%, issued by XYZ plc, redeemable in 2012, is currently trading at £100 per £100 nominal.*

The flat yield is the coupon divided by the price expressed as a percentage, ie:

£5 ÷ £100 x 100 = 5%.

2. *A bond with a coupon of 4%, issued by ABC plc, redeemable in 2020, is currently trading at £78 per £100 nominal. So an investor could buy £100 nominal value for £78.*

The flat yield is the coupon divided by the price expressed as a percentage, ie:

£4 ÷ £78 x 100 = 5.13%.

3. *5% Treasury stock 2028 is currently priced at £104. So an investor could buy £100 nominal value for £104.*

The flat yield on this gilt is the coupon divided by the price, ie:

£5 ÷ £104 x 100 = 4.81%.

The interest earned on a bond is only one part of its total return, however, as the investor may also either make a capital gain or a loss on the bond if it is held until redemption. The redemption yield is a measure that incorporates both the income and capital return – assuming the investor holds the bond until its maturity – into one figure.

⚙ Example

Redemption Yields

Assume an investor purchases £100 nominal of a bond with a coupon of 3% at £80. The bond is repayable in five years.

If the investor holds the stock until redemption, he or she will receive a repayment of £100 – a gain of 25%. Simply averaging the growth over the five years gives an annualised return equivalent to 5% per annum.

The flat yield is 3.75% – that is 3 ÷ 80 x 100 = 3.75%.

Simplistically, the redemption yield is the sum of the two – that is, 3.75% + 5% = 8.75%.

5.3 Rating Agencies

Credit risk – the probability of an issuer defaulting on their payment obligations and the extent of the resulting loss – can be assessed by looking at the independent credit ratings given to most bond issues.

There are more than 70 agencies throughout the world, and preferred agencies vary from country to country. The three most prominent credit rating agencies that provide these ratings are Standard & Poor's; Moody's; and Fitch Ratings.

The table below shows the credit ratings available from the three companies.

Standard & Poor's and Fitch Ratings refine their ratings by adding a plus or minus sign to show relative standing within a category, whilst Moody's do the same by the addition of a 1, 2 or 3.

As can be seen, bond issues that have been subject to credit ratings can be divided into two distinct categories: those given an 'investment

BOND CREDIT RATINGS				
Credit risk		Moody's	Standard & Poor's	Fitch Ratings
Investment Grade				
Highest quality		Aaa	AAA	AAA
High quality	Very strong	Aa	AA	AA
Upper medium grade	Strong	A	A	A
Medium grade		Baa	BBB	BBB
Non-Investment Grade				
Lower medium grade	Somewhat speculative	Ba	BB	BB
Low grade	Speculative	B	B	B
Poor quality	May default	Caa	CCC	CCC
Most speculative		C	CC	CC
No interest being paid or bankruptcy petition filed		C	D	C
In default		C	D	D

grade' rating, and those categorised as non-investment grade, or speculative. The latter are also known as 'high yield' or – for the worst-rated – 'junk bonds'. Investment grade issues offer the greatest liquidity and certainty of repayment.

Bonds will be assessed and given a credit rating when they are first issued and then re-assessed if circumstances change, so that their rating can be upgraded or downgraded with a consequent effect on their price.

Learning Objectives

Chapter Five has covered the following Learning Objectives:

5   Bonds

 Lesson 07

5.1   Government Bonds

 Lesson 13

5.1.1   Know the definition and features of government bonds: DMO maturity classifications, how they are issued

 Lesson 13 (DMO maturity classifications) and Lesson 15 (how they are issued)

5.2.1   Know the definitions and features of the following types of bond: domestic; foreign; eurobond; asset-backed securities including covered bonds; zero coupon; convertible

 Lesson 32 (domestic; foreign; eurobond; asset-backed securities) and Lesson 33 (zero coupon; convertible)

5.3.1   Know the advantages and disadvantages of investing in different types of bonds

 Lesson 31

5.3.2   Be able to calculate the flat yield of a bond

 Lesson 30

5.3.3   Understand the role of credit rating agencies and the differences between investment and non-investment grades

 Lesson 31

Based on what you have learned in Chapter Five, try to answer the following end of chapter questions.

📑 End of Chapter Questions

Think of an answer for each question and refer to the appropriate section for confirmation.

1. What are the alternative terms for the face value of a bond?

    Answer Reference: Section 2

    ....

    ....

2. What is the market convention for quoting bond prices?

    Answer Reference: Section 2

    ....

    ....

3. What is a gilt?

    Answer Reference: Section 3

    ....

    ....

4. What are the four types of government bond?

    Answer Reference: Section 3.1

    ....

    ....

5. What would make an issuing government repay a dual-dated bond early?

    Answer Reference: Section 3.1.2

    ....

    ....

6. What is uplifted by inflation in an index-linked bond?

    Answer Reference: Section 3.1.3

    ....

    ....

7. What makes a UK government stock medium-dated?

    Answer Reference: Section 3.2

    ....

    ....

8. Who handles new issues of gilts?

    Answer Reference: Section 3.3

    ....

    ....

9. What is a secured corporate bond?

    Answer Reference: Section 4.1.1

    ....

    ....

10. What are call and put provisions?

    Answer Reference: Section 4.1.2

    ....

    ....

11. What is a medium-term note?

Answer Reference: Section 4.2.1

....

....

12. What is an FRN and what is used to compute the coupon rate?

Answer Reference: Section 4.2.3

....

....

13. Who issues PIBS?

Answer Reference: Section 4.2.4

....

....

14. Why might convertible bonds enable a company to raise finance cheaply?

Answer Reference: Section 4.2.5

....

....

15. Why would anyone purchase a zero coupon bond?

Answer Reference: Section 4.2.6

....

....

16. What distinguishes a domestic bond from a foreign bond?

    Answer Reference: Section 4.3

    ....

    ....

17. What is a Eurobond?

    Answer Reference: Section 4.4

    ....

    ....

18. How are asset-backed securities created?

    Answer Reference: Section 4.5

    ....

    ....

19. What are the main advantages in investing in bonds?

    Answer Reference: Section 5.1

    ....

    ....

20. What are the main risks involved in investing in bonds?

    Answer Reference: Section 5.1

    ....

    ....

21. How is the flat yield calculated?

Answer Reference: Section 5.2

....

....

22. What does the flat yield ignore that is reflected in the redemption yield?

Answer Reference: Section 5.2

....

....

23. What is the best credit rating that a bond can have?

Answer Reference: Section 5.3

....

....

24. What is the lowest investment grade rating that a bond can have and how does the Moody's rating differ from the rating given by Standard & Poor's or Fitch Ratings?

Answer Reference: Section 5.3

....

....

25. What is a 'junk bond'?

Answer Reference: Section 5.3

....

....

6
Other Retail Financial Products

Other Retail Financial Products

1. Introduction

Having already encountered equities and bonds, this chapter looks at a number of other financial instruments and products that are available – in particular, instruments and activities in the so-called 'money market', the foreign exchange market (or 'forex') plus a detailed look at the property market and the way property purchases can be financed through mortgage loans.

2. Money Markets

The term 'money market' is a little confusing – it can be thought of as the market for shorter term bonds. Remember that bonds are IOU (I owe you) instruments that generally pay a regular coupon and then repay the amount borrowed at the end of a particular period. The period between the issue and the maturity of

a bond is typically years. In contrast, money market instruments are IOUs where the period between issue and maturity is much shorter, often just three months and certainly not exceeding a year.

Bonds and equities are used to raise relatively long term capital for the issuer – they are capital market instruments. Instruments issued to raise cash for shorter term periods of up to a year are referred to as money market instruments.

Direct investment in money market instruments is often subject to a relatively high minimum subscription and therefore tends to be more suitable for institutional investors like pension funds and insurance companies. Because of this, it is often described as a 'wholesale' or institutional market. However, money market instruments are accessible to retail investors indirectly through collective investment funds.

The short-term nature of the money markets means that issuers seek to avoid any excessive administrative costs. For most money market instruments, this is achieved in two ways:

1. By issuing the instruments in 'bearer' form and therefore removing the need to maintain a register of the holders of the instruments.
2. By not paying a coupon and instead issuing the instruments at a discount to their face value, in a similar way to zero coupon bonds.

The main types of UK money market instruments are:

- **Treasury bills** – like gilts, these are issued by the **Debt Management Office (DMO)** on behalf of the UK Treasury. However, Treasury bills are issued much more frequently than gilts, generally every week and the money is used to meet the government's short-term borrowing needs. Treasury bills are non-interest-bearing instruments. Instead of interest being paid out on them, they are issued at a **discount to par** – ie, a price of less than £100 per £100 nominal – and commonly redeem after three months. For example, a Treasury bill might be issued for £990 and mature at £1,000 three months later. The investor's return is the difference between the £990 paid, and the £1,000 received on the Treasury bill's maturity.
- **Certificates of deposit (CDs)** – These are issued by banks in return for deposited money. They can be thought of as tradeable deposit accounts, as they can be bought and sold in the same way as shares and bonds. For example, Lloyds Banking Group might issue a CD to represent a deposit of £1 million from a customer, redeemable in six months. The CD will specify that Lloyds TSB will pay the £1 million back plus interest of, say, 2.5% of £1 million. If the customer needs the money back before six months has elapsed, he can sell the CD to another investor in the money market.
- **Commercial paper (CP)** – This is the equivalent of a Treasury bill issued by

a corporate entity (a company) rather than the government. Commercial paper tends to be issued by large companies to meet their short-term borrowing needs. A company's ability to issue commercial paper is typically agreed with banks in advance. For example, a company might agree with its bank to a programme of £10 million worth of commercial paper. This would enable the company to issue various forms of commercial paper with different maturities (eg, one month, three months and six months) and possibly different currencies, to the bank. As with Treasury bills, commercial paper is zero coupon and issued at a discount to its par value.

Settlement of money market instruments is typically achieved through CREST and is commonly settled on the day of the trade or the following business day.

Money market instruments provide a relatively low-risk way to generate an income or capital return, as appropriate, while preserving the nominal value of the amount invested. As a result, they tend to be particularly popular at times of market uncertainty. However, they are unsuitable for anything other than the short term since, historically, they have underperformed most other asset types over the medium to long term. Indeed, in the long term, returns from money market instruments have barely been positive once tax and inflation have been taken into account.

The money market is a highly professional market that is used by banks and companies to manage their liquidity needs. It is not accessible by private investors, who instead need to utilise either money market accounts offered by banks, or money market funds.

There is a range of money market funds available and they can offer some advantages over pure money market accounts. There is the obvious advantage that the pooling of funds with other investors gives the investor access to assets they would not otherwise be able to invest in. The returns on money market funds should also be greater than a simple money market account offered by a bank.

Placing funds in a money market account means that the investor is exposed to the risk of that bank. By contrast, a money market fund will invest in a range of instruments from many providers, and as long as they are AAA-rated they can offer high security levels.

Under FSA rules, money market funds may only invest in approved money market instruments and deposits with credit institutions and meet other conditions on the structure of the underlying portfolio.

The Investment Management Association (IMA) introduced two money market sectors which came into effect on 1 January 2012. These are based on the European definitions of money market funds that have been adopted by the FSA – short-term money market funds and money market funds.

- **Short-term money market funds** must maintain a constant net asset value which means that the income in the fund is either paid out to the unitholder or used to purchase more units in the scheme.
- **Money market funds** by contrast may have a fluctuating net asset value. It should be noted that money market funds may invest in instruments where the capital is at risk and so may not be suitable for many investors. In addition, money market funds can be differentiated by the currency of issue of their assets.

3. Foreign Exchange

The foreign exchange market, which is also known as the forex or simply the FX market, refers to the trading of one currency for another. It is by far the busiest and most active of the financial markets, with turnover comfortably exceeding that of bonds and equities.

Most currencies are allowed by their central banks to 'float', so that the exchange rate between one currency and another can vary. This clearly creates risks for companies operating internationally, as can be seen in the following example.

Example

A British company, Union Jack plc manufactures and sells goods internationally. Union Jack is negotiating a sale with a large US customer, Stars & Stripes Inc. Because Stars & Stripes is potentially a very valuable client to Union Jack, the sale will be made in US dollars and Stars & Stripes will not be required to pay until a month after the sale is invoiced.

As far as Union Jack is concerned, there is a risk that the number of pounds the dollars will buy in a month's time may be less than when the sale is first made. This risk could be removed by using a foreign exchange forward contract, where Union Jack agrees to sell the US dollars it is anticipating to receive from Stars & Stripes in one month's time at a rate established now.

With currencies allowed to float freely against one another, trading in currencies has become 24-hour, and it can take place in the various time zones of Asia, Europe and America. London, being placed between the Asian and American time zones, is well placed to take advantage of this, and has grown to become the world's largest forex market. Other large centres include the US, Japan and Singapore.

Trading of foreign currencies clearly involves selling one currency and buying another, the two currencies involved are described as 'pairs'. The price at which a pair is bought and sold provides the **exchange rate**. When the exchange rate is being quoted, the name of the each currency is abbreviated to a three letter reference; so, for example, sterling is abbreviated to GBP which is an abbreviation of Great British pounds.

The most commonly quoted currency pairs are:

- US dollar and Japanese yen (USD/JPY);
- Euro and US dollar (EUR/USD);
- US dollar and Swiss franc (USD/CHF);
- British pound and US dollar (GBP/USD).

When currencies are quoted, the first currency is the base currency and the second is the counter or quote currency. The base currency is always equal to one unit of that currency, in other words, one pound, one dollar or one euro. For example, at the time of writing the EUR:USD exchange rate is 1:1.4260 which means that €1 is worth $1.4260. When the exchange rate is described as going up, it means that the value of the base currency is rising relative to the other currency and is referred to as the currency strengthening; where the opposite is the case, the currency is said to be weakening.

The graph below, shows the Great British pound (GBP) against the US dollar over approximately five years showing a general weakening of the pound from being worth more than $2, to around $1.60.

When currency pairs are quoted, the foreign exchange trader will quote a **bid and ask price**. Staying with the example of the EUR:USD the quote might be 1.4260/62 – notice that the euro is not mentioned, as standard convention is that the base currency is always one unit. So if a client wanted to **buy** €100,000 then he

will need to pay the higher of the two prices and deliver $142,620; if a client wanted to **sell** €100,000 then he will get the lower of the two prices and receive $142,600.

The foreign currency market is primarily an over-the-counter (OTC) market, ie, one where brokers and dealers negotiate directly with one another. The main participants are large international banks, which continually provide the market with both bid (buy) and ask (sell) prices. Central banks are also major participants in foreign exchange markets, which they use to try to control money supply, inflation and interest rates.

There are several types of transactions and financial instruments commonly used:

- **Spot transaction** – the 'spot rate' is the rate quoted by a bank for the exchange of one currency for another with immediate effect. However in many cases spot trades are 'settled' – that is, the currencies actually change hands and arrive in recipients' bank accounts – two business days after the transaction date (T+2).

GBP/USD (2007-2011)

- **Forward transaction** – as seen in the earlier example, in a forward transaction money does not actually change hands until some agreed future date. A buyer and seller agree on an exchange rate for any date in the future, for a fixed sum of money, and the transaction occurs on that date, regardless of what the market rates are then. The duration of the trade can be a few days, months or years.
- **Future** – foreign currency futures are a standardised version of forward transactions that are traded on derivatives exchanges for standard sizes and maturity dates. The average contract length is roughly three months.
- **Swap** – the most common type of forward transaction is the currency swap. In a swap, two parties exchange currencies for a certain length of time and agree to reverse the transaction at a later date. These are not exchange-traded contracts and instead are negotiated individually between the parties to a swap. They are a type of OTC derivative that will be covered in more detail in the next chapter.

4. Property

Property is often considered as a separate type of asset in which to invest that is distinct from other asset classes such as shares and bonds. Property that is purchased for rental income and/or to make a profit on sale is generally referred to as commercial property. It includes retail and office developments, industrial property, agricultural land and residential property such as apartment blocks. As an asset class, property has a number of distinguishing features:

- Each individual property is unique in terms of location, structure and design.
- Individuals tend to find different characteristics attractive, so valuation is subjective.
- The transfer of property is subject to complex legal considerations and high transaction costs.

- It can take a considerable amount of time to buy or sell a property making property highly illiquid.
- Property is also illiquid in another sense: the investor generally has to sell all of the property or nothing at all. For example, a residential property owner cannot sell his spare bedroom to raise a little cash!
- Property can only be purchased in discrete and generally sizeable and relatively expensive units, making diversification difficult. In fact, only the largest investors, which generally means institutional investors, can purchase sufficient properties to build a diversified portfolio.
- The supply of land is finite and its availability can be further restricted by legislation and local planning regulations. Therefore, price is heavily driven by changes in demand and not supply.

As an asset class, direct investment in property has at times provided positive real long-term returns with a reliable stream of income and little volatility. An exposure to property can provide diversification benefits within a portfolio of investments due to its low correlation with other asset classes like equities and bonds. Many private investors have chosen to become involved in the property market by purchasing residential properties they intend to rent, known as the buy-to-let market.

Others with less money to invest wanting to include property within a diversified portfolio generally seek indirect exposure via a collective investment scheme, or shares in publicly quoted property companies.

Despite its unique features, investing in property does confer a number of advantages. As an asset class, it has provided positive real long-term returns, combined a reliable stream of income. However, property can also be subject to prolonged downturns, and its lack of liquidity, significant maintenance costs, high transaction costs on transfer and the risk of having commercial property with no tenant (and, therefore, no rental income) makes direct investment in commercial property only suitable for long-term investing institutions such as pension funds.

5. Mortgages

A mortgage is simply a secured loan, with the security taking the form of a property. The mortgage is typically provided to finance the purchase of that property, and for most people their main form of borrowing is the mortgage on their house or flat. Mortgages tend to be taken out over a long term, with most mortgages running for 20 or 25 years.

Whether a mortgage is to buy a house or flat in which the mortgagee will live, or to 'buy-to-let', the factors considered by the lender are much the same. The mortgage lender, such as the building society or bank, will consider each application for a loan in terms of the credit risk – the risk of not being repaid the principal sum loaned and the interest due.

Applicants are assessed in terms of:

- income and security of employment;
- existing outgoings – utility bills, other household expenses, school fees, etc;
- the size of the loan in relation to the value of the property being purchased.

If the borrower fails to make the agreed repayments and/or the interest payments on the mortgage, the borrower is described as 'in default'. The lender can then re-possess the property, sell the property (often at auction) and then reimburse itself with the proceeds. Any money left over after repayment of the outstanding loan is returned to the former property owner.

A second mortgage is sometimes taken out on a single property. If the borrower defaults on his borrowings, the first mortgage ranks ahead of the second one in terms of being repaid out of the proceeds of the property sale.

5.1 Mortgage Interest

There are four main methods by which the interest on a mortgage may be charged. These are:

- variable rate;
- fixed rate;
- capped rate; and
- tracker rate.

In a typical **variable rate mortgage** the borrower pays interest at a rate that varies with prevailing interest rates. The rate is typically the lending bank or building society's 'standard variable rate'. This standard variable rate will reflect increases or decreases in the rates set by the Bank of England. So a borrower on a variable rate mortgage will benefit from rates falling and remaining low, but will suffer the additional costs when rates increase.

In a **fixed rate mortgage** the borrower's interest rate is set for an initial period, usually the first three or five years. If interest rates rise, the borrower is protected from the higher rates throughout this period, continuing to pay the lower, fixed rate of interest. However, if rates fall, and perhaps stay low, the fixed rate loan can only be cancelled if a redemption penalty is paid. The penalty is calculated to recoup the loss suffered by the lender as a result of the cancellation of the fixed rate loan.

It is common for fixed rate borrowers to be required to remain with the lender and pay interest at the lender's standard variable rate for a couple of years after the fixed rate deal ends – commonly referred to as a 'lock in' period.

Capped mortgages protect borrowers from rates rising above a particular rate – the 'capped rate'. For example, a mortgage might be taken out at 6%, with the interest rate based on the lender's standard variable rate, but with a cap at 7%. If prevailing rates fall to 5% the borrower pays at that rate, but if rates rise to 8% the rate paid cannot rise above the cap, and is only 7%.

A **tracker mortgage** is one that is linked to another rate such as the Bank of England base rate. The tracker rate will be set at a percentage above the Bank of England base rate, say 1% above, and will then increase or decrease as base rate changes, hence why it is called a tracker.

Lending institutions often attract borrowers by offering **discounted rate mortgages**. A 6% loan might be discounted to 5% for the first three years. Such deals might attract 'switchers' – borrowers who shop around and remortgage at a better rate; they may also be useful for first-time buyers as they make the transition to home ownership easier for those with a relatively low but growing level of income.

5.2 Types of Mortgage

5.2.1 Repayment Mortgages

The most straightforward form of mortgage is a repayment mortgage. This is simply a mortgage where the borrower will make monthly payments to the lender, with each monthly payment comprising both interest and capital.

⚙ Example

Mr Mullergee borrows £100,000 from XYZ Bank to finance the purchase of a flat on a repayment basis over 25 years. Each month he is required to pay £600 to XYZ Bank.

In the above example, Mr Mullergee will pay in total £180,000 to XYZ Bank (£600 x 12 months x 25 years), a total of £80,000 interest over and above the capital borrowed of £100,000.

Each payment he makes will be partly allocated to interest and partly allocated to capital. In the early years the payments are predominantly interest. Towards the middle of the term the capital begins to reduce significantly, and at the end of the mortgage term the payments are predominantly capital (see graph below).

The key advantage of a repayment mortgage over other forms of mortgage is that, as long as the borrower meets the repayments each

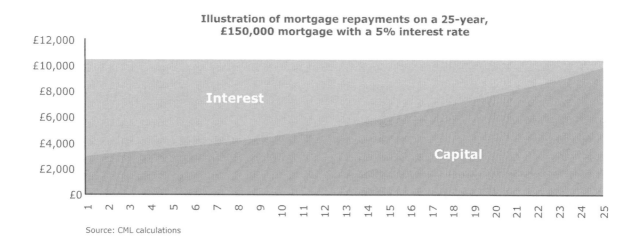

Illustration of mortgage repayments on a 25-year, £150,000 mortgage with a 5% interest rate

Source: CML calculations

month, he is guaranteed to pay off the loan over the term of the mortgage.

The main risks attached to a repayment mortgage from the borrower's perspective are:

- The cost of servicing the loan could increase, where interest is charged at the lender's standard variable rate of interest. This rate of interest will increase if interest rates go up. Mortgage repayments can rise significantly at the end of a fixed rate deal when they revert to the standard variable rate.
- The borrower runs the risk of having the property repossessed if he fails to meet the repayments – remember the mortgage loan is secured on the underlying property.

These risks also apply to other forms of mortgage.

5.2.2 Interest-Only Mortgages

As the name suggests, an interest-only mortgage requires the borrower to make interest payments to the lender throughout the period of the loan. At the same time, the borrower generally puts money aside each month, into some form of investment.

The borrower's aim is for the investment to grow through regular contributions and investment returns (such as dividends, interest and capital growth) so that at the end of the mortgage the accumulated investment is sufficient to pay back the capital borrowed and perhaps offer some additional cash.

⚙ Example

Ms Ward borrows £100,000 from XYZ Bank to finance the purchase of a flat on an interest-only basis over 25 years. Each month she is required to pay £420 interest to XYZ Bank. At the same time,

Ms Ward pays £180 each month into an investment fund run by an insurance company.

At the end of the 25-year period, Ms Ward hopes that the investment in the fund will have grown sufficiently to repay the £100,000 loan from XYZ Bank and offer an additional lump sum.

The main risks attached to an interest-only mortgage from the borrower's perspective are:

- Borrowers with interest-only mortgages still face the risks that repayment mortgage borrowers face – namely that interest rates may increase and their property is at risk if they fail to keep up the payments to the lender.
- There is also an additional risk that the investment might not grow sufficiently to pay the amount owing on the mortgage. In the example above, there is nothing guaranteeing that, at the end of the 25-year term, the investment in the fund will be worth £100,000 – indeed, it might be worth considerably less.

6. Life and Protection Insurance

Life assurance and protection policies are designed and sold by the insurance industry to provide individuals with some financial protection in case certain events occur. Although product details may vary from country to country, the general principles of what the individual (and his adviser) should be looking for in the products and their main features tend to be consistent. The big insurance companies are global operations, so the range of products they offer have common features and are similar whether offered in North America, Europe or the Asia/Pacific regions.

The following table gives some indication of the range of needs and products available.

Areas in need of protection	Protection products
Life and family	Life cover Critical illness cover Life or earlier critical illness cover Medical cover Long-term care
Lifestyle and income	Income protection Accident and sickness cover Unemployment cover
Home and contents	Household cover Mortgage income protection
Business	Key person protection Shareholder protection Partnership protection

6.1 Life Cover

Life assurance is a form of insurance policy where the event insured is a death. Such policies involve the payment of premiums in exchange for life cover – a lump sum that is payable upon death. These life policies are commonly taken out to provide for dependants after death (typically the spouse and children), or, when associated with a mortgage payment, to pay off the loan on the death of the borrower.

There are two types of life cover we need to consider, namely whole-of-life assurance and term assurance. A **whole-of-life policy** provides permanent cover, meaning that the sum assured will be paid whenever death occurs, as opposed to if death occurs within the term of a **term assurance policy**.

Before looking at these, it is important to know some key terms. See the table below.

KEY TERMS	
Proposer	The person who proposes to enter into a contract of insurance with a life insurance company to insure himself or another person on whose life he has insurable interest.
Life Assured	The person on whose life the contract depends is called the 'life assured'. Although the person who owns the policy and the life assured are frequently the same person, this is not necessarily the case. A policy on the life of one person, but effected and owned by someone else, is called a 'life of another' policy. A policy effected by the life assured is called an 'own life policy'.
Single Life	A single life policy pays out on one individual's death.
Joint Life	Where cover is required for two people, this can typically be arranged in one of two ways, through a joint life policy or two single life policies.
	A joint life policy can be arranged so that the benefits would be paid out following the death of either the first, or, if required for a specific reason, the second life assured. The majority of policies are arranged ultimately to protect financial dependants, with the sum assured or benefits being paid on the first death.
	With two separate single life policies, each person is covered separately. If both lives assured were to die at the same time, as the result of a car accident for example, the full benefits would be payable on each of the policies. If one of the lives assured died, benefits would be paid for that policy, with the surviving partner having continuing cover on their life.
Insurable Interest	To buy a life insurance policy on someone else's life, the proposer must have an interest in that person remaining alive, or expect financial loss from that person's death. This is called an insurable interest.

6.1.1 Term Assurance

A **term assurance** policy is for a set period, say 25 years. If the policy holder dies during the term, then his/her beneficiaries receive the insured sum. Term assurance has a variety of uses, such as ensuring there are funds available to repay a mortgage in case someone dies or providing a lump sum that can be used to generate income for a surviving partner or to provide funds to pay any tax that might become payable on death.

When taking out life cover, the individual selects the amount that they wish to be paid out if the event happens and the period that they want the cover to run for. If, during the period when the cover is in place, they die, then a lump sum will be paid out that equals the amount of life cover selected. With some policies, if an individual is diagnosed as suffering from a terminal illness which is expected to cause death within 12 months of the diagnosis, then the lump sum is payable at that point.

The amount of the premiums paid for term assurance will depend on:

- the amount insured;
- age, sex and family history;
- other risk factors, including state of health (for example, whether the individual is a smoker or non-smoker), his occupation and whether he participates in dangerous sports such as hang-gliding; and
- the term over which cover is required.

When selecting the amount of cover, an individual is able to choose three types of cover, namely level, increasing or decreasing cover.

Level cover, as the name suggests, means that the amount to be paid out if the event happens remains the same throughout the period in which the policy is in force, eg, £500,000 cover over the whole 25 years. As a result, the premiums are fixed at the outset and do not change during the period of the policy.

With **increasing cover**, the amount of cover and the premium rise, for example with inflation or by a set percentage each year, on each anniversary of the taking out of the policy.

As you would expect, with **decreasing cover** the amount that is originally chosen as the sum to be paid out decreases each year. The amount by which it decreases is agreed at the outset and, if it is used to repay a mortgage, it will be based on the expected reduction in the outstanding mortgage that would occur if the client had a repayment mortgage. Although the amount of cover will diminish year by year, the premiums payable will remain the same throughout the policy.

Note: 'Insurance' refers to something that *might* happen – for example, an individual might die at some stage in the next 25 years. 'Assurance' relates to something that *will* happen – every individual is going to die at some stage. Technically therefore, life assurance should be used to refer to a whole-of-life policy that will pay out on death, while life insurance should be used in the context of term policies that pay out only if death occurs within a particular period.

6.1.2 Whole-of-Life Assurance

Whole-of-life plans are generally investment-based policies (usually 'with-profits' schemes – see below). Essentially, they combine insurance (a pre-determined payout if the insured dies during a particular period) with savings. The savings part of these policies involves the money being invested in a fund that is often run by the insurance company, and invests in a combination of shares and bonds. A slightly simplistic policy might guarantee to pay out £100,000 if the insured dies during a 25 year period, or alternatively pay the accumulated value of the savings part of the policy at the end of 25 years if the insured survives.

The total paid out, therefore, depends on the guaranteed sum, the date of death and the investment performance of the fund.

There are three main types of whole of life policy:

- non-profit;
- with-profits; and
- unit-linked.

A **non-profit policy** guarantees to pay a set amount of life cover on the death of the person, regardless of when that might occur. It can be thought of as the equivalent of a term policy where the term will only end when the insured dies. There is no 'savings' portion for this type of policy, and the guaranteed amount paid out means that the policy does not depend on investment growth. As a result, the premiums are often very high. The insured sum is chosen at the outset and is fixed, eg, £500,000 whenever death occurs.

With-profits policies usually have a minimum amount of life cover. However, if the insured dies during the policy period, the minimum is increased each year by the addition of annual bonuses. These bonuses are based on the performance of the underlying investment portfolio run by the insurance company, often termed the 'with-profits fund'. However, these annual bonuses are usually spread out over a number of years to smooth the effect of fluctuating stock market returns. In other words, in a good year not all of the positive return will be added to the allocated bonus which should enable the insurance company to add a bonus even in a bad year.

One advantage of with-profits schemes is that profits are locked in each year, ie, the bonuses permanently increase the basic guaranteed sum. So, if the with-profits policy is being used to pay off a loan such as an interest-only mortgage, there is no risk that a general decline in the stock market just before the repayment date will suddenly remove the ability to repay the loan. If the investor had bought shares or bonds directly, or within a collective fund, the value of the investments could fall just before the repayment date.

A typical scheme might pay out:

- the '**sum assured**' or '**guaranteed sum**', which is usually an amount a little less than the premiums paid over the term;
- **annual bonuses**, as seen these are declared each year by the insurance company, and can vary. If the underlying performance of the investments in the fund is better than expected part of the surplus will be held back to enable the insurance company to award an annual bonus when returns are worse than expected. In this way, the returns 'smooth' the peaks and troughs that may be occurring in the underlying stock market;
- a '**terminal bonus**' at the end of the period. The terminal bonus can be substantial, for example 20% of the sum insured, but is not declared until the end of the policy term. It is essentially topping-up the policy to give it the appropriate share of the with-profits fund.

With **unit-linked policies** or a **unitised scheme**, the savings portion of the premium is used to buy units in the insurance company's investment fund rather than just allocated to the with-profits fund. The other portion of the premium is used to pay for the life assurance cover. The eventual return will be dependent upon the performance of the funds selected.

The reason for such policies being taken out is not normally just for the insured sum itself. Usually they are bought as part of a protection planning exercise to provide a lump sum in the event of death to pay off the principal in a mortgage or to provide funds to assist with the payment of any tax that might become payable on death. They can serve two purposes, therefore, both protection and investment.

Purchasing a life assurance policy is the same as entering into any other contract. When a person completes a proposal form and submits it to an insurance company, that constitutes a part of the formal process of entering into a contract. The principle of utmost good faith applies to insurance contracts. This places an obligation on the person seeking insurance to disclose any material facts that may affect how the insurance company may judge the risk of the contract they are entering into. Failure to disclose a material fact gives the insurance company the right to avoid paying out in the event of a claim.

There is a wide range of variations on the basic life policy that are driven by mortality risk, investment and expenses and premium options – all of which impact on the structure of the policy itself.

6.2 Protection Planning

There are four main areas that might be in need of protection – family and personal, mortgage, long-term care and business protection.

Each area is briefly considered below:

Family and Personal

The main wage-earner or another family member might suffer a serious illness. In some cases the illness may be critical. Without protection, the family could lose its main source of income and may have insufficient funds to live on. Additionally, there may be medical bills and care costs arising.

Similarly, the main wage-earner could lose his or her job. The family will lose its main source of income and may have insufficient funds to live on.

Other family and personal issues include the possibility that the family home is burgled, or suffers damage from extreme weather such as flooding or wind. Again, without protection, major expenditure will be required to buy new contents and repair any damage.

Mortgage

Job loss or illness suffered by the main wage-earner could result in difficulty in meeting mortgage payments. Furthermore, the main wage-earner might die before the mortgage

is repaid, saddling the family with ongoing mortgage repayments. Protection policies could be used to address these issues.

Long-Term Care

If an individual suffers mental and/or physical incapacity, the cost of care could drain and perhaps exhaust the individual's savings.

Business Protection

A key person within a business might die or suffer a serious illness. The business will no longer be able to generate sufficient profits without the key person's contribution.

Alternatively, a substantial shareholder or partner within the business may die. Their shareholding or partnership stake may need to be bought out by the remaining shareholders/partners.

6.3 Personal Protection Products

There is a wide range of protection products marketed by insurance companies and the characteristics of some of the more common types of products are considered below.

6.3.1 Critical Illness Insurance Cover

Critical illness cover is designed to pay a lump sum in the event that a person suffers from any one of a wide range of critical illnesses. Looking at how many people suffer from a major illness before they reach 65, its use and value can readily be seen. Illness may force an individual to give up work and so could cause financial hardship, to say nothing of how they will pay for specialist medical treatment or afford the additional costs that permanent disability may bring about.

Some of the key features of such policies include:

- The critical illnesses that will be covered will be closely defined.

- Some significant illnesses may be excluded.
- Illness resulting from certain activities, such as war or civil unrest, will not be covered.

Critical illness cover is available to those aged between 18 and 64 years of age and must end before an individual's 70th birthday. It will pay out a lump sum if an individual is diagnosed with a critical illness and will normally be tax-free. The cover will then cease.

There will be conditions attached to the cover that determine whether any payment will be made. A standard condition applying to all illnesses covered is that the insured person must survive for 28 days after the diagnosis of a critical illness to claim the benefit, and the illness must be expected to cause death within 12 months.

Critical illness cover can usually be taken out on a level, decreasing or increasing cover basis and can often be combined with other cover such as life cover.

6.3.2 Income Protection Cover

Income protection insurance is designed to pay out an income benefit when a person is unable to work for a prolonged period due to sickness or incapacity. Since this may be paid for a significant period of time, the premiums are relatively expensive. Their use and value can be readily appreciated by considering how a family would continue to pay its bills if the main income-earner were to fall ill. Some of the key features of such policies include:

- They run for a set term and an individual must be aged between 18 and 59 when the cover starts and it will stop when they reach 65.
- The circumstances under which a benefit will be payable are clearly defined. The illness or injury that an individual may suffer is referred to as 'incapacity', and the insurance policy will define what constitutes this in relation their occupation.

- They provide a regular income after a certain waiting period but there will be maximum limits on the amount of benefits paid related to a percentage of annual earnings. Payments will differ or cease on return to work.
- The cover pays out a regular monthly benefit if the individual becomes unable to work for longer than a deferred period, which is the time they must wait from when they first become unable to work until benefits start under the cover.
- The benefit starts once the deferred period finishes. The longer the deferred period chosen, the lower the premiums will be; the options available will be periods such as four, eight, 13, 26, 52 and 104 weeks.

Once a claim is made, the insurance company may extend the deferred period or even decline the claim. The claim will not be met if incapacity arises as a result of specific situations including unreasonable failure to follow medical advice, alcohol or solvent abuse, intentional self-inflicted injury and so on.

6.3.3 Mortgage Payment Protection Cover

Mortgage payment protection is designed to ensure that the payments that are due for a mortgage continue to be paid if the borrower is unable to work because of accident, sickness or unemployment.

They tend to be available from the lending institution, as well as insurance companies, although costs need to be carefully compared. They are designed to cover short-term problems, such as covering the costs if an individual loses their job and until they find alternative work, rather than long-term benefits.

The same basic features as reviewed above under income protection cover will apply, along with the following further considerations:

- The protection provided will be on a level basis, so regular reviews are needed so that the cover reflects the payments due as mortgage interest rates change.

- The amount of benefit payable can be reduced to take account of income from other sources and there may be limits on the maximum amounts that will be paid. As a result, the amount of benefit paid may not cover the mortgage payments.

6.3.4 Accident and Sickness Cover

Personal accident policies are generally taken out for annual periods and can provide for income or lump sum payments in the event of an accident. Although they are relatively inexpensive, care needs to be taken to look in detail at the exclusions and limits that apply. These may include:

- The amount of cover may be the lower of a set amount or a maximum percentage of the individual's gross monthly salary.
- The waiting period between when an individual becomes unable to work and when benefits start may be 30 or 60 days.

The insurance company will assess eligibility at the time of the claim and may refuse a claim as a result of pre-existing medical conditions even if they have been disclosed.

6.3.5 Household Cover

House and contents insurance are well established products and are well understood by consumers, so these will only be covered briefly.

Key considerations include:

- Is the cover enough to pay for the complete rebuild of a home?
- To what extent are external features of a house covered, such as walls, gates, drives and pathways?
- What cover is there in case a neighbour sues you for your tree falling on their property or a similar accident?
- What is the extent of cover for personal possessions?
- Is legal cover included?

6.3.6 Medical Insurance

Private medical insurance is obviously intended to cover the cost of medical and hospital expenses. It may be taken out by individuals, or provided as part of an individual's employment.

Some of the key features of such policies include:

- The costs that will be covered are usually closely defined.
- There will be limits on what will be paid out per claim, or even over a period such as a year.
- Standard care that can be dealt with by a person's local doctor may not be included.

Again, there will be exclusions such as for pre-existing conditions.

6.3.7 Long-Term Care

The purpose of long-term care cover is to provide the funds that will be needed in later life to meet the cost of care. Simply considering the cost of nursing home care explains the need for such a policy, but its value to an individual will depend on the amount of state funding for care costs that will be available.

Premiums will be expensive, reflecting the cost of care, and the benefit will normally be paid as an income that can be used to cover the expenditure.

6.3.8 Business Insurance Protection

Business insurance protection can take many forms. Some examples of its use are:

- To provide indemnity cover for claims against the business for faulty work or goods.
- To protect loans that have been taken out and secured against an individual's assets.
- To provide an income if the owner is unable to work and the business ceases.

- To provide payments in the event of a key member of a business dying to cover any impact on its profits.
- To provide money in the event of death of a major shareholder or partner so that the remaining shareholders can buy out his share and his estate can distribute the funds to his family.

Learning Objectives

Chapter Six has covered the following Learning Objectives:

3.2.1 Know the difference between a capital market instrument and a money market instrument

Lesson 17

3.2.2 Know the definition and features of the following: Treasury bill; commercial paper; certificate of deposit; money market funds

Lesson 13 and 17 (Treasury bill), Lesson 16 and 17 (certificate of deposit), Lesson 17 and 31 (commercial paper) and Lesson 17 (money market funds)

3.2.3 Know the advantages and disadvantages of investing in money market instruments

Lesson 17

3.3.1 Know the characteristics of property investment: commercial/residential property; direct/indirect investment

Lesson 39

3.3.2 Know the advantages and disadvantages of investing in property

Lesson 39

3.4.1 Know the basic structure of the foreign exchange market: currency quotes; settlement

Lesson 38

10.2.1 Understand the characteristics of the mortgage market: interest rates

Lesson 52

10.2.2 Know the definition of and types of mortgage: repayment; interest-only

Lesson 52

10.3.1 Understand the basic principles of life assurance

Lesson 51

10.3.2 Know the definition of the following types of life policy: term assurance; whole-of-life

Lesson 51

10.4.1 Know the main areas in need of protection: family and personal; mortgage; long-term care; business protection

Lesson 51

CISI
CHARTERED INSTITUTE FOR
SECURITIES & INVESTMENT

10.4.2 Know the main product features of the following: critical illness insurance; income protection; mortgage payment protection; accident and sickness cover; household cover; medical insurance; long-term care insurance; business insurance protection

 Lesson 51

Based on what you have learned in Chapter Six, try to answer the following end of chapter questions.

📄 End of Chapter Questions

Think of an answer for each question and refer to the appropriate section for confirmation.

1. How do money market instruments differ from capital market instruments?

    Answer Reference: Section 2

    ....

    ....

2. What are the three major types of money market instruments found in the UK and how do they pay their returns?

    Answer Reference: Section 2

    ....

    ....

3. Are exchange rates between most currencies fixed or floating?

    Answer Reference: Section 3

    ....

    ....

4. Where is the world's largest foreign exchange market centre?

    Answer Reference: Section 3

    ....

    ....

5. What are the most commonly quoted currency pairs?

    Answer Reference: Section 3

    ....

    ....

6. The number of US dollars that can be purchased with a £ has increased over a period. Which currency is said to have 'strengthened'?

   Answer Reference: Section 3

   ....

   ....

7. Who are the major participants in the foreign exchange market?

   Answer Reference: Section 3

   ....

   ....

8. Why is property different to other asset classes such as shares and bonds?

   Answer Reference: Section 4

   ....

   ....

9. What is a mortgage loan's typical term and what is it secured on?

   Answer Reference: Section 5

   ....

   ....

10. What is a mortgage default, and what is the likely result?

    Answer Reference: Section 5

    ....

    ....

11. What are the four main methods of charging interest on a mortgage?

    Answer Reference: Section 5.1

    ....

    ....

12. What are the two forms by which a mortgage loan is repaid?

    Answer Reference: Section 5.2

    ....

    ....

13. In a repayment mortgage, what proportion of the monthly payment is capital towards the beginning and end of the term?

    Answer Reference: Section 5.2.1

    ....

    ....

14. How is an interest-only mortgage typically repaid?

    Answer Reference: Section 5.2.2

    ....

    ....

15. What form of term assurance policy is typically used to cover a repayment mortgage loan?

    Answer Reference: Section 6.1.1

    ....

    ....

16. How does a with-profits policy smooth investment returns?

    Answer Reference: Section 6.1.2

    ....

    ....

7

The Economic Environment

The Economic Environment

1. Introduction

This chapter looks at economics. Economics is important as it is a key driver of the performance of both equities and bonds. For example, when the economy is generally doing well, most companies generate healthy profits and their shareholders benefit. When the economy suffers, interest rates tend to fall which boosts the value of bonds.

Initially, the chapter looks at how economic activity is determined in various economic and political systems, and then looks at the role of the central bank, particularly the Bank of England, in the management of that economic activity.

The chapter concludes with an explanation of some of the key economic measures that provide an indication of the state of an economy.

2. Factors Determining Economic Activity

2.1 Factors of Production

Any economic activity, such as running a business, requires four different kinds of input – land, labour, capital and enterprise. In economics these are commonly referred to as the 'factors of production'.

1. The land represents the physical space that is required, such as the fields required for agriculture, the factory for manufacturing, the shop for a retail business and office space.

2. The labour is the workforce, which could be skilled workers, unskilled workers or a mix of both.

3. The capital is the plant and equipment required to run the business, like production machinery in a manufacturing business, or computer equipment and ATMs for a retail bank.

4. Finally enterprise is the 'know how' – the knowledge or ability to put the first three factors to productive use.

The extent to which these factors are in private hands, or government hands, differs from country to country.

2.2 State-controlled Economies

A state-controlled economy is one where the state (ie, the government) decides what is produced and how it is distributed. These are also called 'planned', 'centrally planned', or 'command' economies, because all economic activity is supposed to be carried out according to a plan.

The Soviet Union (formed after the Russian Communist revolution in 1918) was the first modern, centrally planned economy. However, since the fall of Communism in the 1990s, Russia no longer plans its economy.

Similarly, China became a centrally planned economy after their revolution in 1949 and China has adopted market-based policies since the 1980s. North Korea is probably the last-surviving, true centrally-planned economy.

In a centrally planned (or 'command') economy, the factors of production are owned by the state and the motivation of the workforce is presumed to be the collective good of society, not individual gain. Every aspect of the economy is planned by the state in accordance with national priorities. This can result in excessive layers of bureaucracy, and state control inevitably removes a great deal of individual choice.

2.3 Market Economies

In a market economy, the factors of production – land, labour, capital and enterprise – are privately owned. Businesses produce goods and services to meet the demand from consumers. The interaction of demand from consumers and supply from businesses in the market will determine the **market-clearing price**. This is the price that reflects the balance between what consumers will willingly pay for goods and services and what suppliers will willingly accept for them.

If consumers demand more of a good, then shortages may occur. A shortage causes the price to rise, and the price rise provides the signal to the producing firms to produce more and attract new firms into the market.

In contrast, if the firms are producing too much of a particular good and the consumers are not buying all of the products, the price will be driven lower. The result will be that some producers will leave the market, as they will be unable to make a profit at the lower price.

In this way, the market directs resources and in a pure market system, the government merely operates as supervisor by issuing currency and providing a legal system.

Furthermore, there is a market not only for goods and services, but also for productive assets, such as capital goods (eg, machinery), labour and money. For the labour market, it is the wage level that is effectively the 'price', and for the money market it is the interest rate.

So, people compete for jobs and companies compete for customers in a market economy. Scarce resources, including skilled labour, such as a particularly skilful football player, or a financial asset, such as a share in a successful company, will have a high value. In a market economy, competition means that inferior football players and shares in unsuccessful companies will be much cheaper and ultimately competition could bring about the collapse of the unsuccessful company, and result in the inferior football player searching for an alternative career.

2.4 Mixed Economies

A mixed economy combines a market economy with some element of state control. The vast majority of economies are mixed to a greater or lesser extent.

While most would agree that unsuccessful companies should be allowed to fail, people also generally feel that the less able in society should be cushioned from the full force of the market economy. In a mixed economy, the government will provide a welfare system to support the unemployed, the infirm and the elderly, in tandem with the market-driven aspects of the economy. The government will also spend money running key areas such as defence, education, public transport, health and police services.

Governments raise finance for their public expenditure by:

* collecting taxes directly from wage-earners and companies;
* collecting indirect taxes (eg, VAT and taxes on petrol, cigarettes and alcohol); and
* raising money through borrowing in the capital markets.

Civil servants, primarily working for the government to raise money and spend it, tend to be one of the largest groups in the labour market. In the UK it is the civil servants working for the Treasury who raise money and allocate it to the 'spending departments', such as the National Health Service.

Virtually every economy in the world contains a mix of market activity and government intervention and the extent of the mix can be measured by government spending as a percentage of gross domestic product or GDP. GDP is a key measure of economic output and will be explored in more detail later in this

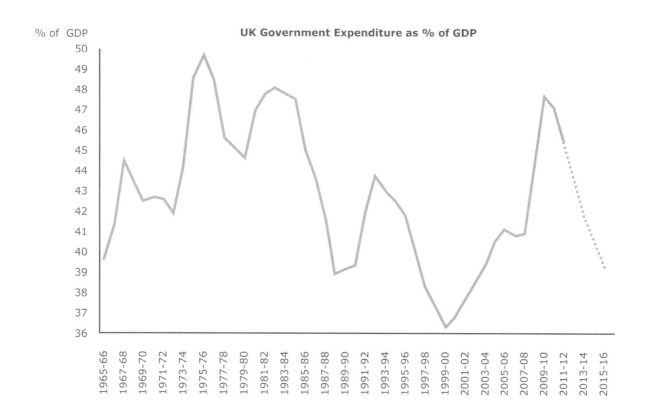

UK Government Expenditure as % of GDP

chapter. Clearly, the bigger the percentage, the more government control within the mixed economy.

2.5 Open Economies

In an open economy there are few barriers to trade or controls over foreign exchange. Most developed nations are relatively open economies. For example, although most western governments create barriers to protect their citizens against illegal drugs and other dangers, they generally have policies to allow or encourage free trade.

From time to time, issues will arise where one country believes another is taking unfair advantage of trade policies and takes some form of retaliatory action, possibly including the imposition of sanctions. These sanctions might take the form of special tariffs that are applied to imports. When a country prevents other countries from trading freely with it in order to preserve its domestic market, it is usually referred to as **protectionism**.

The **World Trade Organisation (WTO)** exists to promote the growth of free trade between economies. It is, therefore, sometimes called upon to arbitrate when disputes arise.

3. Central Banks

Traditionally, the role of government has been to manage the economy through taxation and through economic and monetary policy, and to ensure a fair society by the state provision of welfare and benefits to those who meet certain criteria, while leaving business relatively free to address the challenges and opportunities that arise.

Governments can use a variety of policies when attempting to reduce the impact of fluctuations in economic activity. Collectively these measures are known as stabilisation policies and are categorised under the broad headings of fiscal policy and monetary policy.

Fiscal policy involves making adjustments using government spending and taxation, whilst monetary policy involves making adjustments to interest rates and the money supply. Rather than following one or other type of policy, most governments now adopt a pragmatic approach to controlling the level of economic activity through a combination of fiscal and monetary policy. In an increasingly integrated world, however, controlling the level of activity in an open economy in isolation is difficult, as financial markets, rather than individual governments and central banks, tend to dictate economic policy.

Governments implement their economic policies using their central bank, and a consideration of their role in this implementation is explained below.

3.1 The Role of Central Banks

Central banks operate at the very centre of a nation's financial system. They are public bodies but, increasingly, they operate independently of government control or political interference. They usually have some or all of the following responsibilities:

- Acting as banker to the banking system by accepting deposits from, and lending to, commercial banks.
- Acting as banker to the government.
- Managing the national debt.
- Regulating the domestic banking system.
- Acting as lender of last resort to the banking system in financial crises to prevent the systemic collapse of the banking system.
- Setting the official short-term rate of interest.
- Controlling the money supply.
- Issuing notes and coins.
- Holding the nation's gold and foreign currency reserves.
- Influencing the value of a nation's currency through activities such as intervention in the currency markets.
- Providing a depositors' protection scheme for bank deposits.

3.2 The Bank of England

The Bank of England is the central bank of the UK. It was founded in 1694 and is often referred to as the 'Old Lady of Threadneedle Street' because its headquarters building is situated in Threadneedle Street in the City of London.

The Bank's roles and functions have evolved and changed over its 300-year history. Since its foundation it has been the government's banker and, since the late 18th century, it has been banker to the banking system more generally – the bankers' bank. As well as providing banking services to these customers, the Bank of England also manages the UK's foreign exchange and gold reserves.

The Bank has two core purposes – monetary stability and financial stability.

- **Monetary Stability** – Monetary stability means stable prices and confidence in the currency. Stable prices are defined by the Government's inflation target, which the Bank seeks to meet through its decisions in relation to interest rates.

- **Financial Stability** – A stable financial system is a key ingredient for a healthy and successful economy. People need to have confidence that the system is safe and stable, and functions properly. The Bank of England's role in relation to this involves detecting and reducing threats to the financial system as a whole. Such threats are detected through the Bank's surveillance and market intelligence functions. They are reduced by the Bank overseeing the payments systems, banking and market operations, including, in exceptional circumstances by acting as lender of last resort, and resolution work to deal with distressed banks.

Since the credit crisis, the Bank's role of protecting and enhancing the stability of the financial system has gained greater emphasis and importance. The purpose of preserving financial stability is to maintain the three vital functions which the financial system performs in the economy:

- providing the main mechanism for paying for goods, services and financial assets;
- intermediating between savers and borrowers, and channelling savings into investment, via debt and equity instruments; and
- insuring against, and dispersing, risk.

The government plans a major reform of the UK regulatory regime which will significantly increase and broaden the Bank's role and responsibilities for financial stability. These changes are a result of the weaknesses identified as a result of the credit crisis of which perhaps the most significant failing was that no single institution had responsibility, authority or powers to oversee the financial system as a whole.

In June 2011, the government announced the details of its plans which will include the establishment of a new committee at the Bank of England — the Financial Policy committee (FPC). The FPC will be tasked with monitoring the stability and resilience of the UK financial system and using its powers to tackle those risks.

The Bank is perhaps most visible to the general public through its banknotes and, more recently, its interest rate decisions. The Bank has had a monopoly on the issue of banknotes in England and Wales since the early 20th century. But it is only since 1997 that the Bank has had statutory responsibility for setting the UK's official interest rate. Prior to 1997, the setting of interest rates could be subject to political interference, for example, an existing government could keep the interest rate low in the lead up to a General Election.

Interest rate decisions are taken by the Bank's **Monetary Policy Committee (MPC)**. The MPC's primary focus is to ensure that inflation is kept within a government-set range. Inflation is prices persistently increasing, and the impact of this will be considered in greater detail in the next section.

The MPC can then set the 'base rate', an officially published short-term interest rate, to meet the inflation target. The inflation target is set each year by the Chancellor of the Exchequer.

At its monthly meetings, the MPC must gauge all of those factors that can influence inflation over both the short and medium term. These include the level of the exchange rate, the rate at which the economy is growing, how much consumers are borrowing and spending, wage inflation, and any changes to government spending and taxation plans. When setting the base rate, however, it must also be mindful of the impact any changes will have on the sustainability of economic growth and employment in the UK and the time lag between a change in rate and the effects it will have on the economy. If the Bank fails to keep inflation close to the government target, the Governor of the Bank of England is required to write a letter of explanation to the Chancellor of the Exchequer.

Controlling inflation using the interest rate is a delicate balancing act. Increasing interest rates to curb inflation puts people off borrowing to buy, but can also slow down the economy because reduced demand means less production of goods and services, and less production means less employment, and slower economic growth. In contrast, low interest rates stimulate the economy, but could lead to inflation.

In addition to its short-term interest-rate-setting role, the Bank also assumes responsibility for many other traditional central bank activities, including:

- Acting as banker to the banking system by accepting deposits from, and lending to, commercial banks.
- Acting as banker to the government.
- Acting as lender of last resort to the banking system in financial crises to prevent its systemic collapse.
- Issuing notes and coins.
- Holding the nation's gold and foreign currency reserves.

- Influencing the value of the nation's currency through activities such as intervention in the currency markets.

There are two roles that are often performed by central banks that are not undertaken by the Bank of England. These are:

- Managing the national debt (this is done by the Debt Management Office in the UK).
- Providing a depositors' protection scheme for bank deposits (this is provided by the Financial Services Compensation Scheme in the UK).

3.3 The Federal Reserve (FED)

The Federal Reserve System in the US dates back to 1913. The Fed, as it is known, comprises 12 regional Federal Reserve Banks, each of which monitors the activities of, and provides liquidity to, the banks in its region. Although free from political interference, the Fed is governed by a seven-strong board appointed by the President of the United States. This governing board, together with the presidents of five of the 12 Federal Reserve banks, makes up the Federal Open Market Committee (FOMC). The chairman of the FOMC, also appointed by the US President, takes responsibility for the committee's decisions, which are directed towards its statutory duty of promoting price stability and sustainable economic growth.

The FOMC meets every six weeks or so to examine the latest economic data in order to gauge the health of the economy and determine whether the economically sensitive Fed funds rate should be altered. Very occasionally it meets in emergency session, if economic circumstances dictate. As lender of last resort to the US banking system, the Fed has, in recent years, rescued a number of US financial institutions and markets from collapse. In doing so it has prevented widespread panic, and stopped systemic risk from spreading throughout the financial system.

3.4 The European Central Bank (ECB)

Based in Frankfurt, the ECB assumed its central banking responsibilities upon the creation of the euro, on 1 January 1999. The ECB is principally responsible for setting monetary policy for the entire eurozone, with the sole objective of maintaining internal price stability. Its objective of keeping inflation, as defined by the harmonised index of consumer prices (HICP), 'close to but below 2% in the medium term' is achieved by influencing those factors that may influence inflation, such as the external value of the euro and growth in the money supply.

The ECB sets its monetary policy through its president and council; the latter comprises the governors of each of the eurozone's national central banks. Although the ECB acts independently of European Union member governments when implementing monetary policy, it has on occasion succumbed to political persuasion. It is also one of the few central banks that does not act as a lender of last resort to the banking system.

4. The Impact of Inflation

This section will first consider the way goods and services are paid for, including the ability of banks to create credit, and then move on to look at how this interacts with inflation, and the impact inflation can have on an economy.

4.1 Credit Creation

Most of what is purchased by consumers is not paid for using cash. It is generally more convenient to pay by card or cheque and it is fairly easy (subject to the borrower's credit status) to buy something now and pay later, for example, by going overdrawn, using a credit card or taking out a loan. Loans will often be for more substantial purchases such as a house or a car. Buying now and paying later is generally referred to as purchasing goods and services 'on credit'.

The banking system provides a mechanism in which credit can be created. This means that banks can increase the total amount of spending power in the economy, as shown in the following example.

> ⚙ **Example**
>
> *New Bank plc sets up business and is granted a banking licence. It is authorised to take deposits and make loans. Because New Bank knows that only a small proportion of the deposited funds are likely to be demanded at any one time, it will be able to lend most of the deposited money to others. New Bank will make profits by lending money out and charging a higher rate of interest than it pays depositors.*
>
> *These loans provide an increase in the money supply in circulation – New Bank is creating credit.*

By lending, banks create money and advance this to borrowers that may be businesses, consumers and governments. As soon as the borrowed money is spent on goods and services, the people to whom it is paid (the providers of those goods and services) will then deposit it in their own bank accounts, allowing the banks to use it to create fresh credit all over again.

It is estimated that this 'credit creation' process accounts for 96% of the money in circulation in most industrialised nations, with only 4% being in the form of notes and coins created by the government.

If this process were uncontrolled it could lead to a rapid increase in the money supply and, with too much money chasing too few goods, the result would be an increase in inflation. Understandably, therefore, central banks aim to keep the amount of credit creation under control as part of their overall monetary policy. They aim to ensure that the amount of credit creation is below the level at which it would increase the money supply so much that inflation accelerates.

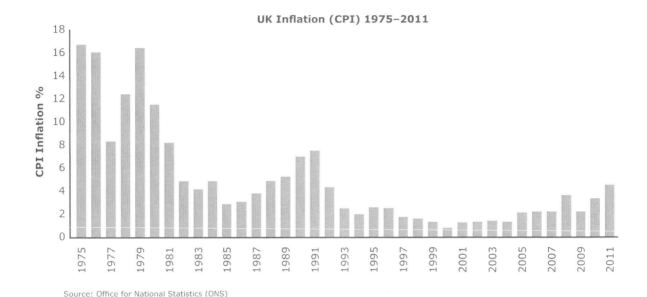

UK Inflation (CPI) 1975–2011

Source: Office for National Statistics (ONS)

As seen earlier, the MPC of the Bank of England does this by influencing people's willingness to borrow by setting the interest rate.

4.2 The Impact of Inflation

As already seen, inflation is a persistent increase in the general level of prices. There are a number of reasons why prices might increase, such as:

- Excess demand in the economy – too much money chasing too few goods.
- Scarcity of resources – when goods or services are in short supply, the prices paid for them tend to increase.
- Rapidly increasing government spending.

Most western governments seek to control inflation at a level of about 2–3% per annum without letting it get too high, or too low.

High levels of inflation can cause the following problems:

- Businesses have to continually update prices to keep pace with inflation.
- Employees find the real value of their salaries eroded.

- Those on fixed levels of income, such as pensioners, will suffer as the price increases are not matched by increases in income.
- Exports may become less competitive.
- The real value of future pensions and investment income becomes difficult to assess, which might act as a disincentive to save.

There are, however, some positive aspects to high levels of inflation:

- Rising house prices contribute to a 'feel good' factor (although this might contribute to further inflation as house owners become more eager to borrow and spend).
- Borrowers benefit, because the value of their debt falls in 'real terms' – ie, after adjusting for the effect of inflation.
- Inflation also erodes the real value of a country's national debt and so can benefit an economy in difficult times.

5. Key Economic Indicators

This section looks at a number of key economic statistics that can provide investors with a guide to the health of the economy and aid long-term investment decisions. These statistics are often called economic 'indicators', because they indicate how well the economy is performing. They are watched carefully by the government as well as by financial analysts.

5.1 Inflation Measures

Inflation is generally measured by selecting a 'basket' of goods and services that are typically purchased by consumers. The basket of goods and services forms the basis for an index to measure inflation. The index simply takes this basket of goods and services and works out how much each price has changed and then weights the price changes according to their importance.

Some price changes have a much bigger impact on people than others. For example, an increase of 5% in the price of bread is likely to affect people much more than a 100% increase in the price of a box of matches. So bread therefore gets a much bigger weighting than matches, and changes in the price of bread will have a bigger effect on the index than changes in the price of matches.

There are various measures of inflation, including the following:

- **Retail Prices Index (RPI)** – the RPI (also known as the 'headline' rate) measures the increase in general household spending, including mortgage and rent payments, food, transport and entertainment.
- **RPIX** – this is the RPI, but excluding mortgage interest payments. This is often referred to as the 'underlying' rate of inflation. Excluding mortgage interest payments removes much of the impact of interest rate changes in general from the measure of inflation.
- **Consumer Prices Index (CPI)** – this is a measure of inflation that is prepared in a standard way throughout the EU. Like the RPIX, it excludes mortgage interest payments, largely because a substantial proportion of the population in continental Europe rent their homes, rather than buy them. Unlike the RPIX, however, it also excludes other housing costs aside from mortgage interest costs (for example, it excludes the 'depreciation component', an amount which the RPI uses to allow for the cost of maintaining a home in a constant condition). It was originally known as the **Harmonised Index of Consumer Prices (HICP)**.

Clearly, the different measures of inflation tend to show similar patterns but will not move perfectly in step as illustrated in the graph below.

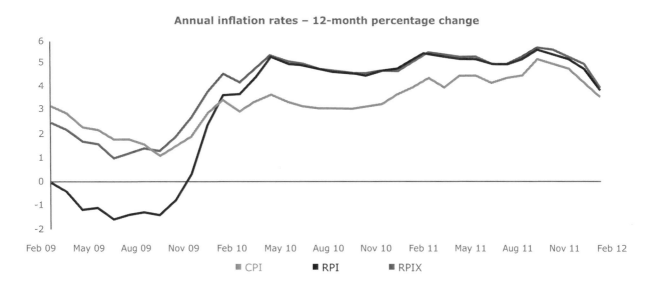

Annual inflation rates – 12-month percentage change

In the UK, the government uses the CPI for a range of purposes, principally those where it needs to measure inflation on a like-for-like basis with other European countries.

5.2 Measures of Economic Data

In addition to inflation measures like the CPI, there are a number of other economic statistics carefully watched by the government and by other market participants as potentially significant indicators of how the economy is performing.

5.2.1 Gross Domestic Product (GDP)

At the very simplest level, an economy comprises two distinct groups: individuals and firms. Individuals supply firms with the productive resources (such as their labour) in exchange for an income. In turn, these individuals use this income to buy the entire output produced by firms employing these resources. This gives rise to what is known as the **circular flow** of income.

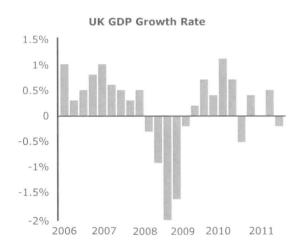

UK GDP Growth Rate

However, as can be seen by the diagram below, there is a little more to the 'circular flow' than just the individuals and firms. The government takes taxes from both firms and individuals and provides benefits to the unemployed and needy in the form of 'transfer payments' as well as spending on areas like

defence and healthcare. There are exports from the firms to overseas economies and imports from overseas economies into the UK and there is money channelled through the financial markets in the form of savings and investment.

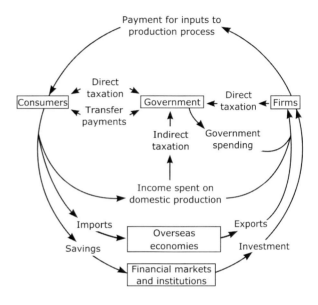

Using the circular flow, economic activity can be measured in one of three ways:

- by the total income paid by firms to individuals;
- by individuals' total expenditure on firms' output; or
- by the value of total output generated by firms.

Gross domestic product is most commonly measured by looking at expenditure to calculate a country's output. This is known as the 'expenditure basis' and is typically calculated quarterly as follows:

Gross Domestic Product	
	consumer spending
+	government spending
+	investment
+	exports
−	imports
=	GDP

Clearly, an increasing level of GDP usually signifies an economy in a healthy state, with economies ideally looking for a consistent **'trend' of growth** over time. Below is a chart of some recent GDP statistics for the UK showing the quarterly and annual GDP percentage growth figures.

If GDP falls, it is described as 'negative growth' and two consecutive quarters of negative growth is defined as a 'recession'. In a recession, consumers spend less, jobs are lost and output falls with the government usually trying to make up for the shortfall by spending more. However, this may be difficult if the government concerned has already built up too much debt and cannot borrow any more money.

The fact that actual growth fluctuates and deviates from trend growth in the short-term is often termed the economic cycle, or business cycle. When an economy is growing in excess of its trend growth rate, actual output will exceed potential output, often leading to inflation. However, when a country's output contracts and the economy is in recession, there is likely to be spare capacity and unemployment.

5.2.2 Balance of Payments

The balance of payments is a summary of all the transactions between the UK and the rest of the world. If the UK imports more than it exports, there is a **balance of payments deficit**. If the UK exports more than it imports, there is a **balance of payments surplus**.

The main components of the balance of payments are the current account and the capital account.

The balance of trade comprises a visible trade balance – the difference between the value of imported and exported goods – and an invisible trade balance – the difference between the value of imported and exported services. The trade balance is detailed in the **current account**, which is used to calculate the total value of goods and services that flow into and out of a country. The results of the current

account calculations provide details of the balance of trade a country has with the rest of the world. The UK typically runs a deficit on visible trade but an invisible trade surplus. Also, being an open economy, imports and exports combined total over 50% of UK GDP.

The **capital account** records international capital transactions related to investment in business, real estate, bonds and stocks. This includes transactions relating to the purchase and sale of domestic and foreign investment assets. These are usually divided into categories such as foreign direct investment where an overseas firm acquires a new plant or an existing business; portfolio investment which includes trading in stocks and bonds; and other investments which include transactions in currency and bank deposits.

For the balance of payments to balance, the current account must equal the capital account plus or minus a balancing item – used to rectify the many errors in compiling the balance of payments – plus or minus any change in central bank foreign currency reserves. In other words, a current account deficit resulting from a country being a net importer of overseas goods and services must be met by a net inflow of capital from overseas, taking account of any measurement errors and any central bank intervention in the foreign currency market.

Having a favourable **exchange rate** can be critical to the level of international trade undertaken, and therefore to a country's economic position. This can be understood by looking at what happens if a country's exchange rate alters.

- If the value of the domestic currency (eg, £ sterling) rises relative to other currencies, then exports will be less competitive unless producers reduce their prices and imports will be cheaper and therefore more competitive. The result will be either to reduce a trade surplus or worsen a trade deficit.

- If the value of the domestic currency falls against other currencies then the reverse happens: exports will be cheaper in foreign markets and thus more competitive, and imports will be more expensive and therefore, less attractive. A trade surplus or deficit is likely to see an improving position.

5.2.3 Public Sector Net Cash Requirement (PSNCR)

A key function of government is to manage the public finances, and so a key economic indicator is the level of public sector debt, or the national debt as it is more frequently referred to.

In the past a state would incur budget deficits, usually as a result of wars, and finance these through taxation. In the UK, this changed in the late 1600s when the government's need to finance another war with France led to the creation of the Bank of England in 1694 and the first issue of state public debt in England.

Following on from this, the early 1700s saw the emergence of banking and financial markets and the ability to raise money by creating debt through the issue of bills and bonds and the beginning of the national debt. Some key statistics from the Office for National Statistics show how the national debt has grown since then:

- The national debt rose from £12 million in 1700 to £850 million by the end of the Napoleonic Wars in 1815.
- The two world wars of the 20th century caused debt levels to rise, from £650 million in 1914 to £7.4 billion by 1919 and from £7.1 billion in 1939 to £24.7 billion in 1946.
- The period of relatively high inflation in the 1970s and 1980s saw debt rise from £33.1 billion in 1970 to £197.4 billion in 1988.

Since then, of course, the national debt has ballooned even further and as the effects of previous overspending and the recent

recession take effect. There are a wide number of measures used as key economic indicators which can be quite confusing. This is due to each measuring different sets of data but essentially they fall into two main types:

- **Government debt** – essentially this is what the government owes. The most widely quoted is the public sector net debt.
- **Government deficit** – essentially the shortfall between what the government receives in tax receipts and what it spends. The most widely quoted is in the Public Sector Net Cash Requirement (PSNCR).

Debt measures are also usually presented as a percentage of GDP since comparisons over time need to allow for effects such as inflation. Dividing by GDP is the conventional way of doing this.

So, the PSNCR is the difference between government expenditure and government income. Government income mainly comes from taxes. In a buoyant economy, government spending tends to be less than income, with substantial tax revenues generated from corporate profits and high levels of employment. This enables the government to reduce public sector (ie, government) borrowing.

In a slowing economy, spending tends to exceed tax revenues and the government will need to raise borrowing by issuing government bonds. This is currently the case in the UK, where the budget deficit has increased substantially as the recession reduced tax receipts and pushed up spending on unemployment benefit. Public sector net debt as a proportion of GDP is forecast to peak at 78.0% in 2014–2015. If left unaddressed, high levels of public borrowing and debt risk undermining growth and economic stability.

5.2.4 Level of Unemployment

The extent to which those seeking employment cannot find work is an important indicator of the health of the economy. There is always likely to be some unemployment in an economy – some people might lack the right skills and/or live in employment black spots. Higher levels of unemployment indicate low demand in the economy for goods and services produced and sold to consumers and therefore low demand for UK people to provide them.

In addition, high unemployment levels will have a negative impact on the government's finances. The government will need to increase social security payments, and its income will decrease because of the lack of any tax revenues from the unemployed.

⭐ Learning Objectives

Chapter Seven has covered the following Learning Objectives:

2.1 Economic Environment

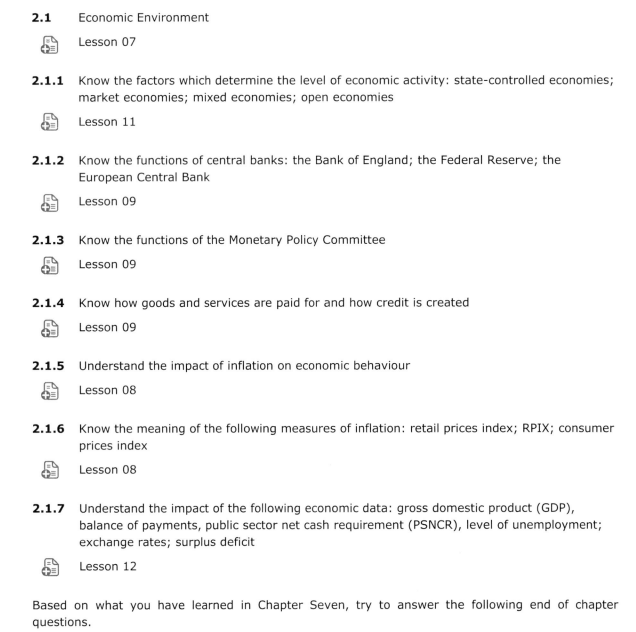

Lesson 07

2.1.1 Know the factors which determine the level of economic activity: state-controlled economies; market economies; mixed economies; open economies

Lesson 11

2.1.2 Know the functions of central banks: the Bank of England; the Federal Reserve; the European Central Bank

Lesson 09

2.1.3 Know the functions of the Monetary Policy Committee

Lesson 09

2.1.4 Know how goods and services are paid for and how credit is created

Lesson 09

2.1.5 Understand the impact of inflation on economic behaviour

Lesson 08

2.1.6 Know the meaning of the following measures of inflation: retail prices index; RPIX; consumer prices index

Lesson 08

2.1.7 Understand the impact of the following economic data: gross domestic product (GDP), balance of payments, public sector net cash requirement (PSNCR), level of unemployment; exchange rates; surplus deficit

Lesson 12

Based on what you have learned in Chapter Seven, try to answer the following end of chapter questions.

🖎 End of Chapter Questions

Think of an answer for each question and refer to the appropriate section for confirmation.

1. What are the four factors of production?

    Answer Reference: Section 2.1

    ....

    ....

2. What are the two alternative terms for a state-controlled economy?

    Answer Reference: Section 2.2

    ....

    ....

3. Give an example of a state-controlled economy.

    Answer Reference: Section 2.2

    ....

    ....

4. In a market economy, how are prices determined?

    Answer Reference: Section 2.3

    ....

    ....

5. The vast majority of countries are neither state-controlled nor market economies. What are they?

    Answer Reference: Section 2.4

    ....

    ....

6. What is an open economy?

    Answer Reference: Section 2.5

    ....

    ....

7. Who arbitrates in disputes over international trade?

    Answer Reference: Section 2.5

    ....

    ....

8. What are the two core functions of the Bank of England?

    Answer Reference: Section 3.1

    ....

    ....

9. Who decides on the UK's official interest rate?

    Answer Reference: Section 3.1

    ....

    ....

10. Who decides on the UK's inflationary target?

    Answer Reference: Section 3.1

    ....

    ....

11. What happens if the Bank of England fails to keep inflation close to target?

    Answer Reference: Section 3.1

    ....

    ....

12. List the seven things for which the Bank of England has responsibility.

    Answer Reference: Section 3.1

    ....

    ....

13. List the two typical central bank roles that are not undertaken by the Bank of England.

    Answer Reference: Section 3.1

    ....

    ....

14. How are most goods and services paid for in the UK?

    Answer Reference: Section 4.1

    ....

    ....

15. What is credit creation?

    Answer Reference: Section 4.1

    ....

    ....

16. What is inflation?

    Answer Reference: Section 4.2

    ....

    ....

17. List at least three problems caused by high levels of inflation.

    Answer Reference: Section 4.2

    ....

    ....

18. What are the three major measures of inflation published in the UK and how do they differ?

    Answer Reference: Section 5.1

    ....

    ....

19. How is GDP usually calculated?

    Answer Reference: Section 5.2.1

    ....

    ....

20. What is a recession?

    Answer Reference: Section 5.2.1

    ....

    ....

21. What is a balance of payments surplus?

    Answer Reference: Section 5.2.2

    ....

    ....

22. What is the current account made up of?

    Answer Reference: Section 5.2.2

    ....

    ....

23. What is the likely impact on the balance of trade if the domestic currency exchange rate weakens?

    Answer Reference: Section 5.2.2

    ....

    ....

24. What is the PSNCR?

    Answer Reference: Section 5.2.3

    ....

    ....

25. What impact is high unemployment likely to have on government finances?

    Answer Reference: Section 5.2.4

    ....

    ....

Derivatives

Derivatives

1. Uses of Derivatives

A derivative is a financial instrument where the value of the instrument is derived from the price of another underlying asset. This underlying asset could be a financial asset, such as those considered in the previous chapters, or a commodity. Examples of financial assets include bonds, shares, stock market indices and interest rates; for commodities they include oil, silver or wheat.

A simple example would be an airline committing to buy jet fuel from an oil company now, with the delivery not taking place until two months later. This is termed a 'forward' contract. The price the airline will have to pay will obviously be closely related to prevailing price of the underlying asset, jet fuel.

The trading of derivatives can take place directly between **counterparties** (such as the airline and the oil company seen above) or on an organised exchange. Where trading takes place directly between counterparties it is referred to as **OTC or over-the-counter** trading. When a derivative is traded on an exchange, it is no longer an OTC trade and is instead referred to as **exchange-traded**.

Derivatives tend to be used for two purposes – hedging and speculating.

Hedging is reducing the risk of adverse price movements. In the brief example outlined above, the airline is removing the risk that the cost of jet fuel may increase in the next two months and the oil company is guaranteeing that it will not suffer if the price of jet fuel falls in the next two months. So, both participants are hedging.

Speculation is where the motivation behind the derivative trade is to make money. Developing the earlier example of the airline hedging its risk in relation to the price of jet fuel, imagine that the deal is done between the airline and a bank, rather than the airline and an oil company. Clearly the airline's motivation is still to hedge, but why would a bank be willing to be involved? Well, if the bank thought that the price of jet fuel was likely to fall over the next two months, then the derivatives contract might make some money for the bank. The bank is speculating. As long as the bank is correct and the price of jet fuel falls over the next two months, the bank will make money because it has agreed to sell jet fuel at a higher price than it needs to pay for the fuel two months later.

As will be detailed in the remainder of this chapter, most derivatives take one of the following forms:

- Forwards.
- Futures.
- Options.
- Swaps.

2. Futures

2.1 Development of Futures

Derivatives are not a new concept and, in fact, have been around for hundreds of years. Their origins can be traced back to agricultural markets where farmers needed a mechanism to guard against price fluctuations caused by gluts of produce or periods of drought. So, in order to fix the price of agricultural produce in advance of harvest time, farmers and merchants entered into forward contracts. Like the jet fuel example encountered above, these agricultural forward contracts set the price at which a stated amount of a commodity (for example a bushel of wheat) would be delivered between a farmer and a merchant at a pre-specified future time.

Because these early derivative contracts removed risks they were very popular and led

to the opening of the world's first derivatives exchange, the Chicago Board of Trade (CBOT), in 1848.

The exchange introduced a **futures contract**. The futures contract involved the purchase or sale of a standardised quantity and quality of grain (such as 100 bushels of wheat containing no more than 5% moisture) for a price agreed now and for delivery on a stated future delivery date, such as three months later. Unlike the forward contracts that preceded it, these futures contract are traded on the exchange, rather than over the counter. These futures contracts have subsequently been extended to a wide variety of commodities and are offered by an increasing number of derivatives exchanges.

It was not until 1975 that CBOT introduced the world's first **financial futures contract**. Rather than being based on a commodity like wheat, oil or metal, financial futures are based on financial assets like shares and bonds.

2.2 Definition and Function of a Future

A future is an agreement between a buyer and a seller. A futures contract is a legally binding obligation between two parties: the buyer agrees to pay a pre-specified amount for the delivery of a particular pre-specified quantity of an asset at a pre-specified future date. The seller agrees to deliver the asset at the future date, in exchange for the pre-specified amount of money.

⚙ Example

A buyer might agree with a seller to pay $100 per barrel for 1,000 barrels of crude oil in three months' time. The buyer might be an electricity-generating company wanting to fix the price it will have to pay for the oil to use in its oil-fired power stations and the seller might be an oil company wanting to fix the sales price of some of its future oil production. Both of the counterparties to the trade are using the futures contract to hedge.

A futures contract has two distinct features:

- It is **exchange-traded** – for example, on the derivatives exchanges such as NYSE Liffe or the IntercontinentalExchange (ICE).
- It is dealt on **standardised terms** – the exchange specifies the quality of the underlying asset, the quantity underlying each contract, the future date and the delivery location – only the price is open to negotiation. In the above example, the oil quality will be based on the oil field from which it originates (eg, Brent crude – from the Brent oil field in the North Sea), the quantity is 1,000 barrels, the date is three months ahead and the location might be the port of Rotterdam.

2.3 Futures Terminology

Derivatives markets have specialised terminology that is important to understand.

Staying with the example above, the buyer of the contract to purchase 1,000 barrels of crude oil at $100 per barrel for delivery in three months is said to go 'long' of the contract, while the seller is described as going 'short'. Entering into the transaction is known as 'opening the trade' and the eventual delivery of the crude oil will **close-out** the trade.

The definition of these key terms that the futures market uses are as follows:

- **Long** – the term used for the position taken by the buyer of the future. The person who is 'long' of the contract is committed to buying the underlying asset at the pre-agreed price on the specified future date.
- **Short** – the position taken by the seller of the future. The seller is committed to delivering the underlying asset in exchange for the pre-agreed price on the specified future date.
- **Open** – the initial trade. A market participant 'opens' a trade when it first enters into a future. It could be buying a future (opening a long position), or selling a future (opening a short position).

- **Close** – the physical assets underlying most futures that are opened do not end up being delivered: they are 'closed-out' instead. For example, an opening buyer will almost invariably avoid delivery by making a closing sale before the delivery date. If the buyer does not close-out, he will pay the agreed sum and receive the underlying asset. This might be something the buyer is keen to avoid, for example because the buyer is actually a financial institution like a bank simply speculating on the price of the underlying asset using futures.
- **Covered** – is where the seller of the future has the underlying asset that will be needed if physical delivery takes place.
- **Naked** – is where the seller of the future does not have the asset that will be needed if physical delivery of the underlying commodity is required.

3. Options

3.1 Development of Options

Options are another form of derivative. They did not really start to flourish until two US academics produced an option pricing model in 1973 that allowed them to be readily priced. This paved the way for the creation of standardised options contracts and the opening of the Chicago Board Options Exchange (CBOE) in the same year. This in turn led to an explosion in product innovation and introduction of options onto other exchanges, such as NYSE Liffe.

3.2 Definition and Function of an Option

An option gives a buyer the right, but not the obligation, to buy or sell a specified quantity of an underlying asset at a pre-agreed **exercise price**, on or before a pre-specified future date or between two specified dates. The seller, in exchange for the payment of a **premium**, grants the option to the buyer.

As further detailed below, an option could be sold by one party (such as a bank) to another (such as an investor). In exchange for a premium, the bank might agree to sell the investor 1000 shares in a particular company (XYZ plc) in three months' time for £5 each, if the investor wishes. In other words, the investor (the buyer of the option) has a choice of either going ahead and buying the shares at the exercise price of £5 each (exercising the option), or deciding not to go ahead and letting the option lapse. Clearly, the choice the investor makes will be driven by whether or not the shares in XYZ plc are worth more or less than £5 in three months. If they are worth more than £5, the investor will go ahead. If they are trading at less than £5, the investor will let the option lapse.

Where options are traded on an **exchange**, they will be in standardised sizes (such as for 1,000 shares) and terms (such as for a period of three months). From time to time, however, investors may wish to trade an option that is outside these standardised terms and they will do so in the **over-the-counter (OTC)** market. Options can therefore also be traded off-exchange, or OTC, where the contract specification is determined by the two counterparties, rather than the exchange.

3.3 Options Terms

There are two classes of options:

- A **call option** is where the buyer has the right to buy the asset at the exercise price, if he chooses to. The seller is obliged to deliver if the buyer exercises the option. The above example relating to XYZ plc shares was a call option.
- A **put option** is where the buyer has the right to sell the underlying asset at the exercise price. The seller of the put option is obliged to take delivery and pay the exercise price, if the buyer exercises the option.

The buyers of options are the owners of those options. They are also referred to as **holders**.

The sellers of options are referred to as the **writers** of those options. Their sale is also referred to as 'taking for the call' or 'taking for the put', depending on whether they receive a premium for selling a call option or a put option.

For exchange-traded contracts, both buyers and sellers contract through the exchange's system rather than directly with each other. The **premium** is the money paid by the buyer to the exchange (and then by the exchange to the writer) at the beginning of the option contract; it is not refundable.

The following exercise is intended to assist in understanding the way in which option contracts might be used. The answer can be found at the end of this chapter.

⚙ Exercise 1

Suppose shares in Beckenham Ventures plc are trading at 125p and an investor buys a 150p call for three months. The investor, Frank Smith, has the right to buy Jersey shares from the writer of the option (another investor – Steve Jones) at 150p if he chooses, at any stage over the next three months.

If Beckenham Ventures shares are below 150p three months later, Frank will abandon the option and Steve will keep the premium. If they rise to, say, 200p, Frank will contact Steve and either:

- *exercise the option (buy the shares at 150p and keep them, or sell them at 200p); or*
- *persuade Steve to give him 200 – 150p = 50p to settle the transaction.*

1. *What does Frank hope will happen to the shares in Beckenham Ventures plc in the next three months?*

2. *What does Steve hope will happen to the shares in Beckenham Ventures plc in the next three months?*

3. *If Frank paid a premium of 20p to Steve, what is Frank's maximum loss and what level does Beckenham Ventures plc have to reach for Frank to make a profit?*

Staying with the Frank and Steve example, there are two more terms that need to be considered in relation to options – 'covered' and 'naked'. The writer of the option (Steve) is hoping that Frank will not exercise his right to buy the underlying shares and then he can simply pocket the premium. This obviously presents a risk because if the price does rise then Steve will need to supply the shares to Frank to meet his obligation. If Steve does not already have the shares to deliver, he may need to buy them in the market and his position is referred to as being **naked**. Alternatively, if Steve does already hold the shares, his position would be referred to as **covered**.

4. Derivatives and Commodity Markets

A derivative is a financial instrument whose price is derived from that of another asset, and the other asset is generally referred to as the 'underlying asset', or sometimes just 'the underlying'.

The physical trading of commodities tends to take place side by side with the trading of derivatives on those commodities. The physical market is simply the buying, selling and subsequent delivery of commodities like oil, wheat, barley and aluminium. This trading is dominated by major international trading houses, governments, and the major producers and consumers. The derivatives markets exist in parallel and enable the participants in the physical markets to hedge the risk of adverse price movements.

4.1 Physical Markets

There are a number of different commodity markets, which are differentiated by the commodity that is traded there. Some of the major commodities are:

- agricultural commodities (such as wheat, potatoes and livestock);
- base metals (such as aluminium and copper);
- precious metals (such as gold and silver);
- energy commodities (such as crude oil and natural gas).

The features of the base and precious metals markets and energy markets are considered in more detail below.

4.1.1 Base and Precious Metals

There are numerous metals produced worldwide and subsequently refined for use in a large variety of products and processes.

As with all other commodity prices, metal prices are influenced by supply and demand. The factors influencing supply include the availability of raw materials and the costs of extraction and production. Demand comes from underlying users of the commodity, for example, the growing demand for metals in rapidly industrialising economies, including China and India.

Demand also originates from investors that might buy metal futures in anticipation of excess demand, or incorporate commodities into specific funds. Producers use the market for hedging their production. Traditionally, the price of precious metals such as gold will rise in times of crisis – gold is seen as a safe haven.

4.1.2 Energy Markets

The energy market includes the market for oil (and other oil-based products like petroleum), natural gas and coal.

Oil includes both crude oil and various 'fractions' produced as a result of the refining process, such as naptha, butanes, kerosene, petrol and heating/gas oil. Crude oil is defined by three primary factors:

- Field of origin, for example, Brent, West Texas Intermediate, Oman.
- Density, ie, low density or 'light', high density or 'heavy'.
- Sulphur content, ie, low sulphur (known as 'sweet') or high sulphur (known as 'sour').

Supply of these commodities is finite, and countries with surplus oil and gas reserves are able to export to those countries with insufficient oil and gas to meet their requirements. Prices can be raised by producers restricting supply, for example, by the activities of the major oil producing countries within the Organisation of the Petroleum Exporting Countries (OPEC).

Demand for oil and gas is ultimately driven by levels of consumption, which in turn is driven by energy needs, for example, from the manufacturing industry and transport requirements.

Prices can react sharply to political crises, particularly in major oil-producing regions of the world such as the Middle East. Furthermore, since the level of demand is directly determined by the consuming economies' growth, economic forecasts and economic data also have an impact on energy prices.

4.2 Derivatives Markets

As seen, there are two distinct groups of derivatives, which are differentiated by how they are traded. These are OTC derivatives and Exchange-Traded Derivatives (ETD).

OTC derivatives are ones that are negotiated and traded privately between parties without the use of an exchange. Products such as interest rate swaps and foreign exchange forwards are traded in this way.

The OTC market is the larger of the two in terms of value of contracts traded daily. Trading takes place predominantly in Europe and, particularly, in the UK.

Exchange-traded derivatives are ones that have standardised features and can therefore be traded on an organised exchange. The main types are futures and options. The role of the exchange is to provide a marketplace for trading to take place as well as to provide some sort of guarantee that the trade will eventually be settled. The exchanges do this by using an intermediary (known as the 'central counterparty') for their trades.

4.2.1 Derivatives Exchanges

Details of some of the main derivatives exchanges in Europe are shown below.

NYSE Liffe

In 2001, Euronext purchased a derivatives exchange in London called LIFFE (pronounced 'life') and renamed it Euronext.liffe. LIFFE was originally an acronym for the London International Financial Futures and Options Exchange, originally set up in 1982.

Euronext is a network of individual European stock exchanges formed by the exchanges in Paris, Amsterdam and Brussels. Euronext has since merged with the New York Stock Exchange to become the NYSE Euronext Group, and the derivatives exchange is now known as NYSE Liffe.

NYSE Liffe is the main exchange for trading financial derivative products in the UK, including futures and options on:

- interest rates and bonds;
- equity indices (eg, FTSE);
- individual equities (eg, BP, HSBC).

NYSE Liffe also trades derivatives on soft commodities, such as sugar, wheat and cocoa. It also runs futures and options markets in Amsterdam, Brussels, Lisbon and Paris.

Trading on NYSE Liffe is on an electronic, computer-based system known as **Liffe CONNECT**.

Eurex

Eurex is the world's leading international derivatives exchange and is based in Frankfurt. Its principal products are German bond futures and options, the most well known of which are contracts on the Bund (a German government bond). It also trades index products for a range of European markets.

Eurex was created by Deutsche Börse AG and the Swiss Exchange. Trading is on the fully computerised Eurex platform, that enables members from across Europe and the US to access Eurex outside Switzerland and Germany.

IntercontinentalExchange (ICE)

ICE operates an electronic global futures and OTC marketplace for trading energy commodity contracts. These contracts include crude oil and refined products, natural gas, power and emissions.

The company's regulated futures and options business, formerly known as the International Petroleum Exchange (IPE), now operates under the name ICE Futures. ICE acquired the London-based energy futures and options exchange in 2001.

ICE Futures is Europe's leading energy futures and options exchange. ICE's products include derivative contracts based on key energy commodities: crude oil and refined oil products, such as heating oil and jet fuel and other products, like natural gas and electric power.

Recently, ICE Futures introduced what has become Europe's leading emissions futures contract in conjunction with the European Climate Exchange (ECX).

ICE's other markets are centred in North America and include trading of agricultural, currency and stock index futures and options.

London Metal Exchange (LME)

The London Metal Exchange is the world's premier non-ferrous metals market and has been operating for over 130 years. Although it is based in London, it is a global market with an international membership and with more than 95% of its business coming from overseas.

Futures and options contracts are traded on a range of metals, including aluminium, copper, nickel, tin, zinc and lead. More recently, it has also launched the world's first futures contracts for plastics.

Trading on the LME takes place across three trading platforms: through open outcry trading in the 'ring', through an inter-office telephone market and through **LME Select**, the exchange's electronic trading platform.

4.3 Investing In Derivatives

Having looked at various types of derivatives and their main uses, we can summarise some of the main advantages and disadvantages of investing in derivatives.

Advantages

- They enable producers and consumers of goods to agree the price of a commodity today for future delivery which can remove the uncertainty of what price will be achieved for the producer and the risk of lack of supply for the consumer.
- They enable investment firms to hedge the risk associated with a portfolio or an individual stock.
- They offer the ability to speculate on a wide range of assets and markets to make large bets on price movements.

Drawbacks and Risks

- Some types of derivatives investment can result in the investor losing more than their initial outlay.
- Derivatives markets thrive on price volatility, meaning that professional investment skills and experience are required.

- In the OTC markets, there is a risk that the counterparty may default on their obligations, and so it requires great attention to detail in terms of counterparty risk assessment, documentation and the taking of collateral.

5. Swaps

5.1 Description of Swaps

Swaps are a form of OTC derivative and are negotiated between the parties – usually a bank and a customer of the bank. A swap is an agreement to exchange one set of cash flows for another. They are most commonly used to switch financing from one currency to another (foreign currency swaps) or to replace floating interest with fixed interest (interest rate swaps). Interest rate swaps are considered in more detail below, including an example as to why they might be used.

5.2 Interest Rate Swaps

Interest rate swaps are the most common form of swaps. They involve an exchange of interest payments and are usually constructed whereby one side of the swap requires the payment of a fixed rate of interest and the other side requires the payment of a floating rate of interest.

They are usually used to hedge exposure to interest rate changes and can be easily appreciated by looking at an example.

⚙ Example

Company A is embarking on a three-year project to build and equip a new manufacturing plant and needs to borrow funds to finance the cost. Because of its size and credit status, it has no choice but to borrow at variable rates from banks.

Company A can reasonably estimate what additional returns its new plant will generate but, because the interest it is paying will be

variable, it is exposed to the risk that the project may turn out to be uneconomic if interest rates rise unexpectedly.

If the company could secure fixed rate finance, it could remove the risk of interest rate variations and more accurately predict the returns it can make from its investment.

To do this, Company A could enter into an interest rate swap with an investment bank. Under the terms of the swap, Company A pays a fixed rate of interest to the investment bank and in exchange receives an amount of interest from the investment bank calculated on a variable rate. With the amount it receives from the investment bank, it then has the funds to settle its variable rate lending, even if rates increase.

In this way, it has hedged its concerns about interest rates rising.

The two exchanges of cash flow are known as the 'legs' of the swap and the amounts to be exchanged are calculated by reference to a 'notional' amount. The notional amount in the above example would be the amount that Company A has borrowed to fund its project. It is referred to as the notional amount as it is needed in order to calculate the amounts of interest due, but is neither paid nor received by Company A or the investment bank.

Typically, one party (Company A in the example) will pay an amount based on a fixed rate to the other party (the investment bank), who will pay back an amount of interest that is variable and usually based on the quoted interest rate LIBOR (London Inter-Bank Offered Rate). The two legs will typically be paid quarterly, with the variable rate reset to the appropriate prevailing LIBOR rate each quarter. The variable rate is often described as the 'floating' rate.

⚙ Answers to Chapter Exercises

⚙ Exercise 1

Suppose shares in Beckenham Ventures plc are trading at 125p and an investor buys a 150p call for three months. The investor, Frank Smith, has the right to buy Jersey shares from the writer of the option (another investor – Steve Jones) at 150p if he chooses, at any stage over the next three months.

If Beckenham Ventures shares are below 150p three months later, Frank will abandon the option and Steve will keep the premium.

If they rise to, say, 200p, Frank will contact Steve and either:

*   *exercise the option (buy the shares at 150p and keep them, or sell them at 200p); or*
*   *persuade Steve to give him 200–150p = 50p to settle the transaction.*

1. *What does Frank hope will happen to the shares in Beckenham Ventures plc in the next three months?*

    Frank hopes the shares in Beckenham Ventures plc will rise and he will make a profit. Frank is speculating on Beckenham Ventures plc shares increasing in value in the next three months.

2. *What does Steve hope will happen to the shares in Beckenham Ventures plc in the next three months?*

    Steve has the opposite view to Frank. He is hoping that shares in Beckenham Ventures plc will not rise in value over the next three months and he is able to keep the premium received from Frank as profit.

3. *If Frank paid a premium of 20p to Steve, what is Frank's maximum loss and what level does Beckenham Ventures plc have to reach for Frank to make a profit?*

    The most Frank can lose is 20p, the premium he has paid. If the Beckenham Ventures plc shares rise above 150 + 20p, or 170p, then he makes a profit. If the shares rise to say 151p then Frank would exercise his right to buy – better to make a penny and cut his losses to 19p than lose the whole 20p.

Learning Objectives

Chapter Eight has covered the following Learning Objectives:

6.1.1 Understand the uses and application of derivatives

Lesson 34

6.2.1 Know the definition and function of a future

Lesson 34

6.3.1 Know the definition and function of an option

Lesson 36

6.3.2 Understand the following terms: calls, puts

Lesson 36

6.4.1 Understand the following terms: long, short, open, close, holder; writing; premium; covered, naked, OTC, exchange-traded

Lesson 34 (long, short, open, close, holder; writing; premium; covered, naked) and Lesson 36 (OTC, exchange-traded)

6.5.1 Know the characteristics of the derivatives and commodity markets: trading (metals, energy)

Lesson 35

6.5.2 Know the advantages and disadvantages of investing in the derivatives and commodity markets

Lesson 35

6.6.1 Know the definition and function of an interest rate swap

Lesson 37

Based on what you have learned in Chapter Eight, try to answer the following end of chapter questions.

End of Chapter Questions

Think of an answer for each question and refer to the appropriate section for confirmation.

1. Define a derivative.

    Answer Reference: Section 1

    ....

    ....

2. What is the 'underlying' in relation to a derivative?

    Answer Reference: Section 1

    ....

    ....

3. What are the two trading possibilities for derivatives?

    Answer Reference: Section 1

    ....

    ....

4. What are the two primary purposes for which derivatives can be used?

    Answer Reference: Section 1

    ....

    ....

5. What are the four major forms of derivative?

    Answer Reference: Section 1

    ....

    ....

6. How does a futures contract differ from a forward?

   Answer Reference: Sections 2.1/2.2

   ....

   ....

7. What are the 'short' and the 'long' in relation to a futures contract?

   Answer Reference: Section 2.3

   ....

   ....

8. What are 'opening' and 'closing' in relation to a futures contract?

   Answer Reference: Section 2.3

   ....

   ....

9. What are 'covered' and 'naked' in relation to a futures contract?

   Answer Reference: Section 2.3

   ....

   ....

10. How does an option differ from a future?

    Answer Reference: Section 3.2

   ....

   ....

11. What is the 'exercise price' in relation to an option?

    Answer Reference: Section 3.2

    ....

    ....

12. How does a call option differ from a put option?

    Answer Reference: Section 3.3

    ....

    ....

13. Explain the 'holder' and the 'writer' in relation to an option.

    Answer Reference: Section 3.3

    ....

    ....

14. What is the 'premium' in relation to options?

    Answer Reference: Section 3.3

    ....

    ....

15. The physical trading of commodities is generally driven by two factors, what are they?

    Answer Reference: Section 4.1

    ....

    ....

16. Where is NYSE Liffe?

    Answer Reference: Section 4.2.1

    ....

    ....

17. Where is Eurex and what is its most well-known contract?

    Answer Reference: Section 4.2.1

    ....

    ....

18. Where is ICE Futures and what trades there?

    Answer Reference: Section 4.2.1

    ....

    ....

19. What is traded on the LME?

    Answer Reference: Section 4.2.1

    ....

    ....

20. What are the two legs of an interest rate swap?

    Answer Reference: Section 5.2

    ....

    ....

Investment Funds

Investment Funds

1. Introduction

Investment management is a vital part of the financial services industry. In essence, investment managers select the most appropriate investments (mainly shares, bonds and money market instruments) for their clients. The investment managers tend to do this by creating 'funds' in which their clients can choose to invest and, since each fund includes a collection of investors, the funds are often referred to as **collective investment' funds or collective investment schemes**.

Investment management is also referred to using alternative terms, such as 'asset management' or 'fund management' and its importance in the financial services industry is illustrated in the diagram below.

As shown, the financial services sector can be divided into two main functions – the 'sell side' and the 'buy side', and at the heart of it are the investment managers.

The sell side is involved in the selling of investment ideas, strategies, advice and

services to either those with money to invest, or more likely those managing the investments on behalf of others – the investment managers. Typical sell side participants are the stockbrokers providing advice as to which are the best shares to buy and then arranging the purchase of those shares through stock exchange trading systems.

The buy side is the owners or managers of money that are paying for the sell side services with fees or commission, such as an investment manager choosing to buy a particular company's shares through a broker, and paying a commission for doing so.

Ultimately, the buy side is individuals investing their money, however much of this investment is done indirectly perhaps by a financial adviser persuading an individual to invest in a particular fund run by an investment manager, or an individual having monthly contributions deducted from his salary and paid into a pension fund run on behalf of the employees by an investment management company.

The UK Investment Market

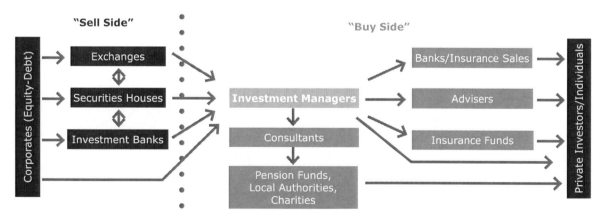

Source: Investment Management Association (IMA)

The size and scale of the industry can be seen in the regular reports issued by the Investment Management Association (IMA). The IMA is the trade body for the UK-based asset management industry and its recent Asset Management Survey showed that the assets managed by investment management firms in the UK at the end of December 2009 totalled an estimated £3.4 trillion.

1.1 The Benefits of Collective Investment

When investors decide to invest in a particular asset class, such as equities, there are two ways they can do it – direct investment or indirect investment.

Direct investment is where an individual personally buys shares in a company, such as Apple, the technology giant. Indirect investment is where an individual buys a stake in an investment fund, such as a mutual fund that invests in the shares of a range of different types of companies, perhaps including Apple.

A more formal description of a fund is that it is a collective investment scheme that pools the resources of a large number of investors, with the aim of pursuing a common investment objective. The investors could be individuals (retail investors) putting their money into a UK equity fund, run by a fund manager, that aims to make money by investing in UK company shares.

The pooling of resources into funds brings a number of benefits, including:

Economies of scale

The fund manager will place larger orders to buy or sell investments than most retail investors, and these large investment orders will attract much more competitive dealing fees and commissions. The managers of large funds also tend to get much more attention from brokers and investment bankers, meaning that investment information can be more timely and comprehensive.

Diversification

As summarised by the phrase 'don't put all your eggs in one basket', a diversified portfolio contains a substantial number of investments and will be less risky than a portfolio with just one or two investments in it.

The value of shares and most other investments can fall as well as rise. Some might fall spectacularly, for example, shares in a company that suddenly collapses, such as Northern Rock and Lehman Brothers. However, where an investor holds a diversified pool of investments in a portfolio, the risk of single constituent investments falling spectacularly will normally be offset by outperformance on the part of other investments. In other words, risk is lessened when the investor holds a diversified portfolio of investments.

However, to create a diversified portfolio directly, an investor would require a substantial amount of money, as illustrated in the following example.

⚙ Example

John Wiltshire has £5000 to invest. He wants to invest in top, UK company shares and is aware of the old adage of not putting all of his eggs in one basket. As a result John would like at least 50 different company shares in his portfolio.

Investing directly in shares of John's own choosing will incur stockbrokers' commission charges. Even using online brokers will probably incur a minimum commission of £12.50 per trade, irrespective of the size of the deal. So his £5,000 invested across 50 different shares would incur charges of 50 x £12.50 or £625–12.5% of the entire investment!

Alternatively, John could put his £5,000 into a UK equity fund, which is likely to be spread over comfortably more than 50 different company shares, and only incur an initial fee of 5%.

Diversification can also come from a fund investing in a mix of different types of asset, such as a mix of cash, equities, bonds and property. A collective investment scheme could also put limited amounts of investment into bank deposits and even into other funds, when it would be termed a 'fund of funds'.

Access to professional investment management

Collective investment schemes also give investors access to professional investment management and geographical areas or asset classes with which they may be unfamiliar. The great majority of private investors have very little knowledge of stock markets outside their own country and some of the best performance can be found in some of the least accessible markets around the world. Professional fund management firms usually maintain teams of fund managers who specialise in investing in specific areas of the world. They will follow their chosen markets closely and will consider carefully what to buy or sell and more importantly when to buy or sell – with timing often being the key to successful investment.

Regulatory oversight

Another benefit of investing in funds rather than directly is the fact that many funds are carefully vetted by financial services regulators before they can be marketed to potential investors. The regulators generally ensure the fund is suitably diversified and does not take any excessive risks.

Tax deferral

Investing in funds can be tax efficient. For example, many funds do not pay any tax on the income and gains they generate, and the investor only pays tax when she sells the investment. This is known as 'tax deferral' because the investor's requirement to pay tax is being deferred until such a time as she decides to sell her investment.

However, fund managers do not manage portfolios for nothing. As seen in the earlier example, they might charge investors fees to become involved in their funds (known as entry fees or initial charges). They also may charge investors when they leave the fund (known as exit charges), and they will charge annual management fees. Clearly, these fees are needed to cover the investment managers' salaries, technology, research, their dealing, settlement and risk management systems, and to provide them with a profit.

1.2 Investment Styles

There is a wide range of funds available with many different investment objectives and investment styles. Each of these funds has an investment portfolio managed by a fund manager according to a clearly stated set of objectives. An example of an objective might be to invest in the shares of UK companies with above-average potential for capital growth and to outperform the FTSE All Share index. Another fund's objective could be to maximise income or to achieve steady growth in capital and income.

In each case it will also be made clear what the fund manager will invest in, ie, shares and/or bonds and/or property and/or cash or money market instruments, and whether derivatives will be used to hedge currency or other market risks.

It is also important to understand the investment style the fund manager adopts. This refers to the fund manager's approach to choosing investments and meeting the fund's objectives. The investment styles can be either 'active' or 'passive'.

1.2.1 Active Management

Active management seeks to out-perform a predetermined benchmark over a specific time period. So, for example, a fund could be created that invests in large, UK-listed company shares and aims to do better than the index for large UK-listed companies, the FTSE 100.

If the FTSE 100 rose by 15% in one year and the value of a fund's UK large-cap share portfolio rose by 20%, it can be said to have outperformed its benchmark. The active management has paid off for the fund's investors.

The active manager can use fundamental analysis or technical analysis to select the investments. Fundamental analysis involves forecasting what is likely to happen, and the impact that this might have on a company and its shares. So, anticipating an increase in unemployment, an active fund manager might decide to invest more heavily in retail stores selling staple goods at discount prices.

Technical analysis at its simplest involves deciding whether to buy or sell based on the past pattern of an investment's prices. For example, if a chart of a share's price over time is exhibiting a particular pattern, the technical analyst might conclude that the next movement in the share's price is likely to be upwards. He would therefore buy in anticipation of this.

Two commonly used terms in the context of active management are 'top-down' or 'bottom-up'.

Top-down means that the manager focuses on economic and industry trends rather than the prospects of particular companies. So, a top down investment manager might decide that investment needs to be concentrated on growing economies like China, and with its growing middle class perhaps invest in luxury goods companies selling into the Chinese market.

In contrast, bottom-up means that the analysis of a company's financial statements, strategy and management is the priority. This might involve looking at the company's net assets, future profitability and cash flow to decide whether that company is likely to do better than its peers.

Included in the bottom-up approach is a range of investment styles:

- **Growth investing** – picking the shares of companies that are most likely to grow in the medium and long term.

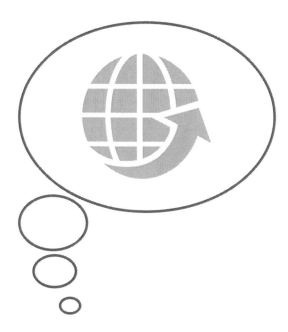

The rationale of passive, index tracking funds is that relatively few active fund managers actually outperform their benchmarks. Investors in most actively managed funds would have been better off simply investing in the index, because the index actually performed better than the active fund manager's stock selections.

Passive fund management recognises phenomenon by constructing a portfolio which simply replicates the index itself. It simply buys the index constituents which means that the performance of the portfolio is designed to 'track' the up-and-down movements of the index.

No attempt is made to forecast future events and, once set up, passive portfolios are generally less expensive to run than active portfolios. This is because the ratio of staff to funds managed is lower than for actively managed portfolios and the turnover of the portfolio is lower, leading to lower dealing costs.

Passive management does have certain disadvantages such as:

- Performance is impacted by the need to rebalance the portfolio to replicate changes in the index constituent weightings and to adjust for stocks being promoted into – and being relegated from – the index.
- Most indices assume that dividends from the constituent equities are re-invested on the ex-dividend (xd) date but a passive fund can only re-invest dividends when those dividends are actually received, which is usually around six weeks after the share has been declared ex-dividend.
- A passively managed Index-based portfolios will clearly follow the index down in bear markets.

- **Value investing** – picking the shares of companies that are consider cheap, in other words that are under-valued relative to their present profits or cash-flows.

- **Momentum investing** – picking those shares where the price is rising, on the assumption that this will continue.

- **Contrarian investing** – picking the shares that are out of favour and may have value the rest of the market may not have spotted.

There is also a significant range of styles used by managers of hedge funds. Hedge funds will be considered later in this chapter.

1.2.2 Passive Management

In contrast to active management that seeks to out-perform a benchmark index, passive management is seen in funds where the aim is perform in line with, or 'track' the benchmark index. As a result, passively managed funds are often described as index-tracker funds. Index-tracking, or indexation, involves constructing a portfolio in such a way that it will track, or mimic, the performance of an index, such as the FTSE 100.

1.2.3 Combining Active and Passive Management

Active and passive management are not mutually exclusives. Some funds employ both styles, known as **core-satellite management**.

This is achieved by putting a large proportion of a portfolio into index tracking passive funds, say, 70% to 80% of the portfolio's value (the 'core'), so as to minimise the risk of underperformance, and then fine tuning this by investing the remainder in a number of specialist actively managed funds or individual securities. This is the 'satellite' element of the fund.

1.3 Range of Funds Available

With well over 2,000 authorised investment funds available to investors, it is not surprising that a method of classifying them is needed in order to allow investors to compare funds with similar objectives.

The trade body the **Investment Management Association (IMA)** maintains a system for classifying certain funds and a similar role is occupied by the **Association of Investment Companies (AIC)** for certain investment companies.

The IMA's classification system contains over 30 sectors grouping similar funds together. Most sectors are broadly categorised between those designed to provide 'income' and those designed to provide 'growth'. Those funds that do not fall easily under these two headings are in a third category entitled 'specialist funds'.

Each of the sectors is made up of funds investing in similar asset categories, in the same stock market or in the same geographical region. So, for example, under the heading of funds principally targeting income includes sectors that for UK gilts, UK corporate bonds and global bonds.

Clearly, the classification of funds into sectors is targeted at the needs of the investor, to enable the comparison of funds on a like-for-like basis. Each sector provides groups of similar funds whose performance can be fairly compared by an investor and their adviser.

An example of how the IMA sectors work can be seen on the following page.

1.4 Regulation of Funds

The investment industry has many regulations that are designed to protect investors, and some of these regulations govern where and how a fund manager can invest and the documentation an investor can expect to receive.

The regulatory regime for UK funds is heavily influenced by EU directives that have been issued in order to promote a single market in investment funds.

1.4.1 Authorised versus Unauthorised Funds

In the UK, some collective investment schemes are authorised, while others are unauthorised. Authorisation is granted by the FSA. Broadly, the FSA will only authorise those schemes that are sufficiently diversified and which invest in a range of permitted assets.

It is only authorised collective investment schemes that can be freely marketed to the general public in the UK.

Collective investment schemes that have not been authorised by the FSA cannot be marketed to the general public. These unauthorised schemes are perfectly legal, but their marketing is subject to certain restrictions which mean that the funds can only be marketed to certain types of investor such as investment professionals or sophisticated investors.

A useful example of how the IMA sectors work can be seen by looking at bond funds and how the content of each differs.

UK Gilts	*Funds which invest at least 95% of their assets in sterling-denominated (or hedged back to sterling) triple AAA-rated, government-backed securities, with at least 80% invested in UK government securities (gilts).*
UK Index Linked Gilts	*Funds which invest at least 95% of their assets in sterling-denominated (or hedged back to sterling) triple AAA-rated government-backed index-linked securities, with at least 80% invested in UK index-linked gilts.*
£ Corporate Bonds	*Funds which invest at least 80% of their assets in sterling-denominated (or hedged back to sterling), triple BBB-minus or above corporate bond securities (as measured by Standard & Poor's or an equivalent external rating agency). This excludes convertibles, preference shares and permanent interest-bearing shares (PIBS).*
£ Strategic Bond	*Funds which invest at least 80% of their assets in sterling-denominated (or hedged back to sterling) fixed interest securities. This includes convertibles, preference shares and permanent interest- bearing shares (PIBS). At any point in time, the asset allocation of these funds could theoretically place the fund in one of the other fixed interest sectors. The funds will remain in this sector on these occasions since it is the manager's stated intention to retain the right to invest across the sterling fixed interest credit risk spectrum.*
£ High Yield	*Funds which invest at least 80% of their assets in sterling-denominated (or hedged back to sterling) fixed interest securities and at least 50% of their assets in below BBB-minus fixed interest securities (as measured by Standard & Poor's or an equivalent external rating agency), including convertibles, preference shares and permanent interest-bearing shares (PIBs).*
Global Bonds	*Funds which invest at least 80% of their assets in fixed interest securities. All funds which contain more than 80% fixed interest investments are to be classified under this heading regardless of the fact that they may have more than 80% in a particular geographic sector, unless that geographic area is the UK, when the fund should be classified under the relevant UK (sterling) heading.*

1.4.2 UCITS

UCITs is the acronym for 'Undertakings for Collective Investment in Transferable Securities'. It refers to a series of EU regulations that were aimed at making it easier to promote funds to retail investors across Europe. The EU plan was to create a 'single market' that enabled collective investment schemes to operate freely throughout the EU on the basis of a single authorisation from one member state. In other words, if a local regulator, such as the FSA in the UK, authorised a scheme as complying with UCITS then that scheme could be freely marketed in other European states such as France and Germany without needing to gain similar authorisation is France or Germany.

The original EU directive was issued in 1985 establishing a set of EU-wide rules governing collective investment schemes. Funds set up in accordance with these rules could then be sold across the EU, subject to local tax and marketing laws.

Since then, further UCITs directives have been issued which have broadened the range of assets a fund can invest in – in particular allowing managers to use derivatives more freely. Other directives introduced a consistent marketing document – the **simplified prospectus**. A fourth directive is currently being implemented.

While UCITS regulations are not directly applicable outside the EU, other jurisdictions, such as Switzerland and Hong Kong, recognise UCITS when funds are applying for registration to sell into those countries. In many countries, UCITS is seen as a brand signifying the quality of how a fund is managed, administered and supervised by regulators.

1.5 Onshore versus Offshore Funds

Unsurprisingly, UK collective investment schemes that are established and operated in the UK are generally described as being **onshore funds**, to contrast them with funds that are established and operated in other jurisdictions. Collective investment schemes that are established outside the UK are commonly described as **offshore funds**.

Offshore locations include several 'British-sounding' territories such as the Isle of Man,

Jersey and Guernsey. Other common offshore locations for funds include Luxembourg and Dublin, Ireland.

Some, but not all, offshore vehicles are less heavily regulated than their UK equivalents, which potentially enables the funds to pursue a more risky strategy.

In addition, offshore funds are likely to be subject to different tax treatment from their onshore equivalents. While some are regarded as more tax-efficient, others are not. For example, a UK investor investing in an offshore fund which has not been granted **reporting status** by the UK tax authority HMRC could suffer punitive taxes on any gains realised on the sale of the fund investment.

This is because, unless an offshore fund is certified by HMRC as a reporting fund, UK investors are subject to income tax rather than capital gains tax on any gain arising from the disposal of their interests in the fund. Since the current highest rate of income tax of 50% is significantly higher than the capital gains tax rate of 18%, obtaining reporting status is of crucial importance to most UK individual investors.

At the time of writing, HMRC has a list of 12,600 offshore collective investment schemes that have been granted 'reporting status'.

Offshore funds that seek to market into the UK may do so if the FSA is satisfied they meet the FSA's criteria for authorised funds, in which case they are known as 'recognised schemes'.

2. Unit Trusts

2.1 Introduction

A unit trust is a particular form of collective investment scheme. As its name suggests, a unit trust is established as a trust and the investors buy units in the fund. In basic terms, a trust is a particular type of entity that is often used to hold assets such as investments on behalf of another person, or group of

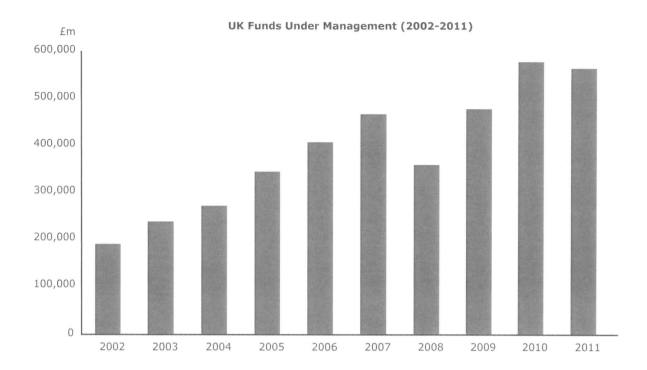

UK Funds Under Management (2002-2011)

persons. The persons who receive the benefit of the trust are known as the beneficiaries and trusts appoints one or more trustees as the legal owner of the investments, holding those investments for the benefit of the beneficiaries.

So, in a unit trust, the trustee is the legal owner of the underlying assets and the unit holders are the beneficial owners. Each unit trust may be authorised and marketable to retail investors, or unauthorised and restricted in the way it is marketed. Remember that a UK collective investment scheme such as a unit trust must be authorised by the FSA before it can be offered to the general public.

Investors pay money into the trust in exchange for units. The more people invest, the bigger the trust will grow. Unit trusts are often described as open-ended collective investment schemes because each trust can grow as more investors buy into the fund, or shrink as investors sell units back to the fund and they are cancelled.

The investors' money is invested in a diversified portfolio of assets, usually consisting of shares

or bonds or a mix of the two. If the diversified portfolio increases in value, the value of the units will increase. Of course, there is a possibility that the portfolio might fall in value, in which case the units will decrease in value.

The unit trust industry started in 1931, when M&G launched the first unit trust. Today the industry manages £3 trillion in over 2,000 funds across over 30 different investment sectors.

2.2 The Function of a Unit Trust Manager

Each unit trust has a **unit trust manager** who will decide, within the rules of the trust and the various regulations, which investments are included within the unit trust to meet its investment objectives. This will include deciding what to buy and when to buy it, as well as what to sell and when to sell it. The unit trust manager may (and commonly does) outsource this decision-making to a separate investment management company.

In summary, the unit trust manager is responsible for a number of functions including the following:

- The day-to-day management of the trust fund, which will involve either deciding which investments to buy and sell in the financial markets or delegating day-to-day investment decisions to separate fund managers.
- Offering the units for sale, including valuing and fixing the price of the units. The valuation is always based on the underlying value of the investments, so if the investments were worth £1 million in total, and there were 1 million units in issue, each unit would be priced at £1. This is known as the '**net asset value**' or just the NAV.
- Purchasing units back from those unit holders that choose to sell. The price at which the units will be purchased (the bid price) is always lower than the price at which units will be sold to investors (the offer price). The difference between the two prices is referred to as the spread, and is generally around 5-7%, however unit trusts are permitted to widen this gap to more than 10% if they wish to.

2.3 The Trustee

Every unit trust must also appoint a **trustee**. The trustee is the legal owner of the assets in the trust, holding the assets for the benefit of the underlying unit holders. The trustee has an important policing role, ensuring that the manager complies with the terms of the legal document that created the trust, the 'trust deed'.

So, the trustee has the responsibility of overseeing the unit trust. This will typically include:

- Holding and controlling the trust assets (the portfolio of investments).
- Collecting and distributing income from trust assets.

- Issuing unit certificates to unit trust investors.
- Approving any advertisements and marketing material.

In most cases, the role of the trustee will be carried out by either a bank, or an insurance company. These trustees are organisations that the unit holders can 'trust' with their assets because they are heavily regulated financial institutions.

3. Open-Ended Investment Companies (OEICs)

Unit trusts are gradually being replaced by a more modern equivalent, the Open-Ended Investment Company (OEIC). The FSA often refers to OEICs as **Investment Companies with Variable Capital (ICVCs)**, and in continental Europe, they are known as **SICAVs (Société d'Investissement a Capital Variable)**.

An OEIC is another form of authorised collective investment scheme, but in contrast to a unit trust, an OEIC is a collective investment scheme structured as a company, with the investors holding shares. The OEIC invests shareholders' money in a diversified pool of investments and has the ability to issue more shares or redeem shares as demanded by investors.

Although OEICs are companies, they differ from conventional companies because they are established under special legislation that enable them to create new shares and redeem existing ones according to investor demand, unlike ordinary companies. This means they are open-ended in nature, in the same way as unit trusts.

When an OEIC is set up, it is a requirement that an **authorised corporate director (ACD)** and a depository are appointed. The ACD is responsible for the day-to-day management of the fund, including managing the investments, valuing and pricing the fund and dealing with investors. It may undertake these activities itself or delegate them to suitable third parties. Effectively, the ACD is the OEIC equivalent of the unit trust manager of an authorised unit trust.

The OEIC's investments are held by an independent depository, responsible for looking after the investments on behalf of the OEIC shareholders and overseeing the activities of the ACD. The depository occupies a similar role to that of the trustee of an authorised unit trust and is subject to similar regulatory requirements.

The OEIC is the legal owner of the investments and shareholders are the beneficial owners of the value of the company. The register of shareholders is maintained by the ACD.

4. Pricing, Dealing and Settlement

4.1 Pricing and Charges

The prices at which authorised unit trusts and OEICs are bought and sold are based on the value of the fund's underlying investments – the net asset value or NAV. The authorised fund manager is, however, given certain flexibility in relation to the prices quoted to investors.

Unit trusts are traditionally dual-priced. Investors are quoted a higher offer price at which they can buy units and a lower bid price at which they can sell their units back to the manager. The difference between the two prices is known as the spread. So, for an investor to make a positive return on her investment the bid price must rise above the offer price before she sells the units.

An OEIC is single-priced that is directly linked to the value of the fund's underlying investments. All shares are bought and sold at this single price, so there is no need to calculate the spread. The OEIC has been described as a 'what you see is what you get product'.

Although authorised unit trusts traditionally used **dual pricing** and OEICs use **single pricing**, all funds now have a choice of which pricing methodology they use; whichever is chosen must be disclosed in the fund's prospectus.

The maximum price at which the fund manager is able to sell new units is prescribed by the FSA. It is the fund manager's offer price, but it tends to be referred to from the perspective of the investor as the **maximum buying price**. Under dual pricing, the maximum buying price comprises the creation price plus the fund manager's upfront 'initial' charge. The creation price is broadly the net asset value plus an allowance for dealing costs such as brokers' commission and stamp duty. This is illustrated in the example below.

⚙ Example

- *Value of the portfolio (at offer prices) divided by the number of units = 100.00p.*
- *Add, allowance for dealing costs: brokerage at, say, ¼% = 0.25p.*
- *Stamp duty at ½% = 0.50p.*
- *Subtotal (= creation price) = 100.75p*
- *Add, fund manager's initial charge at, say, 6.55% = 6.55p.*
- *Maximum buying price = 107.30p.*

The actual buying price offered to new investors does not have to be 107.30p and, because of the sensitivity of investors to charges, the fund manager may feel that a lower price of, say, 103p per unit is more appropriate.

The bid price at which the fund manager will repurchase units is calculated in a similar manner. From the investor's viewpoint it is referred to as the selling price, and the minimum selling price is also known as the cancellation price, using as its starting point the value of the portfolio at bid prices. Again, the manager has some flexibility about the price that is set, subject to its being no less than the minimum selling price.

Where a fund is single-priced, it is important to note that an initial charge will still be charged but will be separately identified. Indeed single pricing can and generally does involve the investors paying more than the single price when they buy, due to the addition of an initial charge. Single pricing can also result in the investors getting less than the single price when they sell, because the manager can deduct a separate charge known as the 'dilution levy' to make sure dealing expense are recouped. Essentially, single pricing is much more transparent about how the buying and selling prices are arrived at. Dual-pricing lacks the same transparency because it disguises the charges within the spread.

The prices of most individual funds are provided in broadsheet newspapers each day. The telephone numbers and addresses of the fund managers are normally provided alongside the prices.

4.2 Dealing and Settlement

Whether an investor wants to buy or sell units in a unit trust or shares in an OEIC, they will be either bought from, or sold back to, the authorised fund manager. There is no active secondary market in units or shares, except between the investors (or their advisers/intermediaries) and the fund manager. The key point to note, therefore, is that units in authorised unit trusts and shares in OEICs are bought from the managers themselves and not via a stock market.

Investors can buy or sell units in unit trusts or shares in OEICs in a number of ways:

- direct with the fund manager (either by telephone, via the internet or by post); or
- via their broker or financial adviser; or
- through a fund supermarket.

A **fund supermarket** is an organisation that specialises in offering investors easy access to a range of unit trusts and OEICs from different providers. They are usually based around an internet platform which takes the investor's order and processes it on their behalf, usually at reduced commission rates. Fund supermarkets tend to offer online dealing, valuations, portfolio planning tools and access to key features documents and illustrations. Investors can look at their various holdings in different funds in one place, analyse their performance and easily make switches from one fund to another.

Settlement currently takes place directly with each fund group. For **purchases**, once the investment has been made and the amount invested has been received, the fund group will record ownership of the relevant number of units or shares in the fund's share register. When the investor decides to sell, he/she need to instruct the fund manager (or ask his/her adviser or the supermarket to instruct the fund manager), who then has four days from receipt of the instruction in which to settle the sale and remit the proceeds to the investor. Traditionally, this instruction had to be in writing, but since 2009 managers, supermarkets or advisers have been able to accept instruction via the internet or over the telephone, using appropriate security checks.

Where an order to buy or sell units is undertaken by an organisation that provides dealing services, such as a fund supermarket, it is likely to use a systems platform to place those orders with the fund management group. One widely used system is EMX, which can be used by firms to enter customer orders, aggregate these and then send them electronically to the fund group. The firm then receives an electronic confirmation of receipt and, once the deal is traded at the next valuation point, EMX will send an electronic dealing confirmation showing the price at which the deal was done.

EMX was taken over by Euroclear UK & Ireland, the parent company that owns CREST, in late 2006.

5. Investment Trusts

Despite its name, an investment trust is actually a company, not a trust. It is a **listed company** and, like other companies it has directors and shareholders.

However, like unit trusts and OEICs, an investment trust invests in a diversified portfolio of investments, allowing its shareholders to diversify and lessen their risk.

When a new investment trust is established and launched, it issues **shares** to new investors. Unlike an authorised unit trust or OEIC, the number of shares is likely to remain fixed for many years. As a result, investment trusts are **closed-ended**, in contrast with authorised unit trusts and OEICs which are open-ended.

The cash from the issue of shares will be invested in a number of other investments, mainly the shares of other companies. If the value of the investments grows, then the value of the investment trust company's shares should rise too.

5.1 Share Classes

Some investment trust companies have more than one type of share, and where this is the case they are known as **split-capital investment trusts**. For example, an investment trust might issue both ordinary shares and preference shares.

Preference shares may be issued on different terms and may, for example, be issued as **convertible preference shares** that are convertible into the ordinary shares or as **zero dividend preference (ZDP) shares**. As the name suggests, ZDPs receive no dividends and the investor instead receives their return via the difference in the price they paid and the amount they receive when the ZDP is repaid at a fixed future date.

5.2 Gearing

In contrast with OEICs and authorised unit trusts, investment trust companies are allowed to borrow money on a long-term basis by taking out bank loans and/or issuing bonds. This can enable them to invest the borrowed money in more stocks and shares – a process known as 'gearing'. This approach can improve returns when markets are rising, but when markets are falling it can exacerbate losses. As a result, the greater the level of gearing used by an investment trust, the greater will be the risk.

Below are some key statistics drawn from XYZ Investment Trust showing that it has borrowed money on a long term basis. At the time, it had gross gearing of 111% (ignoring the fact that the fund also held some cash that could be used to repay some of the borrowing) and net gearing of 108% (assuming the cash is used to reduce the borrowing).

Financial make-up	
Total assets (£m):	248.4
Market capital (£m)	204.5
Number of shares:	154,643,542
Gross gearing	111
Net gearing:	108

5.3 Pricing, Discounts and Premiums

The price of a share (except in the case of an OEIC share, where the price is based on the net asset value) is what someone is prepared to pay for it. The price of a share in an investment trust is no different.

The share price of an investment trust is thus arrived at in a very different way from the unit price of an authorised unit trust or the share price of an OEIC.

Remember that units in an authorised unit trust are bought and sold by its fund manager at a price that is based on the underlying value of the constituent investments. Similarly, shares in an OEIC are bought and sold by the authorised corporate director (ACD), at the value of the underlying investments.

The share price of an investment trust company, however, is not necessarily the same as the value of the underlying investments. The value of the underlying investments determined on a per share basis is referred to as the **net asset value** and, because the share price is driven by supply and demand factors, it may be above or below the net asset value.

When the investment trust share price is **above the net asset value**, it is said to be trading at a premium. This is illustrated in the following example.

⚙ Example

Investment Trusts Trading at a Premium

ABC Investment Trust shares are trading at £2.30. The net asset value per share is £2.00. ABC Investment Trust shares are trading at a premium. The premium is 15% of the underlying net asset value.

At the end of 2010, Fidelity China Special Situations Trust was standing at a premium to its net asset value in response to demand for the shares. Its net asset value was 112.7p per share, but it was trading at 119.5p – a premium of 6.1%.

In contrast, when the investment trust share price is **below the net asset value**, it is said to be trading at a discount. This is illustrated in the following example.

⚙ Example

Investment Trusts Trading at a Discount

XYZ Investment Trust shares are trading at 95p. The net asset value per share is £1.00. XYZ Investment Trust shares are trading at a discount. The discount is 5% of the underlying net asset value.

Investment trust company shares generally trade at a discount to their net asset value and the extent of the discount is calculated daily and shown in the business pages of most newspapers.

A number of factors contribute to the extent of the discount and it will vary across different investment trust companies. The discount tends to be a function of the market's view of the quality of the management of the investment trust portfolio, and its choice of underlying investments.

Some investment trusts have a predetermined date at which they will be wound up, with all the investments sold and the cash distributed to the shareholders. A smaller discount tends to be displayed where investment trusts are nearing their winding-up, or where the investment trust is subject to a takeover bid by another company.

5.4 Trading in Investment Trust Shares

In the same way as other listed company shares, shares in investment trust companies are bought and sold on the London Stock Exchange's trading systems.

6. Real Estate Investment Trusts (REITs)

Real Estate Investment Trusts (REITs) are investment trust companies that pool investors' funds to invest in property, mainly commercial property and possibly residential property. Having been popular for sometime in other markets such as the US, REITs became available to UK investors from January 2007. Since then many major quoted property companies, such as Land Securities and British Land, have converted to REIT status.

One of the main features of REITs is that they provide investors access to property returns without the previous disadvantage of double taxation. Prior to the introduction of REITs, where an investor held property company shares, not only would the company pay corporation tax, but the investor would be liable to income tax on any dividends from the shares and capital gains tax on any growth when the shares are sold. Under the rules, REIT pays no corporation tax on property income or capital gains on property disposals, providing that at least 90% of that income (after expenses) is distributed to shareholders. These property income distributions are then taxed in the hands of the investor as if he/she had received that income directly himself/herself.

REITs give investors access to professional property investment and provide new opportunities, such as the ability to invest in commercial property. This allows investors to diversify the risk of holding direct property investments. This type of investment trust company also removes a further risk from holding direct property, namely liquidity risk or the risk that the investment will not be able to be readily realised.

REITs are closed-ended funds; like other investment trusts, they are quoted on the London Stock Exchange and other trading venues and dealt in the same way.

Some major REITs listed in the UK	
Big Yellow	Self storage
British Land	Diversified
Capital Shopping Centres Group PLC	Retail
Derwent London	Offices
Hammerson	Retail, offices
Highcroft Investments	Diversified
London & Stamford Property Plc	Offices, Retail
McKay Securities	Offices
Primary Health Properties	Health care
SEGRO	Industrial
Workspace Group	Offices, Industrial

Source: REITA.org

7. Exchange-Traded Funds (ETFs)

An exchange-traded fund (ETF) is an investment fund usually designed to track a particular index. This is typically a stock market index, such as the FTSE 100. ETFs are similar to investment trusts in that the investor buys shares in the ETF that are quoted on the stock exchange. However, unlike investment trusts, ETFs are '**open-ended funds**'. This means that, like OEICs, the fund will get bigger as more people invest and smaller as people withdraw their money.

ETFs are a recent addition in Europe and have grown very rapidly.

ETF shares may trade at a premium or discount to the underlying investments, but the difference is minimal and the ETF share price essentially reflects the value of the investments in the fund. The investor's return is in the form of dividends paid by the ETF and the possibility of a capital gain (or loss) on sale.

In London, ETFs are traded on the London Stock Exchange, which has established a special subset of the Exchange for ETFs, called extraMARK. Shares in ETFs are bought and sold via stockbrokers and exhibit the following charges:

- There is a spread between the price at which investors buy the shares and the price at which they can sell them. This is usually very small, for example, just 0.1 or 0.2% for, say, an ETF tracking the FTSE 100.
- An annual management charge is deducted from the fund. Typically, this is 0.5% or less.

- The investors pay stockbroker's commission when they buy and sell. However, unlike other shares, there is no stamp duty to pay on purchases.

8. Summary: Comparison Between Investment Companies

The table below summarises the main points about each type of collective investment scheme that has been encountered in the chapter so far.

	Authorised Unit Trusts	OEICs	Investment Trusts/ REITs	Exchange-Traded Funds	Key Points
Legal Structure	Trust	Company	Company	Company	Despite the name 'investment trust', only unit trusts are truly structured as a trust.
Management	Authorised Manager (company)	Authorised Corporate Director (company)	Board of Directors	Management Company	The companies that act as manager tend to be investment management companies.
Supervision	Trustee	Depository	Board of Directors	Depository	Supervision for open-ended companies (OEICs and ETFs) is provided by a depository.
Regulation	FSA	FSA	UK Listing Authority	FSA and UK Listing Authority	In order to be listed on the exchange, companies have to satisfy the UK Listing Authority.
Open- or closed-ended	Open	Open	Closed	Open	Only investment trust companies are closed-ended.
Pricing	Single- or dual-priced	Single- or dual-priced	Dependent on demand and supply	Based on net asset value	It is only investment trust companies where the price can exhibit a substantial discount or premium to NAV.
Trading	Authorised Manager	Authorised Corporate Director	Stock Market	Stock Market	Trading for unit trust and OEICs is with the investment manager, not on the stock market.
Settlement	Authorised Manager	Authorised Corporate Director	CREST	CREST	Stock market traded funds are settled via CREST.

9. Hedge Funds

Hedge funds are generally unauthorised funds that cannot be marketed to retail investors. This is because there are few restrictions as to what they do with their investors' money to provide them with a return. It is not unusual for hedge funds to be heavily invested in derivatives, or to create a portfolio that is not well diversified. As a result of this, hedge funds are reputed to be high-risk. However, in some cases this perception stands at odds with reality. There are many different styles of hedge fund – some risk-averse, and some employing highly risky strategies.

One of the most obvious risks faced by investors in equities is market risk – as the broad market moves down, the investor's shares also fall in value. Traditional **absolute return** hedge funds attempt to profit regardless of the general movements of the market, by carefully selecting a combination of asset classes, including derivatives, and by holding both long positions and short positions. A long position is owning an asset, such as shares. In contrast, a short position is selling an asset that the fund does not own, in the hope of buying them asset more cheaply if the market falls.

Some of the common aspects of hedge funds are as follows:

- **High investment entry levels** – many hedge funds have high minimum initial investment levels, meaning that access is effectively restricted to wealthy investors and institutions like pension funds and insurance companies. Most hedge funds require minimum investments in excess of £50,000; some exceed £1 million. However, investors can also gain access to hedge funds through **funds of hedge funds** which can involve lower minimum investment levels.

- **Structure** – as mentioned above, most hedge funds are established as unauthorised, and therefore unregulated, collective investment schemes, meaning that they cannot be generally marketed to private individuals because they are considered too risky for the less financially sophisticated investor.

- **Investment flexibility** – subject to complying with the restrictions in their constitutional documents, the lack of regulation means that hedge funds are able to invest in whatever assets they wish. In addition to being able to take long and short positions in securities such as shares and bonds, some take positions in commodities and currencies. As seen, the investment style is generally aimed at producing 'absolute returns' – positive returns regardless of the general direction of market movements.

- **Gearing** – many hedge funds can borrow funds and use derivatives to potentially enhance their returns.

- **Prime broker** – hedge funds buy and sell investments from, borrow from and, often, entrust the safekeeping of their assets to one main wholesale broker, called their prime broker. The prime broker is commonly one of the large investment banks.

- **Liquidity** – to maximise the hedge fund manager's investment freedom, hedge funds usually impose 'lock-in' periods that prevent the investors cashing in on their investments for a minimum of say, three months.

- **Cost** – hedge funds typically charge performance-related fees which the investor pays if certain performance levels are achieved over and above the annual management fees that are comparable to the fees charged by other collective investment schemes like unit trusts and OEICs. These performance fees can be substantial, with 20% of the performance above certain levels (often termed 'net new highs' or the 'high water mark') being common.

⭐ Learning Objectives

Chapter Nine has covered the following Learning Objectives:

7.1.1 Understand the benefits of collective investment

📑 Lesson 42

7.1.2 Understand the range of investment strategies – active versus passive

📑 Lesson 42

7.1.3 Know the differences between authorised and unauthorised funds

📑 Lesson 43

7.1.4 Know the purpose and principal features of UCITS

📑 Lesson 43

7.1.5 Know the differences between onshore and offshore funds

📑 Lesson 43

7.2.1 Know the definition of a unit trust

📑 Lesson 49

7.2.2 Know the types of funds and how they are classified

📑 Lesson 49

7.2.3 Know the roles of the manager and the trustee

📑 Lesson 49

7.3.1 Know the definition and legal structure of an OEIC

📑 Lesson 49

7.3.2 Know the roles of the authorised corporate director and the depository

📑 Lesson 49

7.3.3 Know the terms ICVC, SICAV and the context in which they are used

📑 Lesson 49

7.4.1 Know how unit trusts and OEIC shares are priced

📑 Lesson 49

7.4.2   Know the ways in which charges can be made by the fund manager

   Lesson 49

7.4.3   Know how shares and units are bought and sold

   Lesson 49

7.4.4   Know how collectives are settled

   Lesson 49

7.5.1   Know the characteristics of an investment trust: share classes; gearing

   Lesson 50

7.5.2   Understand the factors that affect the price of an investment trust

   Lesson 50

7.5.3   Know the meaning of the discounts and premiums in relation to investment trusts

   Lesson 50

7.5.4   Know how investment trust shares are traded

   Lesson 50

7.6.1   Know the basics characteristics of REITs: tax efficient; property diversification; liquidity; risk

   Lesson 50

7.7.1   Know the main characteristics of exchange-traded funds

   Lesson 45

7.7.2   Know how exchange-traded funds are traded

   Lesson 45

7.8.1   Know the basic characteristics of hedge funds: risk and risk types; cost and liquidity; investment strategies

   Lesson 60

Based on what you have learned in Chapter Nine, try to answer the following end of chapter questions.

📝 End of Chapter Questions

Think of an answer for each question and refer to the appropriate section for confirmation.

1. Give two alternative terms for investment management and detail which 'side' of the financial services industry the investment manager sits on.

   Answer Reference: Section 1

   ....

   ....

2. Give at least three benefits of pooling investment into a collective investment scheme.

   Answer Reference: Section 1.1

   ....

   ....

3. What are the two major investment styles adopted by investment managers?

   Answer Reference: Section 1.2

   ....

   ....

4. Active investment management usually uses one of two approaches. What are they?

   Answer Reference: Section 1.2

   ....

   ....

5. A portfolio managed in a way that combines both active and passive is commonly described as what?

   Answer Reference: Section 1.2.3

   ....

   ....

6. What are the trade bodies that represent investment managers and investment companies?

    Answer Reference: Section 1.3

    ....

    ....

7. How does an authorised fund differ from an unauthorised fund?

    Answer Reference: Section 1.4.1

    ....

    ....

8. What is UCITS?

    Answer Reference: Section 1.4.2

    ....

    ....

9. How does an onshore fund differ from an offshore fund?

    Answer Reference: Section 1.5

    ....

    ....

10. A unit trust is what form of entity and what do investors purchase?

    Answer Reference: Section 2

    ....

    ....

11. What are the respective roles of a unit trust manager and trustee?

    Answer Reference: Sections 2.2 & 2.3

    ....

    ....

12. What is an OEIC and what are the equivalent terms used by the FSA and in continental Europe?

    Answer Reference: Section 3

    ....

    ....

13. What are the equivalents to the unit trust manager and trustee in an OEIC?

    Answer Reference: Section 3

    ....

    ....

14. OEICs and unit trusts are generally priced on what basis?

    Answer Reference: Section 4.1

    ....

    ....

15. If an investor wants to buy or sell units/shares in an existing unit trust/OEIC, with whom does she do the trade?

    Answer Reference: Section 4.2

    ....

    ....

16. An investment trust is what form of entity and what do investors purchase?

    Answer Reference: Section 5

    ....

    ....

17. How is an investment fund described if it has more than one type of share in issue?

    Answer Reference: Section 5.1

    ....

    ....

18. Can an investment trust 'gear up'?

    Answer Reference: Section 5.2

    ....

    ....

19. How is it described if an investment trust's shares are trading above their net asset value?

    Answer Reference: Section 5.3

    ....

    ....

20. What particular problem is removed if an investor buys shares in a REIT rather than in a conventional property company?

    Answer Reference: Section 6

    ....

    ....

21. What is an ETF, what form of entity is it, and what do investors purchase?

    Answer Reference: Section 7

    ....

    ....

22. Are hedge funds generally authorised or unauthorised?

    Answer Reference: Section 9

    ....

    ....

23. What is 'absolute return' in the context of hedge funds?

    Answer Reference: Section 9

    ....

    ....

24. What is a prime broker?

    Answer Reference: Section 9

    ....

    ....

25. What are the usual forms of fees paid to a hedge fund manager?

    Answer Reference: Section 9

    ....

    ....

Financial Services Regulation and Professional Integrity

Financial Services Regulations and Professional Integrity

1. Financial Services Regulation

1.1 The Need for Regulation

The financial services industry is all about money and investment, and things can go wrong. The risk of losing money due to sharp practice or just poor decisions in a financial transaction has meant that financial services have always needed rules and regulations to protect investors and the general public.

As markets developed, market participants began to set rules so that there were agreed standards of behaviour, and to provide a mechanism so that disputes could be settled readily. This is known as **self-regulation**, where, for example, a stock exchange would set rules for its members and police their

implementation, as well as providing a secondary market for shares.

As markets, financial institutions and financial services developed further, and the potential impact that they could have on both the economy and society grew, self-regulation became increasingly untenable, and most countries moved to a statutory approach – formalising rules in law – and established their own **regulatory bodies**.

The comments of the chairman of the UK's regulator, the Financial Services Authority, in December 2005, captured this succinctly: *'Regulation exists because of the potential economic and social effects of major financial instability, the desirability of maintaining markets which are efficient, orderly and fair and the need to protect retail consumers in their dealings with the financial services industry.'*

The development of global markets and a series of crises such as the collapses of Barings Bank, Enron and WorldCom, emphasised not only the need for improved regulation and standards, but for **international co-operation** to develop a common approach in a whole range of areas. This was further exacerbated in 2008 as the global community battled against the effects of the credit crunch.

This increasing globalisation of financial markets means there is a demand from governments and investment firms for a common approach to regulation in different countries. As a result, there is a significant level of co-operation between financial services regulators worldwide and, increasingly, common standards. Anti-money laundering rules are probably the best example of this, and these will be considered in detail later in this chapter.

The main purpose and aims of financial regulation are:

- to maintain and promote the fairness, efficiency, competitiveness, transparency and orderliness of the markets;
- to provide protection for members of the public investing in, or holding financial products;
- to minimise crime and misconduct in the industry;
- to reduce systemic risks in the industry; and
- to assist in maintaining the financial stability.

1.2 European Regulation

As well as aiming to ensure that the Europe has world class regulatory standards, the EU is also particularly concerned with the development of a **single market** in financial services across Europe. Broadly, this single market will enable financial services firms to compete freely throughout the European Union without being hampered by significant differences in national regulation.

This has been a major feature of European financial services legislation for some time, and is the cornerstone of the **Financial Services Action Plan (FSAP)**.

The way the EU introduces new financial services regulation and how this gets translated into new rules in each EU country follows an innovative approach devised by a Belgian banking expert, Alexandre Lamfalussy. The approach is aimed at cutting out much of the negotiation between countries that could otherwise delay implementation.

The '**Lamfalussy Process**' for EU regulation comes about by way of a four level, tiered approach to the creation and implementation of rules. The four levels are as follows:

- The first level of the Lamfalussy Process involves the European Council and the European Parliament adopting a 'framework directive' that establishes the core elements of the legislation and sets guidelines for its implementation.
- The second level seeks technical advice from specialist committees and the national regulators of EU member states. The European Commission then issues detailed rules without going through any further consultation.

- At the third level, national regulators work with each other to co-ordinate the new regulations.
- The fourth level sees implementation, overseen by the European Commission.

On legislation related to securities markets, the Commission is guided in its implementation by the **European Securities and Markets Authority (ESMA)**. This is an EU authority which is responsible both for drafting the legislation and for guiding it through EU implementation, overseeing national implementation and enforcement.

This process was used to introduce the Markets in Financial Instruments Directive (MiFID), which has introduced more extensive rules and regulations regarding the conduct of business and organisation of firms within the financial industry.

1.3 UK Regulation

In the UK, the financial services sector underwent a radical change on 1 December 2001 when the **Financial Services and Markets Act of 2000 (FSMA 2000)** came into force. Before FSMA 2000, UK regulation was covered by a hotch-potch of different laws, and enforcement was carried out by a number of statutory and self-regulating organisations. This was considered to be unnecessarily complex and confusing, and it was FSMA 2000 that simplified things.

Under FSMA 2000, the government delegated overall responsibility for the regulation of the financial services industry to the **Financial Services Authority (FSA)**.

FSMA 2000 sets out what is expected from the FSA by giving it four **statutory objectives**. The objectives are:

- **market confidence** – maintaining confidence in the UK financial system;

- **financial stability** – contributing to the protection and enhancement of stability of the UK financial system;
- **consumer protection** – securing the appropriate degree of protection for consumers; and
- **the reduction of financial crime** – reducing the extent to which it is possible for a regulated business to be used for a purpose connected with financial crime.

The FSA is accountable to HM Treasury (and therefore ultimately to Parliament) for the way it conducts its operations.

In July 2009, HM Treasury published a consultation paper titled *Reforming Financial Markets* in a response to the causes of the financial crisis. It proposed a series of sweeping policy initiatives around a number of core issues, one of which is the need to strengthen the UK's regulatory framework so that it is better equipped to deal with all firms and, in particular, globally interconnected markets and firms.

As part of this approach, the new coalition government is looking to transfer operational responsibility for prudential regulation from the FSA to a new subsidiary of the Bank of England. Following a second consultation in February 2011, titled *A New Approach to Financial Regulation: Building a Stronger System*, HM Treasury issued its proposals for how the new regulatory system will operate. The government's reforms focus on three key institutional changes:

Financial Policy Committee (FPC)

A new committee has been established in the Bank of England, with responsibility for 'macro-prudential' regulation, or regulation of the stability and resilience of the financial system as a whole. Its role is:

'*Contributing to the Bank's objective to protect and enhance financial stability, through identifying and taking action to remove or reduce systemic risks, with a view to protecting and enhancing the resilience of the UK financial system.*'

Prudential Regulation Authority (PRA)

The new Prudential Regulation Authority (PRA) will be responsible for prudential regulation of financial firms that manage significant risks on their balance sheets – in other words, it will be responsible for the regulation and supervision of 'significant' individual firms including all deposit-taking institutions, insurers and other prudentially significant firms.

The PRA will have a primary objective of enhancing financial stability by promoting the safety and soundness of PRA-authorised firms in a way which minimises the disruption caused by any firms which do fail. In fulfilling its objective, it will take an intrusive approach to regulation and supervision.

Financial Conduct Authority (FCA)

The new Financial Conduct Authority will focus on regulation of all firms in retail and wholesale financial markets, as well as the infrastructure that supports these markets. In effect it will have responsibility for firms that do not fall under the PRA's scope (approximately 25,000 firms). The FCA's role will include: supervision of investment exchanges and monitoring firms' compliance with the Market Abuse Directive (MAD); powers to investigate and prosecute insider dealing; responsibility for overseeing the Financial Ombudsman Service (FOS), Consumer Financial Education Body (CFEB) and Financial Services Compensation Scheme (FSCS); working closely with the FPC and PRA. Its role will also include:

'*Enhancing confidence in the UK financial system by facilitating efficiency and choice in services, securing an appropriate degree of consumer protection, and protecting and enhancing the integrity of the UK financial system.*'

Changes are under way to put the new regulatory architecture in place by the end of 2012.

1.3.1   Authorisation

FSMA 2000 makes it an offence for a firm to provide financial services in the UK without being authorised to do so. There are some exemptions from this requirement. For example, the Bank of England does not require FSA authorisation.

Under the terms of the FSMA 2000, the FSA must look at each applicant firm and determine whether it is 'fit and proper' to provide financial services. By only allowing 'fit and proper' firms to be involved in the financial services industry, the FSA begins to satisfy its statutory objectives of maintaining confidence in the financial system and of providing appropriate investor protection.

The FSA's assessment of fitness and properness includes determining whether the firm meets certain **threshold conditions**. Before granting authorisation, the FSA considers the quality of the company's management, its financial strength and the calibre of its staff. The latter is particularly important in certain key roles, which the FSA refers to as '**controlled functions**'.

This is because firms are ultimately operated by individuals – the directors and employees of that firm. Particular individuals, fulfilling the key roles that are 'controlled functions' (see Section 1.3.2 below), have to be approved by the FSA. An individual is only permitted to perform a controlled function after they have been granted **approved person** status by the FSA. The FSA will only grant approval

[9] whether the *person* has been a *director*, *partner*, or concerned in the management, of a business that has gone into insolvency, liquidation or administration while the *person* has been connected with that organisation or within one year of that connection;

[10] whether the *person*, or any business with which the *person* has been involved, has been investigated, disciplined, censured or suspended or criticised by a regulatory or professional body, a court or Tribunal, whether publicly or privately;

[11] whether the *person* has been dismissed, or asked to resign and resigned, from employment or from a position of trust, fiduciary appointment or similar;

Source: FSA – The Fit and Proper Test for Approved Persons handbook

if it is satisfied that the candidate is a fit and proper person to perform the controlled function applied for. In assessing the fitness and propriety of a person, the FSA will look at a number of factors against three main criteria:

* **Honesty, integrity and reputation** – here the FSA will consider such issues as any criminal record or history of regulatory misconduct.
* **Competence and capability to fulfil the role** – this often includes achieving success in certain regulatory examinations.
* **Financial soundness** – here the FSA will consider the applicant's current financial situation and his/her financial history; for instance, an undischarged bankrupt would be unlikely to be approved for many roles.

The extract from the FSA's rulebook above provides some further insight into the reasons why an applicant may not be granted 'approved person' status.

1.3.2 Controlled Functions

The controlled functions are those involved in dealing with customers or their investments,

key managers in the firm including finance, compliance and risk and those exercising a measure of control over the firm as a whole.

The FSA classifies controlled functions into five groups, four of which are '**significant influence functions**'. The significant influence functions are:

* **Governing functions** – for example, the directors of the firm.

* **Significant management functions** – senior managers in the larger firms, such as the head of equity dealing.

* **Systems and control functions** – mainly those responsible for risk management and internal audit.

* **Required functions** – specific roles, such as the director or senior manager responsible for compliance oversight.

The fifth group comprises:

* **Customer functions** – for example, those individuals managing investments or providing advice to customers. Customer functions are not significant influence functions.

2. Money Laundering

2.1 Definition and Stages of Money Laundering

Crime generates large amounts of cash and criminals like cash, particularly because it is difficult to trace. The cash could be generated through a variety of activities such as drug trafficking, arms trafficking or handling stolen goods.

However, legitimate business transactions, particularly large ones such as buying a car or a property, are not commonly done in cash. This is because cash is a security risk and has to be counted. So, for money to be really useful, it needs to be in electronic form, in a bank account. This poses a problem for criminals – how do they convert large amounts of illegal cash into legal bank account balances? The answer is to 'launder' the money and make it appear like legitimate money that is 'clean'.

So, money laundering is the process of turning money that is derived from criminal activities – '**dirty money**' – into money which appears to have been legitimately acquired – '**clean money**' – and which can therefore be more easily invested and spent.

There are three stages to a successful money laundering operation:

- **Placement** – the first stage and typically involves placing the criminally derived cash into some form of bank or building society account.
- **Layering** – the second stage and involves moving the money around in order to make it difficult for the authorities to link the placed funds with the ultimate beneficiary of the money. Disguising the original source of the funds might involve buying and selling foreign currencies, shares or bonds.

- **Integration** – the third and final stage. At this stage, the layering has been successful and the ultimate beneficiary appears to be holding legitimate funds ('clean' money rather than 'dirty' money). The money has been integrated back into the financial system and can be dealt with as if it were legitimate.

2.2 Legal and Regulatory Framework

The cross-border nature of money laundering has led to international co-ordination to ensure that countries have legislation and regulatory processes in place to enable the identification and prosecution of those involved. In particular the **Financial Action Task Force (FATF)** has been established as an inter-governmental body to develop and promote national and international policies to combat money laundering. It is based at the OECD in Paris and has issued recommendations aimed at setting minimum standards for countries to ensure that anti-money laundering efforts are consistent internationally.

At its most basic level, the requirements expect staff at firms to be able to identify suspicions of money laundering, and to report these suspicions. Initially the reporting is made to a central point within the firm, the Money Laundering Reporting Officer (MLRO), and the MLRO will then report all relevant suspicions to the appropriate authorities.

The main laws and regulations relating to money laundering in the UK are:

* Proceeds of Crime Act 2002.
* Money Laundering Regulations 2007.

The **Proceeds of Crime Act 2002** has consolidated and extended existing UK legislation regarding money laundering and established three broad groups of offences related to money laundering that firms and the staff working for them need to avoid committing:

* knowingly assisting in concealing, or arranging for the acquisition, use or possession of criminal property;
* failing to report knowledge or suspicions of possible money laundering;
* tipping off another person that a money laundering report has been made.

The Proceeds of Crime Act 2002 also made it an offence to impede any investigation, for example by destroying or disposing of any documents that are relevant to an investigation.

The maximum prison terms that can be imposed under the Proceeds of Crime Act are 14 years for the offence of money laundering and five years for failing to make a report, tipping off or destroying relevant documents. In each case, the penalties can be imprisonment and/or an unlimited amount of fine.

The **Money Laundering Regulations 2007** implemented the EU directive on money laundering, specifying the arrangements firms must have in place covering areas including record-keeping, internal controls and reporting requirements.

2.3 Action Required by Firms and Individuals

The Proceeds of Crime Act and the Money Laundering Regulations require a court to take account of industry guidance when considering whether a person or firm has committed an offence or has complied with the money laundering regulations.

This guidance is provided by the **Joint Money Laundering Steering Group (JMLSG)**, an industry body made up of 17 financial sector trade bodies.

Its latest guidance sets out what is expected of firms and their staff. It emphasises the responsibility of senior management to manage the firm's money laundering risks, and advises that this should be carried out using a risk-based approach. It sets out a standard approach to the identification and verification of customers, separating out basic identity from other aspects of customer due diligence measures, as well as giving guidance on the obligation to monitor customer activity.

The following sections highlight some of the principal features of the latest guidance.

2.3.1   Internal Controls

There is a requirement for firms to establish and maintain appropriate and risk-based policies and procedures in order to prevent operations related to money laundering. These controls are expected to be appropriate to the risks faced by the firm. So a small independent firm of stockbrokers in Tunbridge Wells would not be expected to maintain the same level of controls as a multi-national with branches in Latin America and the Middle East.

2.3.2   Money Laundering Reporting Officer (MLRO)

Firms are expected to appoint a director or senior manager to be the Money Laundering Reporting Officer (MLRO), who is responsible for overseeing the firm's compliance with the FSA's rules on systems and controls against money laundering.

The MLRO must receive and review the internal disclosure reports, and make external reports to the Serious Organised Crime Agency (SOCA) where required. The MLRO is also required to carry out regular assessments of the adequacy of the firm's systems and controls and to produce a report at least annually to senior management on its effectiveness.

The MLRO must have authority to act independently, and senior management must ensure that the MLRO has sufficient resources available to effectively carry out his or her responsibilities.

2.3.3   Risk-Based Approach

As seen, senior management are expected to ensure that they have appropriate systems and controls in place to manage the risks associated with the business and its customers.

This requires them to assess their money laundering risk and decide how they will manage it. It also means they must determine the identification and vetting procedures required to make sure that the customers of the firm are not involved in money laundering.

This is referred to as appropriate customer due diligence measures, and the procedures should reflect the risk characteristics of customers, based on the type of customer and the business relationship, product or transaction.

2.3.4   Customer Due Diligence (CDD)

The Money Laundering Regulations 2007 set out a firm's obligations to conduct customer due diligence, and describe those customers and products where no, or limited, CDD measures are required, and those customers and circumstances where enhanced due diligence is required. The CDD measures that must be carried out involve:

- identifying the customer and verifying their identity, for example by seeing the customer's passport and council tax bills;
- if a customer is acting for another beneficial owner, then also verifying the identity of the beneficial owner;
- obtaining information of the purpose and intended nature of the business relationship.

Firms must also conduct ongoing monitoring of the business relationship with their customers to identify any unusual activity that may be suspicious.

For some particular customers, products or transactions, **simplified due diligence (SDD)** may be applied. Firms must have reasonable grounds for believing that the customer, product or transaction falls within one of the allowed categories, and be able to demonstrate this to their supervisory authority. Examples of instances where SDD may be applied include where the customer is another regulated firm in the financial sector, or a company listed on a regulated stock market, such as the London Stock Exchange.

In cases of higher risk and if the customer is not physically present when their identities are verified then **Enhanced Due Diligence (EDD)** measures must be applied on a risk-sensitive basis.

The JMLSG Guidance Notes provide extensive guidance on the customer due diligence to be applied and the above is only a very brief summary.

2.3.5 Staff Awareness and Training

The regulations require reports to be made of potential money-laundering activities. So, staff working in the financial sector are required to make reports where they know, or where they suspect, or where they have reasonable grounds for knowing or suspecting, that a person is engaged in money laundering.

Each firm is expected to provide a framework within which such suspicion reports may be raised and considered by a nominated officer, who is usually the MLRO. The nominated officer must consider each report and determine whether there are grounds for knowledge or suspicion for a report to be made to the **Serious Organised Crime Agency (SOCA)**.

However, the best-designed control systems cannot operate effectively without staff who are alert to the risk of money laundering and who are trained in the identification of unusual activities or transactions which may prove to be suspicious. Firms are therefore required to:

* provide appropriate training to make staff aware of money laundering issues and how these crimes might take place through the firm;
* ensure staff are aware of the law, regulations and relevant criminal offences;
* consider providing case studies and examples related to the firm's business;
* train employees in how to operate a risk-based approach.

2.3.6 Record-Keeping

Record-keeping is an essential component of the audit trail that the money-laundering regulations and FSA rules require to assist in any financial investigations. Firms are therefore required to maintain appropriate systems for maintaining records and making these

available when required and, in particular, should retain:

* copies of the evidence obtained of a customer's identity for five years after the end of the customer relationship;
* details of customer transactions for five years from the date of the transaction or five years from when the relationship with the customer ended, whichever is the later;
* details of actions taken in respect of internal and external suspicion reports;
* details of information considered by the nominated officer in respect of an internal report where no external report is made.

2.4 Bribery

The Bribery Act 2010 came into force in July 2011 as part of a complete reform of corruption law to provide a modern and comprehensive scheme of bribery offences that will enable courts and prosecutors to respond more effectively to bribery at home or abroad.

The Bribery Act replaces offences at common law and under legislation dating back to the early 1900s. Its key provisions are:

* Two general offences are created covering the offering, promising or giving of an advantage, and the requesting, agreeing to receive or accepting of an advantage.
* There is a discrete offence of bribery of a foreign public official to obtain or retain business or an advantage in the conduct of business.
* A new offence is created, of failure by a commercial organisation to prevent a bribe being paid for or on its behalf.
* Penalties include a maximum of ten years' imprisonment, unlimited fines, confiscation of proceeds, debarment from public sector contracts and director disqualification.

For companies, the most important point to note is that there is a new offence of failing to prevent bribery, which does not require any corrupt intent. This offence will make it easier for the Serious Fraud Office (SFO) to prosecute companies when bribery has occurred.

The only defence available to commercial organisations charged with the corporate offence will be for the organisation to show that it had adequate procedures in place to prevent an act of bribery being committed in connection with its business. This requires firms to have an effective compliance programme that has to meet six principles:

- Develop well-designed policies, procedures and controls to ensure compliance.
- Top-level commitment is required with the board and senior management making a commitment to conduct business in a fair, honest and ethical manner.
- Risk assessments should be undertaken on an ongoing basis to identify the external and internal risks faced by the company.
- Due diligence should be undertaken on suppliers who undertake services for the company.
- Policies and procedures should be communicated internally along with training of employees and policy statements or a code of conduct published externally.
- Bribery risks should be monitored, evaluated and reassessed regularly and staff surveys undertaken. Results should be reported regularly to top management and the process independently audited.

2.5 Identity Fraud

All firms may unwittingly find themselves targeted by criminals and have to be aware of this possibility and one area that staff working in financial services need to be aware of is the theft of customer data to facilitate identity fraud.

Identity fraud or identity theft is one of the fastest growing types of fraud in the UK.

- **Identity fraud** is the use of a misappropriated identity in criminal activity, to obtain goods or services by deception. This usually involves the use of stolen or forged identity documents such as a passport or driving licence.

- **Identity theft** (also known as impersonation fraud) is the misappropriation of the identity (such as the name, date of birth, current address or previous addresses) of another person, without his or her knowledge or consent. These identity details are then used to obtain goods and services in that person's name.

A person's identity (and their ability to prove it) is central to almost all commercial activity. Organisations need to verify that the person applying for credit or investment services is who they say they are and lives where they claim to live. The procedures used by organisations to check the information supplied by customers help to detect and prevent most identity fraud. however, some fraudulent applications are accepted due to the sophisticated techniques used by the fraudsters.

When opening accounts in banks and other financial organisations, criminals will use data from legitimate persons to provide information for applications and other purposes which, when checked against normal credit reference, postal and other databases, will seem to confirm the genuine nature of the application.

Key to this is accessing what are known as 'breeder' documents – those documents that allow those who possess them to apply for or obtain other documentation and thus build up a profile or 'history' that can satisfy basic Customer Due Diligence (CDD) processes. The information may either be used quickly before the source of the data is alerted or used for example, as a facilitator for other identities so as not to alert the source.

3. Insider Dealing

When directors or employees of a listed company buy or sell shares in that company, there is a possibility that they may be committing a criminal act – that of insider dealing. The following example illustrates the possible circumstances where insider dealing might arise.

⚙ Example

Carlton Murray is the sales director of Quickdeal plc, a substantial retail company with its shares listed on the LSE. He is aware that sales have gone particularly well in the last two months, however the latest results have not yet been released to the general public. If Carlton were to buy some shares in Quickdeal for himself in order to profit from the anticipated market reaction to the positive performance he would be breaking the law. He would be 'insider dealing', using information he gained from 'inside' the company for personal gain.

Insider dealing is a criminal offence in the UK under the Criminal Justice Act 1993, and it is punishable by a fine and/or a jail term.

To be found guilty of insider dealing, the Criminal Justice Act 1993 defines who is deemed to be an insider, what is deemed to be inside information and the situations that give rise to the offence.

Inside information is information that relates to particular securities or a particular issuer of securities (and not to securities or securities issuers generally) and which:

- is specific or precise;
- has not been made public; and
- if it were made public, would be likely to have a significant effect on the price of the securities.

This is generally referred to as 'unpublished price-sensitive information' and the securities are referred to as 'price-affected securities'.

Information becomes public when it is published, for example, a UK-listed company announcing its results. Furthermore, information can be treated as public even though it may be acquired only by persons exercising diligence or expertise (for example, by careful analysis of published accounts, or by scouring a library of press cuttings).

An **insider** is a person that has this price-sensitive information and knows that it is inside information from an inside source. The person may have:

- gained the information through being a director, employee or shareholder of the issuer of the securities;
- gained access to the information by virtue of his employment, office or profession (for example, the auditors to the company);
- sourced the information from either of the above, either directly or indirectly.

The **offence of insider dealing** is committed when an insider acquires or disposes of price-affected securities while in possession of unpublished price-sensitive information. It is also an offence to encourage another person to deal in price-affected securities, or to disclose the information to another person (other than in the proper performance of employment). The acquisition or disposal must occur on a regulated market or through a professional intermediary.

The instruments covered by the insider dealing legislation in the Criminal Justice Act are described as '**securities**'. For the purposes of this piece of law, securities are any of the following:

- shares;
- bonds (includes government bonds and others issued by a company or a public sector body);
- warrants;
- depositary receipts;
- options (to acquire or dispose of securities);
- futures (to acquire or dispose of securities);
- contracts for differences (based on securities, interest rates or share indices).

Note that the definition of 'securities' does not embrace commodities (like oil or aluminium) or derivatives on commodities (such as options and futures on agricultural products, metals or energy products). Units/shares in open-ended collective investment schemes (such as OEICs, unit trusts and SICAVs) are also excluded from the definition of securities for insider dealing purposes.

4. Market Abuse

As seen in the previous section, insider dealing typically occurs when an insider (or someone who gained information from an insider) deals in price affected securities whilst aware of unpublished price sensitive information. It does not embrace other situations such as the following example.

⚙ Example

Helen Moran is a private investor and she realises that the price of shares is often impacted by rumour rather than fact. Helen spreads a false rumour that a particular listed company – Pylon Technology – is being considered as a takeover target in the hope that the shares she holds in Pylon Technology increase in value. If it works, Helen will sell her shares at a profit.

Since Helen is not an employee or director of Pylon Technology, and the rumours she is spreading are known by her to be false, Helen is not guilty of insider dealing. However, she is guilty of a more recent and widely drafted offence of market abuse.

Market abuse is an offence introduced by the Financial Services and Markets Act 2000 (subsequently amended in the Market Abuse Directive 2005). It relates to behaviour by a person (or a group of people working together), which occurs in relation to qualifying investments, on a prescribed market, that satisfies one or more of the following three conditions:

- The behaviour is based on information that is not generally available to those using the market and which, if it were available, would have an impact on the price.
- The behaviour is likely to give a false or misleading impression of the supply, demand or value of the investments concerned.
- The behaviour is likely to distort the market in the investments.

In all three cases the behaviour is judged on the basis of what a **regular user** of the market would view as a failure to observe the standards of behaviour normally expected in the market.

The Treasury has determined the 'qualifying investments' and 'prescribed markets' – broadly, they are the investments traded on any of the UK's exchanges such as the London Stock Exchange's main market, AIM and PLUS Markets.

5. Data Protection Act 1998

Inevitably, most financial services firms collect data in relation to their clients. An obvious example is a bank that gathers details about receipts into, and payments out of, their customers' bank accounts. The Data Protection Act 1998 details how personal data should be dealt with to protect its integrity and to protect the rights of the persons concerned.

In order to comply with the Act, firms have a number of legal responsibilities, including:

- notifying the Information Commissioner that it is processing information;
- processing personal information in accordance with the eight principles of the Data Protection Act;
- answering subject access requests received from individuals.

Any firm that is holding and processing personal data must be registered with the Information Commissioner. The firm is described as a **data controller**, and is required to comply with the Data Protection Act.

The Data Protection Act lays down eight data protection principles:

- Personal data shall be processed fairly and lawfully.

- Personal data shall be obtained for one or more specified and lawful purposes, and shall not be further processed in any manner that is incompatible with those purposes.
- Personal data shall be adequate, relevant and not excessive in relation to the purpose or purposes for which it is processed.
- Personal data shall be accurate and, where necessary, kept up-to-date.
- Personal data shall not be kept for longer than is necessary for its purpose or purposes.
- Personal data shall be processed in accordance with the rights of the subject under the Act.
- Appropriate technical and organisational measures shall be taken against unauthorised or unlawful processing of personal data, and against accidental loss or destruction of, or damage to, the personal data.
- Personal data shall not be transferred to a country or territory outside the European Economic Area unless that country or territory ensures an adequate level of protection in relation to the processing of personal data.

Under these principles, firms are therefore required to take particular care where financial or medical information is held on a laptop or other portable device. Data held on portable devices should be encrypted and organisations must have policies on the appropriate use and security of portable devices and ensuring their staff are properly trained in these policies.

Other steps that can be taken to keep data safe include the following FSA recommendations:

- Employees should not have access to data beyond that necessary for them to perform their job. Where possible, data should be segregated and information such as passport numbers, bank details and social security numbers should be blanked out.
- The firm should look to monitor and control all flows of information into and out of the company.

- All forms of removable media should be disabled, except where there is a genuine business need. There should be no physical means available for unauthorised staff to remove information undetected.
- Where laptops or other portable devices are in use, these should be encrypted and wiped afterwards. Usage of such devices should be logged and monitored under the authority of an appropriate individual. Watertight policies on using such devices should be in place.
- Software that tracks all activities, as well as web surfing and email traffic, should be installed on every single terminal on the firm's network, and staff should be aware of this.
- The firm should completely block access to all internet content that allows web-based communication. This includes all web-based email, messaging facilities on social networking sites, external instant messaging and 'peer-to-peer' file sharing software.
- The firm should conduct due diligence of data security standards of its third party suppliers before contracts are agreed. This should also be reviewed periodically. If the firm chooses to outsource its IT, conduct checks should be made on the outsource provider's staff as well as the firm's own staff, since they have access to the firm's network.
- All visitors to the firm's premises should be logged in and out, and be supervised while on site. Logs should be kept for a minimum of 12 months.

If a firm outsources at all, there are data protection implications. Firms must assess that the organisation can carry out the work in a secure way, check that they are doing so and take proper security measures. The firm must also have a written contract with the organisation that lays down how it can use and disclose the information entrusted to it.

6. Breaches, Complaints and Compensation

6.1 Complaints

It is almost inevitable that customers will raise complaints against a firm providing financial services. Sometimes these complaints will be valid and sometimes not. The FSA requires authorised firms to deal with complaints from **eligible complainants** promptly and fairly. Eligible complainants are, broadly, individuals and small businesses.

In essence, the firm needs to have written procedures that the staff must follow in the event of a complaint. These procedures require the firm to provide a definitive response to the complaint within a reasonable timescale, and to also make the complainant aware that, should he or she be unhappy with the response, there is a possibility of obtaining an independent view from the **Financial Ombudsman Service (FOS)**.

So, the FSA requires firms to have appropriate written procedures for handling expressions of dissatisfaction from eligible complainants. These procedures should be utilised regardless of whether the complaint is oral or written and whether the complaint is justified or not, as long as it relates to the firm's provision or failure to provide a financial service. If the complaint came from an 'ineligible' complainant, such as a large business client, the firm is still able to apply these procedures, if it so chooses.

These internal complaints-handling procedures should provide for the receiving of complaints, acknowledgement of complaints in a timely manner, responding to those complaints, appropriately investigating the complaints and notifying the complainants of their right to go to the FOS where relevant. Among other requirements, the complaints-handling procedures must require the firm to issue its final response to the complainant. This **final response** must follow within **eight weeks** of the date of the original complaint and the complainant must be notified of his/her right to refer their complaint to the FOS if dissatisfied with the firm's response.

Under the internal complaints-handling procedures, the complaints must be investigated by an employee of sufficient competence who was not directly involved in the matter that is the subject of the complaint. The person charged with responding to the complaints must have the authority to settle the complaint, including offering redress where appropriate, or should have access to someone with the necessary authority.

The responses should adequately address the subject matter of the complaint and, where a complaint is upheld, to offer appropriate redress. Where the firm decides that redress is appropriate, the firm must provide the complainant with fair compensation for any acts or omissions for which it was responsible and comply with any offer of redress the complainant accepts. Any redress for financial loss should include consequential or prospective loss, in addition to actual loss.

The firm must take reasonable steps to ensure that all relevant employees are aware of the firm's complaints-handling procedures and endeavour to act in accordance with these. This includes anyone that is not directly employed by the firm but is acting as an appointed representative to the firm.

6.2 Breaches

A 'breach' is doing something that the regulations do not allow. Formally it is any action (or inaction) which conflicts with regulatory requirements.

The term is most commonly used in relation to a breach of the FSA's rules, but the term is equally valid for all other regulations, such as a breach of the requirements laid down by the tax authorities, such as the UK's HMRC. Indeed, many firms will regard a failure to follow internal rules as a breach.

A breach is therefore a failure to follow rules and regulations, while a complaint is an expression of dissatisfaction by a customer. Clearly, it is possible that the two are linked. For example, an investigation into a customer complaint may well reveal a breach of regulations or the firm's internal rules.

Breaches need to be recorded by authorised firms. The purpose of recording breaches is both to ensure that corrective and preventative action can be taken and to determine whether the mistake needs to be reported to the FSA or another regulatory body. Recording can also be used to identify trends so that further corrective and preventative action can be considered and implemented. Breaches may be identified either through internal checks or through a customer complaint.

6.3 The Financial Ombudsman Service (FOS)

The Financial Ombudsman Service (FOS) was mentioned above as the independent view that can be utilised by eligible complainants if they are dissatisfied with the firm's final response to their complaint. Under the provisions of the Financial Services and Markets Act 2000, the FSA was given the power to make rules relating to the handling of complaints, and the FOS was established as an independent body to administer and operate a dispute resolution scheme. It is funded by compulsory contributions from authorised firms.

The Financial Ombudsman Service is designed to resolve complaints about financial services firms quickly and with minimum formality. Eligible complainants are able to refer complaints to the FOS where they are not satisfied with the response of the financial services firm. The decision of the FOS is binding on firms, although not binding on the person making the complaint.

The Financial Ombudsman can require the firm to pay over money as a result of a complaint. This money award against the firm will be of such amount that the Ombudsman considers to be fair compensation; however, the sum cannot exceed £150,000. Where the decision is made to make a money award, the Ombudsman can award compensation for financial loss, pain and suffering, damage to reputation and distress or inconvenience.

6.4 The Financial Services Compensation Scheme (FSCS)

Imagine a bank, authorised by the FSA and serving retail customers, were to collapse and its retail customers were unable to recover any of their deposited money. It would create uproar and undermine confidence in the financial system – depositors would begin to consider keeping cash under the mattress to be a more viable alternative! Thankfully, the Financial Services Compensation Scheme (FSCS) has been established to pay compensation or arrange continuing cover to eligible claimants in the event of a default by an authorised person. Default is, typically, the firm suffering insolvency.

Eligible claimants are, broadly speaking, the less knowledgeable clients of the firm, such as individuals and small organisations. These less knowledgeable clients are generally the firm's 'private customers' and exclude the more knowledgeable 'professional customers'. The scheme is similar to an insurance policy that is paid for by all authorised firms and provides protection to some clients in the event of a firm collapsing. The claims could come from money on deposit with a bank, or claims in connection with investment business, such as the collapse of a fund manager or stockbroker.

The maximum level of compensation for claims against firms declared in default on or after 1 January 2010 is 100% of the first £50,000 per person per firm for investments, and since 31 December 2010 has been £85,000 for bank deposits. (Prior to January 2010, the maximum level of compensation for claims was 100% of the first £30,000 and 90% of the next £20,000 up to £48,000 per person per firm.)

7. Integrity and Ethics in Professional Practice

The following section will not be examined.

7.1 Ethical or Unethical Practice?

Take the following example, if you buy a car, you can see it, you can try it out and you will discover very quickly whether it performs in the manner advertised and which you expect. You will also be provided, in the case of a new car, with a warranty from the manufacturer. You can thus make your purchase decision with considerable confidence, despite knowing that the reward system in the motor industry means that the salesman will almost certainly receive a commission as a result of your purchase.

Contrast this with an imaginary financial product. This may be an arena in which you are less than knowledgeable, and the product may be one to which, once committed, you can have no idea about its quality for many years to come, by which time it may be too late to make changes or seek redress.

An ethical salesman should therefore take you through the structure of, say, a long-term investment instrument in such a manner that you may be reasonably assured that you understand what it is and from whom you are buying the product. He should explain the factors which determine the rate of return that is offered, and tell you whether that is an actual rate or an anticipated rate which is dependent upon certain other things happening, over which the product originator may have no control. He should also tell you what he is being paid if you buy the product.

In other words he will give you all the facts that you need to make an informed decision as to whether you wish to invest. He will be **open**, **honest**, **transparent** and **fair.**

7.2 Assessing Dilemmas

Many firms and individuals maintain the highest ethical standards without feeling the need for a plethora of formal policies and procedures documenting conformity with accepted ethical standards. Nevertheless, it is apparent that it cannot be assumed that ethical awareness will be absorbed through a sort of process of osmosis. Accordingly, if we are achieve the highest standards of ethical behaviour in our industry, and industry more generally, it is sensible to consider how we can create a sense of ethical awareness.

There will often be situations, particularly at work, where we are faced with a decision where it is not immediately obvious whether what we are being asked to do is actually right. A simple checklist will help to decide; is it: open, honest, transparent, fair?

- **Open** – is everyone whom your action or decision involves fully aware of it, or will they be made aware of it?
- **Honest** – does it comply with applicable law or regulation?
- **Transparent** – is it clear to all parties involved what is happening/will happen?
- **Fair** – is the transaction or decision fair to everyone involved in it or affected by it?

7.3 Codes of Ethics, Codes of Conduct, and Regulation

For any industry in which trust is a central feature, demonstrable standards of practice and the means to enforce them are a key requirement. Hence the proliferation of professional bodies in the fields of health and wealth – areas in which consumers are more sensitive to performance and have higher expectations than in many other fields.

It should be noted that, although the terms 'code of ethics' and 'code of conduct' are often used synonymously, using the term 'ethics' to describe the nature of a code whose purpose is to establish standards of behaviour does, undoubtedly, imply that it involves commitment to and conformity with standards of personal morality, rather than simply complying with rules and guidance relating to professional dealings. Such 'instructions' may be contained more appropriately within a document described as a 'code of conduct'. Where it is considered that more specific guidance of standards of professional practice would be beneficial, such standards might be set out in an appropriately entitled document, or in regulatory standards.

Within financial services we have a structure where, in most countries, detailed and prescriptive regulation is imposed by regulatory bodies.

In the UK it is the FSA, which when initially established, other than through the high-level medium of the Principles for Businesses and Principles for Approved Persons, did not impose any stated standards of ethical behaviour.

Nevertheless, professional bodies operating in the field of financial services have developed codes of conduct for their members.

7.3.1   FSA Principles

From the outset of its role as the sole regulator for the UK financial services industry on 1 December 2001, the FSA has operated without a formal code of ethics, since the original view was that establishing ethical standards and the policing of ethical behaviour was not an appropriate responsibility for a regulator.

However, there were 'Principles' established both for FSA-regulated business itself and also for 'approved persons', and both sets of Principles were capable of being invoked when considering the behaviour of industry participants that, while not being breaches of actual regulation, were considered to be inappropriate or damaging to the industry.

Events since 2001 have caused the FSA to revise its belief in the adequacy of the approach that combines regulation with principles, since it is felt that this results in an overly black and white approach. Such an approach is popular

in a number of countries, but is now felt to fall short of what is required in order to produce properly balanced decisions and policies.

Consequently, the FSA consulted with a number of professional bodies including the CISI, as well as consulting the financial adviser community, as a result of which the FSA has proposed a code of conduct for financial advisers.

7.3.2   CISI Code of Conduct

For any industry in which trust is a central feature, demonstrable standards of practice and the means to enforce them are a key requirement

Financial services is one such industry, and the CISI already has in place its own code of conduct. Membership of the Chartered Institute for Securities & Investment (CISI) requires members to meet the standards set out within the Institute's Principles. These words are from the introduction: *'Professionals within the securities and investment industry owe important duties to their clients, the market, the industry and society at large. Where these duties are set out in law, or in regulation, the professional must always comply with the requirements in an open and transparent manner. Members of the Chartered Institute for Securities & Investment (CISI) are required to meet the standards set out within the Institute's Principles. These Principles [...] impose an obligation on members to act in a way beyond mere compliance and to support the underlying values of the Institute.'*

They set out clearly the expectations upon members of the industry 'to act in a way beyond mere compliance'. In other words, we must understand the obligation upon us to act with integrity in all aspects of our work and our professional relationships. Accordingly, it is appropriate at this stage to examine the code of conduct and to remind ourselves of the stakeholders in each of the individual principles.

The code of conduct is intended to provide direction to members of the professional bodies and, via the FSA code, other members of the

	The Principles	Stakeholder
1.	To act honestly and fairly at all times when dealing with clients, customers and counterparties and to be a good steward of their interests, taking into account the nature of the business relationship with each of them, the nature of the service to be provided to them and the individual mandates given by them.	Client
2.	To act with integrity in fulfilling the responsibilities of your appointment and to seek to avoid any acts, omissions or business practices which damage the reputation of your organisation or the financial services industry.	Firm/industry
3.	To observe applicable law, regulations and professional conduct standards when carrying out financial service activities, and to interpret and apply them to the best of your ability according to principles rooted in trust, honesty and integrity.	Regulator
4.	To observe the standards of market integrity, good practice and conduct required or expected of participants in markets when engaging in any form of market dealing.	Market participant
5.	To be alert to and manage fairly and effectively and to the best of your ability any relevant conflict of interest.	Client
6.	To attain and actively manage a level of professional competence appropriate to your responsibilities, to commit to continuing learning to ensure the currency of your knowledge, skills and expertise and to promote the development of others.	Client Colleagues Self
7.	To decline to act in any matter about which you are not competent unless you have access to such advice and assistance as will enable you to carry out the work in a professional manner.	Client
8.	To strive to uphold the highest personal and professional standards.	Industry Self

financial services industry, as to what are their behavioural requirements in dealing in all areas and with all stakeholders involved in the activity of financial services.

At the corporate and institutional level this means operating in accordance with the rules of market conduct, dealing fairly (honestly) with other market participants and not seeking to take unfair advantage of either. That does not mean that you cannot be competitive, but that rules and standards of behaviour are required to enable markets to function smoothly, on top of the actual regulations which provide direction for the technical elements of market operation. At the individual client relationship level, we are reminded of our ethical responsibilities towards our clients, over and above complying with the regulatory framework and our legal responsibilities.

⭐ Learning Objectives

Chapter Ten has covered the following Learning Objectives:

8.1.1 Understand the need for regulation

Lesson 53

8.1.2 Know the function of UK and European regulators in the financial services industry

Lesson 53

8.1.3 Understand the reasons for authorisation of firms and approved persons

Lesson 53

8.1.4 Know the five groups of activity (controlled functions) requiring approved person status

Lesson 53

8.2.1 Know what money laundering is the stages involved and the related criminal offences

Lesson 55

8.2.2 Know the purpose and the main provisions of the Proceeds of Crime Act 2002 and the Money Laundering Regulations 2007

Lesson 56

8.2.3 Know the action to be taken by those employed in financial services if money laundering activity is suspected and what constitutes unsatisfactory evidence of identity

Lesson 56

8.2.4 Know the purpose of the Bribery Act

Lesson 56

8.2.5 Know how firms can be exploited as a vehicle for financial crime: theft of customer data to facilitate identity fraud

Lesson 56

8.3.1 Know the offences that constitute insider dealing and the instruments covered

Lesson 57

8.3.2 Know the offences that constitute market abuse and the instruments covered

Lesson 57

8.4.1   Understand the impact of the Data Protection Act 1998 on firms' activities

   Lesson 58

8.5.1   Know the difference between a breach and a complaint

   Lesson 59

8.5.2   Know the responsibilities of the industry for handling customer complaints and dealing with breaches

   Lesson 59

8.5.3   Know the role of the Financial Ombudsman Service

   Lesson 59

8.5.4   Know the circumstances under which the financial services compensation scheme pays compensation and the compensation payable for investment claims

   Lesson 59

Based on what you have learned in Chapter Ten, try to answer the following end of chapter questions.

📑 End of Chapter Questions

Think of an answer for each question and refer to the appropriate section for confirmation.

1. What is the global approach to regulating financial services?

    Answer Reference: Section 1.1

    ....

    ....

2. What is the Financial Services Action Plan?

    Answer Reference: Section 1.2

    ....

    ....

3. Who is Alexandre Lamfalussy and what did he advocate?

    Answer Reference: Section 1.2

    ....

    ....

4. What is ESMA?

    Answer Reference: Section 1.2

    ....

    ....

5. What are the four statutory objectives of the FSA?

    Answer Reference: Section 1.3

    ....

    ....

6. What must be satisfied before a UK firm can become authorised?

   Answer Reference: Section 1.3.1

   ....

   ....

7. Broadly, what is a 'controlled function' and what is expected of persons fulfilling such functions?

   Answer Reference: Section 1.3.1

   ....

   ....

8. What five groups of functions are 'controlled'?

   Answer Reference: Section 1.3.2

   ....

   ....

9. What are the three stages of a successful money laundering operation?

   Answer Reference: Sections 2.1

   ....

   ....

10. What is FATF?

    Answer Reference: Section 2.2

    ....

    ....

11. What are the three groups of offences laid down in the Proceeds of Crime Act 2002?

    Answer Reference: Section 2.2

    ....

    ....

12. What is the maximum prison sentence under the Proceeds of Crime Act 2002?

    Answer Reference: Section 2.2

    ....

    ....

13. What is the JMLSG?

    Answer Reference: Section 2.3

    ....

    ....

14. What is the role of the MLRO?

    Answer Reference: Section 2.3.2

    ....

    ....

15. Due diligence could be any one of three possibilities in relation to anti-money laundering procedures – what are they?

    Answer Reference: Section 2.3.4

    ....

    ....

16. Insider dealing covers price-affected securities – what are securities in this context?

    Answer Reference: Section 3

    ....

    ....

17. Market abuse must satisfy one or more of three conditions – what are they?

    Answer Reference: Section 4

    ....

    ....

18. The Data Protection Act 1988 requires firms holding personal data to be registered with whom?

    Answer Reference: Section 5

    ....

    ....

19. How do complaints differ from breaches?

    Answer Reference: Sections 6.1 & 6.2

    ....

    ....

20. What are the FOS and the FSCS, and what are their roles?

    Answer Reference: Sections 6.3 & 6.4

    ....

    ....

11

Taxation, Investment Wrappers and Trusts

Taxation, Investment Wrappers and Trusts

1. Introduction

The old proverb says that 'nothing is certain but death and taxes', highlighting the fact that, in the developed world, taxes are as inevitable as death! This chapter starts by outlining the main types of tax and how the tax to be paid is calculated.

Generally taxes need to be paid, however there are certain schemes which government has introduced to encourage people to save and invest by reducing the tax burden. These are often in the form of 'investment wrappers', a little like parcelling away certain investments and freeing them from tax.

The chapter details the major wrappers - Individual Savings Accounts (ISAs) and Child Trust Funds (CTFs) - and then how the government encourages people to save for their retirement by giving tax incentives on pension

contributions. After considering investment bonds, the chapter concludes with a review of trusts. Trusts are often used to achieve certain ends, like transferring ownership to others in as tax efficient a manner as possible.

2. Taxation

This section reviews the main taxes that affect individuals, with particular focus on the impact of tax on the money made from investments. The main taxes are income tax, capital gains tax, stamp duty and inheritance tax.

2.1 Income Tax

Individuals have to pay income tax on the money they earn from their work and also on any interest or dividends that arise from their savings and investments.

The UK tax authority – Her Majesty's Revenue & Customs or simply HMRC - classifies income into three types:

- **Non-savings income** – this category includes earnings from work and pension income.
- **Savings income** – this includes interest from bank accounts and bonds.
- **Dividend income** – this final category includes dividends paid by companies and investment funds.

As stated above, individual, private investors are liable to pay tax on the income generated from their savings and investments. In this context, taxable income includes interest on bank deposits, the dividends from shares, income distributed by unit trusts and the interest on government and corporate bonds.

In simple terms, the calculation of the tax payable by each individual is done in the following three steps:

Step 1

All of the income from the three categories is added up for the year, first non-savings income (such as wages) and then savings income (interest) and finally dividend income.

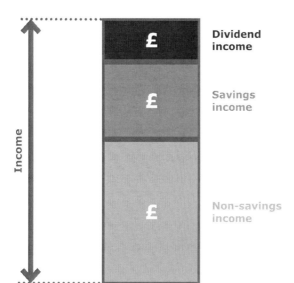

Step 2

Deduct the annual personal allowance from the bottom of the 'pile' of income in step 1. All individuals have an **annual personal allowance** on which no tax is due, and the remaining income is grouped into bands and taxed at different rates. The personal allowance for 2012–13 is £8,105, up to an earnings limit of £100,000, after which it is gradually reduced.

Dividends are treated as the 'top slice' of taxable income, savings as the next slice and other non-savings income as the lowest slice. This means that the personal allowance will always be deducted first from the other (eg, earned) income, and, if there is any remaining, then from savings income, and finally from dividend income.

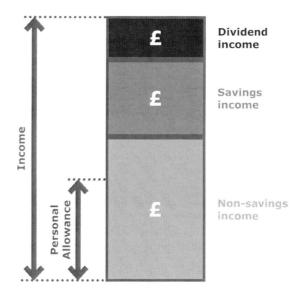

Step 3

Calculate the tax due on the remaining income after deducting the personal allowance, using the following bands and rates:

The rates of income tax for 2012–13 are:

Band of taxable income	Dividend	Savings	Other
£0–£2,710	10%	10%	20%
£2,711–£37,370	10%	20%	20%
£34,371–£150,000	32.5%	40%	40%
Over £150,000	42.5%	50%	50%

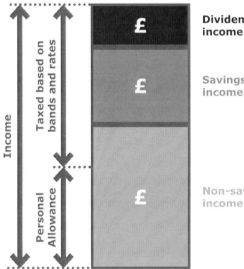

There are a number of deductions that an individual is allowed to make from income before tax is payable; for example, subject to certain limitations, contributions made to a personal or corporate pension scheme; and charitable donations made by individuals on or after 6 April 2000.

There are also some forms of income that are tax-free, including Premium Bond prizes; interest on National Savings Certificates; income from individual savings accounts (ISAs, which will be covered later in this chapter); gambling and National Lottery wins; compensation for loss of employment of up to

£30,000 and statutory redundancy payments; and dividends on ordinary shares of a Venture Capital Trust (VCT). A venture capital trust is a collective investment that invests primarily in start up companies.

2.1.1 Savings Income

Interest income is referred to by HMRC as **non-dividend savings income** and, as seen above, it is treated as the second slice and taxed **after** earned income.

Technically, non-dividend savings income applies to UK and overseas savings income from the following sources:

*   interest from banks and building societies;
*   interest from gilts and corporate bonds;
*   the income component from purchased life annuities;
*   the taxable amount on deep-discounted securities (eg, zero-coupon bonds);
*   distributions from unit trusts and OEICs that principally invest in bonds.

Interest income can be paid either gross or net, that is, either without tax deducted (gross) or with tax deducted (net). For example, interest on bank deposits or other savings accounts is usually paid net of tax and will have 20% tax deducted. Obviously, the deducted tax will form part of the settlement of the tax liability for the individual concerned. If the individual receiving interest is a non-taxpayer, he or she can apply to a bank or building society to have the interest paid gross of tax by filling in form R85.

Interest on gilts can be paid either gross or net; if it is paid net, then it too will have tax at 20% deducted.

Dividends are paid with a 10% tax 'credit', which can simplistically be thought of as a deduction before the dividend is paid. This tax credit applies to dividends paid by companies and from distributions from equity unit trusts and OEICs.

How much tax is then due will depend upon the rate at which the investor pays tax. The table earlier showed that the income tax rates and taxable bands for the 2010/11 tax years are as follows:

2012–2013	
Starting rate for savings: 10%	£0–£2,710
Basic rate: 20%	£0–£34,370
Higher rate: 40%	£34,371–£150,000
Additional rate: 50%	Over £150,000

As you can see from the above, there is a 10% starting rate of tax which is for **savings income only**. If any non-savings income is above this limit (after deducting the personal allowance), then the 10% starting rate for savings will not apply.

So, if an individual has **only** savings income of say, £10,000, then the first £2,440 will be taxed at 10% and the balance at the basic rate. If the same person had non-savings income (say, a pension) of, say, £9,000, then the starting band would not apply and the whole amount would be taxable at the basic rate.

The following examples highlight the way tax is calculated for individuals in a little more detail.

⚙ Example

Alvin is a UK taxpayer who is less than 65 years old. He receives earned income of £6,630 and gross savings income of £3,000 in the year. The personal allowance is first applied against the earned income, so none of the earned income is taxable. After deducting the personal allowance from the combined earned and savings income, there is a total taxable income of £1,525 which enables Alvin to qualify for the 10% starting rate on savings income.

Income Tax Calculation for 2012–13	£
Earnings income	6,630
Non-dividend savings income (grossed up)	3,000
Pension contribution	0
Statutory total income	9,630
Personal allowance	(8,105)
Total taxable income	1,525
Taxable earnings income	0
Taxable non-dividend savings income	1,525
Starting rate, ie, tax on first £2,710 of savings income only @ 10%	152.50
Basic rate, ie, tax on next £34,370 @ 20%	0
Higher rate, ie, tax on taxable income above £34,370 @ 40%	0
Total tax liability	152.50

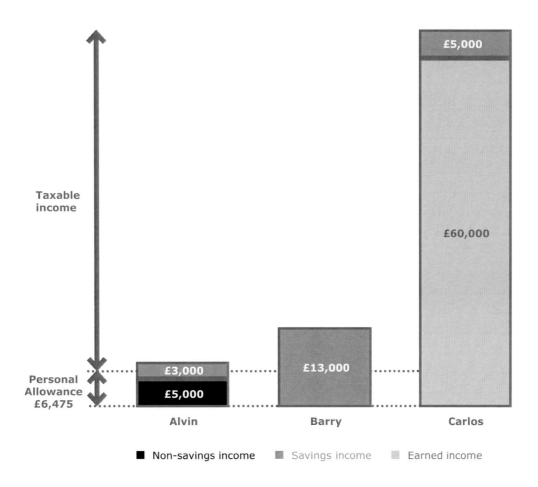

Barry has only gross savings income of £13,000 and no earned income during the year. The absence of any earned income means that, even though Barry has a taxable income (after deduction of the personal allowance) of £4,895, it will be subject to the lower rate of 10% on the first £2,710 of taxable income.

Income Tax Calculation for 2011–12	£
Earnings income	0
Non-dividend savings income (grossed up)	13,000
Pension contribution	0
Statutory total income	13,000
Personal allowance	(8,105)
Total taxable income	4,895
Taxable earnings income	0
Taxable non-dividend savings income	4,895
Starting rate, ie, tax on first £2,710 of savings income only @ 10%	271
Basic rate, ie, tax on next £2,185 @ 20%	437
Higher rate, ie, tax on taxable income above £34,370 @ 40%	0
Total tax liability	708

Carlos is a higher-rate taxpayer. Carlos is single, self-employed, with earned income of £60,000 and gross non-dividend savings income of £5,000.

The earned income is in excess of the £2,710 threshold amount, so the 10% rate for savings income no longer applies. The first £34,370 of taxable income is taxed at the 20% rate, and the amount of taxable income above £34,370 is taxed at the higher rate of 40%.

Income Tax Calculation for 2012–13	£
Earnings income	60,000
Non-dividend savings income (grossed up)	5,000
Statutory total income	65,000
Personal allowance	(8,105)
Total taxable income	56,895
Taxable earnings income	51,895
Taxable non-dividend savings income	5,000
Starting rate, ie, tax on first £2,710 of savings income only @ 10%	0
Basic rate, ie, tax on next £34,370 @ 20%	6,874
Higher rate, ie, tax on taxable income above £34,370 @ 40%	9,010
Total tax liability	15,884

⚙ Example

Dermot is a higher-rate taxpayer and pays tax at 40%. He is entitled to gross interest of £10,000 and tax has been deducted at 20% so that the net payment to him is £8,000.

Dermot will be liable to pay tax at 40% on the gross amount amounting to £4,000 and can set off the tax already paid of £2,000, leaving him with a further liability of £2,000 to pay.

Where an individual's income exceeds £150,000, the excess will be chargeable to income tax at 50%.

⚙ Example

Eric is an additional rate taxpayer and pays tax at 50%. He is entitled to gross interest of £10,000 and tax has been deducted at 20% so that the net payment to him is £8,000.

As Eric is liable to pay tax at 50% on the gross amount, this amounts to £5,000 and he can set off the tax already paid of £2,000, leaving him with a further liability of £3,000 to pay.

2.1.2 Dividends

With **dividends** the position is different to savings income (interest). When a company pays a dividend, the dividend is paid from the company's net profits, on which it will have paid corporation tax. Shareholders are the owners of the company and, recognising this, a credit for some of the tax already paid is given. This takes the form of a tax credit of 10% being applied to all dividends, which can be used to offset any further liability to income tax that the shareholder may have.

Although the tax credit can be used to offset any further liability, it is important to be aware that it cannot be reclaimed should the taxpayer not be liable to tax. So, for example, a pension fund or a charity would not normally be liable to income tax but would be unable to reclaim the tax credit.

⚙ Example

Fred holds 1,000 shares in a company which announces a dividend of 15p per share. When the dividend is paid Fred will receive a cheque for the net dividend of £150.

Accompanying the dividend cheque will be a tax voucher which will show a tax credit of £16.66, that is £150 grossed up and then taxed at 10%. This tax credit can then be used to meet the income tax that is due.

The tax credit for Fred is calculated as follows:

Net dividend representing 90% of the total	*150.00*
Tax credit (10/90th of the net – 10 ÷ 90 x 150)	*16.66*
Gross dividend	*166.66*

The amount of income tax that will be due will depend on the rate of tax that the shareholder is liable to pay. It is here where the treatment of dividends differs significantly from interest.

The rate of tax on dividends is 10% for income up to the basic rate limit. So, for an individual, other than a higher rate taxpayer, no further tax is due, as the tax credit fully meets the tax liability that they are due to pay.

The position is completely different for higher and additional rate taxpayers, who will pay tax at either 32.5% or 42.5% respectively. They can, however, set off the 10% tax credit against their liability, which means there is either a further 22.5% tax or 32.5% tax due.

⚙ Example

Gemma is a higher-rate taxpayer and receives dividend income of £9,000.

To find out how much additional tax is payable by Gemma, first gross up the amount received.

The net dividend payable represents 90% of the gross amount and so the gross amount received is £10,000.

Higher-rate tax on £10,000 at 32.5%	*3,250.00*
Less 10% tax credit	*(1,000.00)*
Additional tax due	*2,250.00*

Note that the additional amount of tax due is calculated as a percentage of the gross amount of the dividend.

2.2 Capital Gains Tax (CGT)

Capital gains tax (CGT) is a tax charged on the increase in the capital value of an asset, normally only paid when the asset is disposed of. So, if an individual bought shares for £2,000 and later sold them for £17,000, then that individual has made a capital gain of £15,000.

CGT may be payable when an asset is sold or otherwise disposed of which includes when a person:

- sells, gives away, exchanges, or transfers – 'dispose of' – all or part of an asset;
- receives a capital sum, such as an insurance payout for a damaged asset.

Most types of assets are liable to CGT and include items such as:

- shares;
- unit trusts;
- certain bonds;
- property (except the person's main home, or principal private residence, see below).

As you can see from the list above, nearly all types of assets are caught by capital gains tax.

There are, however, a number of notable **exemptions**:

- Although property is chargeable to CGT, any gain on the sale of the person's main home is exempt. For CGT purposes, the main home is referred to as the 'principal private residence'.
- Gains on gilts and certain other sterling bonds, called 'qualifying corporate bonds', are exempt when held for more than a year.
- Gains on assets held in accounts that benefit from tax exemptions, such as an Individual Savings Account (ISA), Child Trust Fund (CTF) or approved pension.
- Transfers between spouses.

In addition, individuals have an annual tax-free allowance which is known as the **annual exempt amount** and which allows them to make a certain amount of gains tax-free each year.

For the tax year 2012–13, there is an annual tax free allowance of £10,600. Any net gains in excess are chargeable as follows:

- 18% and 28% for individuals (the rate used will depend on the amount of their total taxable income and gains);

- 28% for trustees or personal representatives;
- 10% for gains qualifying for Entrepreneurs' Relief.

2.3 Inheritance Tax (IHT)

Inheritance tax (IHT) is usually paid on the assets (known as the estate) that someone leaves when they die. It is also sometimes payable on trusts or gifts made during someone's lifetime.

IHT is based on the value of assets that are transferred during the individual's lifetime or that are remaining at death, known as the estate of the deceased.

Each individual has a nil rate band which is currently set at £325,000; and any transfers in excess of the **nil-rate band** are then charged at 40%.

Inheritance tax is a complex area but some of the major **exemptions** are:

- assets left to the deceased person's spouse;
- assets left to registered charities;
- gifts made more than seven years before death can be exempt if certain conditions are met.

Since October 2007, it has also been possible to transfer any unused nil-rate band from a late spouse or civil partner to the second spouse or civil partner when they die. The percentage that is unused on the first death can then be used to reduce the IHT liability on the second death and can increase the inheritance tax threshold of the second partner from £325,000 to as much as £650,000 in 2012–13.

At the time of writing, the government proposes to include provisions in the Finance Bill 2012 to provide for a reduction in the rate of IHT from 40% to 36% where 10% or more of a deceased person's net estate (after deducting IHT exemptions, reliefs and the nil-rate band) is left to charity. The measure will apply to deaths on or after 6 April 2012.

2.4 Stamp Duty and Stamp Duty Reserve Tax (SDRT)

Stamp duty is a tax paid on the purchase of shares where a stock transfer form is used. Stamp duty reserve tax (SDRT) is payable when shares are purchased electronically and no stock transfer form is used. The rate is 0.5% of the purchase price and is paid only by the purchaser.

There is no stamp duty payable on the purchase of foreign shares, bonds, OEICs or unit trusts or on ETFs. However, for OEICs and unit trusts the fund will pay duty when it buys shares and the cost may be passed on to the investor in the difference between the buying and selling price.

2.5 Value Added Tax (VAT)

VAT is chargeable by firms and individuals whose turnover exceeds a certain amount, when they supply what are known as taxable goods or services. Although this affects all firms except those below the VAT threshold, they are allowed to deduct tax they have paid on purchases, so reducing their liability.

The standard rate of VAT is currently 20%. It is relevant to a number of investment services. For example, fees charged for providing an investment management service to an authorised unit trust would be VAT-exempt, while those charged to clients (eg, private individuals) would be VATable. There are also exceptions where no VAT is payable, such as with broker's commission for the execution of a stock market trade.

3. Investment Wrappers

As part of their economic policies, many governments wish to encourage both savings and share ownership. One of the ways this is achieved in the UK is by giving tax advantages to make certain savings and investment products attractive to savers and investors alike. Some of the principal schemes available are known as investment 'wrappers': the term includes products such as:

- Individual Savings Accounts (ISAs);
- Child Trust Funds (CTFs)/Junior ISAs (JISAs);
- Pensions;
- Investment bonds.

As a result of their attractiveness, they are subject to a range of rules set by HMRC prescribing areas such as, who can invest, the amount of annual contributions that can be made and what are permissible investments.

3.1 Individual Savings Accounts (ISAs)

An ISA is an acronym for 'Individual Savings Account'. The ISA itself is often referred to as an investment wrapper because it is essentially an account that holds other investments, such as deposits, shares, OEICs and unit trusts, and allows them to be invested in a tax-efficient manner.

Their tax advantages have made them very popular and, as at the end of 2010, there was approximately £172 billion held in cash ISAs and £177 billion in stocks and shares ISAs.

Firms offering investments in ISAs, such as banks, building societies and fund management companies, must be approved by HMRC. The approved entity is known as the 'ISA manager'. HMRC is also responsible for setting the detailed rules applicable to ISAs.

3.1.1 Eligibility

Stocks and shares ISAs are available only to residents of the UK over the age of 18.

Cash ISAs are available to those aged 16 or over.

3.1.2 Tax Position

ISAs were set up by the government to encourage individual investment. The particular incentive for investment was that the investments held within an ISA were free of income tax and capital gains tax.

This changed from 6 April 2005, when the government withdrew part of the tax advantage; it is now no longer possible to reclaim the tax credit on dividends paid on shares held within an ISA. However, the tax advantage remains for investments earning interest, such as cash deposits and government and corporate bonds. They are also still attractive for higher-rate taxpayers, who are not liable to any additional income tax on interest or dividends held within an ISA.

3.1.3 Types of ISA

Over the years, the rules surrounding the types of ISA had become complex and this made them less than straightforward for investors to understand and caused firms difficulties in administering them.

As a result, the government has simplified the rules and there is now simply one ISA, and savers are able to contribute to two components: cash; and stocks and shares.

Under these new rules, savers are able to hold one of each component per year, with either the same or different providers. In the year when a subscription is made, therefore, an investor can open an ISA to hold the cash component with one manager and a separate one to hold the stocks and shares component with another. However, an investor cannot open an ISA to hold part of the cash component and then later in the year open one

with another manager to hold the balance of the cash component; each component must all be with one manager. The same is the case for the stocks and shares component.

3.1.4 Subscription Limits

Every eligible investor has an annual ISA investment allowance known as a subscription limit. There is an annual maximum overall subscription limit and within that overall limit, no more than 50% may be placed in the cash component. Investors can therefore choose to invest in two separate ISAs with potentially different providers subject to the maximum limits or subscribe the maximum amount to a stocks & shares ISA.

Until 2011, the annual subscription limit was announced annually and so there was uncertainty about how it would increase, if at all. This was changed from 6 April 2011 so that the ISA annual subscription limit is increased in line with inflation on an annual basis. In the event that inflation is negative, the ISA limits remain the same. The first change used RPI as the measure of inflation, but the March 2011 budget announced that the annual ISA subscription limit will be increased on an annual basis by reference to the Consumer Prices Index (CPI) from the 2012–13 tax year. The new limits are calculated by reference to the inflation index for the September before the start of the following tax year.

For 2012–13, HMRC announced that as the CPI data for September 2011 showed inflation was 5.2% then the 2012–13 limits will be an overall ISA subscription limit of £11,280, of which up to £5,640 can be subscribed to a cash ISA. The new annual limits are rounded to the nearest multiple of 120, so that individuals who save monthly are able to calculate their monthly savings more easily.

Investors are also allowed to transfer shares which they have received from approved profit-sharing schemes, share incentive plans or SAYE share options. They have to transfer such shares at market value within 90 days of receipt. The value of these transfers will reduce the remaining ISA subscription balance available to the investor for that year.

3.1.5 Transfers

Investors are able to transfer an existing ISA from one manager to another manager provided that the receiving manager is prepared to accept it. Transfers of previous years' subscriptions can be in whole or just in part. Transfers of the same year's subscriptions, however, must be for the full amount.

Since April 2008, savers are able to transfer some or all of the money saved in previous years from cash ISAs to stocks and shares ISAs without affecting their annual ISA investment allowance.

It is also possible to transfer money saved in the current tax year in cash ISAs to stocks and shares ISAs. Such transfers must be the whole amount saved in that tax year in that cash ISA up to the day of the transfer. The individual is then able to save up to the full remaining balance of their annual ISA investment allowance in ISAs in that tax year.

> ### ⚙ Example
>
> *Henrietta has invested £2,000 into a cash ISA at the beginning of the tax year. She can transfer that amount to a stocks and shares ISA before the end of the tax year. The cash ISA is then treated as if it had never existed. Henrietta could then make further investments into the stocks and shares ISA of up to £8,200 in 2010–11, which, along with her initial investment, would fully use up her annual allowance.*

It should be noted that, whilst a transfer from a cash ISA to a stocks and shares ISA can be made, a transfer the opposite way round cannot be made.

3.1.6 Withdrawals

Withdrawals of any cash or investments from an ISA are permanent. Once withdrawn the

amounts cannot be re-deposited. The only way in which funds can be added to an ISA is by using the current year's subscription. For example, if an investor withdraws funds from their cash ISA they cannot change their mind later and redeposit all or part of the amount if they have already used their current year's subscription.

3.2 Child Trust Funds (CTFs) and Junior ISAs (JISAs)

The Child Trust Fund (CTF) was introduced by the government to help and encourage parents to save for their child's future. The government's intention was that when the child reached 18, they would have some money to give them a start to life as an adult. At 18, they could carry on saving or use the money for other things – such as driving lessons or training courses.

The coalition government, however, announced on 24 May 2010 its plans to reduce and then stop government payments to CTF accounts. The changes required legislation to be passed by Parliament, which was introduced in September, and from 1 January 2011 no further government contributions have been made.

No new accounts can be opened; however, existing accounts can continue. This means that further contributions can be made by parents, family and friends into the account subject to the same maximum limit as apply for Junior ISAs.

The main characteristics of the CTF are as follows:

- It is a long-term savings and investment account that is available to children born on or after 1 September 2002.
- Money invested in a CTF belongs to the child and cannot be withdrawn until the child turns 18.
- There will be no tax on any interest or gains made on the money in the CTF.
- At 16, the child will be able to manage his or her CTF account, for example by deciding to change provider or type of account.
- At 18, young people with CTF accounts will be able to decide for themselves how best to use the money.
- CTFs are treated in the same way as ISAs in respect of tax benefits.

Providers offer up to three forms of CTF account: a savings account, an account that invests in shares or a stakeholder account. The **savings account** is a deposit account and offers a secure type of investment but one whose value will be affected by inflation. The **accounts that invest in shares** offer the potential for growth, but the risk of falling in value. The **stakeholder accounts** invest in shares but the government has set certain rules to reduce risk – in particular, when the child reaches the age of 13, the money starts to be moved from shares into safer investments.

The first CTF accounts will mature in 2020, and if the child does not take the money out it will automatically roll over into an ISA on maturity. The aim is to encourage young people to maintain a saving habit into adulthood.

3.2.1 Junior ISAs (JISAs)

The government announced in October 2010 that it intended to create a new tax-free children's savings account to replace the Child Trust Fund. The new accounts, described as Junior ISAs, offer a simple and tax-free way to save for a child's future. The start date for the new Junior ISA (or JISA as HMRC refers to them) was 1 November 2011 and the key features are below.

- **Eligibility** – all UK resident children (aged under 18) who do not have a CTF will be eligible.
- **Types of account** – both cash and stocks & shares Junior ISAs will be available. The qualifying investments for each of these will be the same as for existing ISAs and children will be able to hold up to one cash and one stocks & shares Junior ISA at a time.
- **Annual subscription limit** – each eligible child will be able to receive contributions of up to £3,600 each year into their Junior ISA or ISAs. The subscription limit will be indexed by CPI from 6 April 2013 onwards.
- **Account opening** – anyone with parental responsibility for an eligible child will be able to open Junior ISAs on their behalf. Eligible children over the age of 16 will also be able to open Junior isAs for themselves.
- **Account operation** – until the child reaches 16, accounts will be managed on their behalf by a person who has parental responsibility for that child. At age 16, the child assumes management responsibility for their account. Withdrawals will not be permitted until the child reaches 18 except in cases of terminal illness or death.
- **Transfers** – it will be possible to transfer accounts between providers, but it will not be possible to hold more than one cash or stocks and shares Junior ISA at any time. it will not be possible to transfer CTFs into Junior ISAs or vice versa.
- **Maturity** – at the age of 18, the Junior ISA will automatically become a normal adult ISA. The funds will then be accessible to the child.

Having a Junior ISA will not affect an individual's entitlement to adult ISAs. it will be possible for Junior ISA account holders to open adult cash ISAs from the age of 16 and Junior ISA contributions will not impact upon their adult ISA subscription limits.

3.3 Pensions

3.3.1 Retirement Planning

For many people their pension and their house are their main assets.

Pensions are becoming increasingly important as people live longer and commentators speak of a 'pensions time bomb', where the pension provided by the state, the individuals and their employers will be inadequate to meet needs in retirement. As an example, it is predicted that by 2040 over 50% of the people in the UK will be over 65. When the state pension was introduced in the UK, the initial need was funding for the rare event of people living beyond the age of 65. Today this is very common.

3.3.2 Tax Incentives

A pension is an investment fund where contributions are made, usually during the individual's working life, to provide a lump sum on retirement plus an annual pension payable thereafter. Pension contributions are tax-effective, as tax relief is given on contributions. In other words, the contributions to a pension made by an individual reduce the total on which income tax in charged in each tax year.

Some of the main tax incentives of pensions include:

- Tax relief on contributions made.
- Pension funds are not subject to income tax and CGT and so the pension fund can grow tax-free.
- The ability to take a pension from age 55.
- An option to take a tax-free lump sum at retirement.
- The option to include death benefits as part of the scheme.

These tax advantages were put in place by the government to encourage people to provide for their own old age. Pensions are subject to income tax when they are received.

3.3.3 State Pension Scheme

The state pension comes in two parts:

- Basic state pension.
- Additional state pension or State Second Pension (S2P).

The government pays state pensions from current National Insurance contributions, and makes no investment for future needs. This is a problem as dependency ratios (the proportion of working people to retired people) are forecast to fall from 4:1 in 2002 to 3:1 by 2030 and 2.5:1 by 2050. This means that by 2050 either each worker will have to support almost twice as many retired people, or the support per head will need to fall substantially, or some combination of these changes.

Currently, the state pension is payable from age 65 for men and 60 for women but this is being changed so that both will receive the state pension at the same age. The pension age for women is being gradually increased from 60 on 5 April 2010 so that the pension age for both men and women will be 65 from 6 April 2018, ie, everyone will draw their pensions at the same age. The pension age is also being increased, and men and women born on or after 6 October 1954 but before 6 April 1968 will now draw their pensions from the age of 66. Of those born after 1968, the pension age will increase from 66 to 67 and then to 68.

The **basic state pension** is paid at a flat rate to people who have made sufficient National Insurance contributions during their working life. Even if people have had long periods of unemployment or invalidity, which might mean that they are not entitled to a full pension, there is provision for the amount of basic state pension to which an individual may be entitled to be topped up through a system known as the **Pension Credit Guarantee**. The Pension Credit Guarantee is a means-tested benefit that is also available to those in receipt of a full basic state pension.

The additional state pension or **State Second Pension** – also known as 'S2P' – was previously known as the State Earnings-Related Pensions (SERPS) until 2002. As the name implies, SERPS was earnings related – the higher the earnings, the bigger the pension. It was reformed in 2002 to become the State Second Pension, to provide a more generous additional state pension for those on low to moderate income levels and for certain carers and disabled individuals; it is still earnings-related.

Workers used to be able to **contract out** of the State Second Pension scheme and put more into their occupational pension scheme, personal pension scheme or stakeholder scheme (see below). Workers who did contract out by joining their employer's contracted-out occupational pension scheme still pay reduced National Insurance contributions that should enable them to pay more into their pension scheme.

3.3.4 Occupational Pension Schemes

One of the earliest kinds of scheme supplementing state funding was the occupational pension scheme.

Occupational pension schemes are run by companies for their employees. In an occupational pension scheme, the employer makes pension contributions on behalf of its workers. The occupational pension scheme could take the form of a defined benefit scheme, also known as a 'final salary scheme', where the pension received is related to the number of years of service and the individual's final salary. For example, an occupational pension scheme might provide an employee with 1/40th of their final salary for every year of service; the employee could then retire with an annual pension the size of which was related to the number of years' service.

The advantages of occupational pension schemes are:

- Employers generally contribute to the fund (some pension schemes do not involve any

contributions from the employee – these are called **non-contributory** schemes).
- Running costs are often lower than for personal schemes and the costs are often met by the employer.
- The employer must ensure the fund is well run and for **defined benefit schemes** must make up any shortfall in funding.

Employers have generally stopped providing defined benefit schemes to new employees because of rising life expectancies and volatile investment returns, and the implications these factors have on the funding requirement for defined benefit schemes.

Instead, occupational pension schemes are now typically provided to new employees on a **defined contribution** basis – where the size of the pension is driven by the contributions paid and the investment performance of the fund. Under this type of scheme, an investment fund is built up and the amount of pension that will be received at retirement will be determined by the value of the fund and the amount of pension it can generate.

The higher cost of providing a defined benefit scheme is part of the reason why many companies have closed their defined benefit schemes to new joiners and make only defined contribution schemes available to staff.

Over half of the defined benefit schemes have closed to new joiners since 2001 as the stock market decline has caused companies problems with the under-funding of their schemes. A key advantage of defined contribution schemes for employers over defined benefit schemes is that poor performance is not the employer's problem; it is the employee who will end up with a smaller pension.

Occupational pension schemes are structured as **trusts**, with the investment portfolio managed by professional asset managers. The asset managers are appointed by, and report to, the trustees of the scheme. The trustees will typically include representatives from the company (eg, company directors) as well as employee representatives.

3.3.5 Private Pensions or Personal Pensions

Private pensions or personal pensions are individual pension plans. They are **defined contribution** schemes that might be used by employees of companies that do not run their own scheme or where employees opt out of the company scheme or in addition to an existing pension scheme. They are also used by the self-employed.

Many employers actually organise **group personal pension schemes** for their employees, by arranging the administration of these schemes with an insurance company or an asset management firm. Such employers may also contribute to the personal pension schemes of their employees.

Employees and the self-employed who wish to provide for their pension and do not have access to occupational schemes or employer-arranged personal pensions have to organise their own personal pension schemes. These will often be arranged through an insurance company or an asset manager, where the individual can choose from the variety of investment funds offered.

Individuals also have the facility to run a **Self-Invested Personal Pension (SIPP)**, commonly administered by a stockbroker or IFA on their behalf. In a SIPP, it is the individual who decides which investments are included in the scheme, subject to HMRC guidelines.

Smaller companies can also make independent pension arrangements by setting up a **Small Self-Administered Scheme (SSAS)**. Under these schemes, the directors keep full control of the scheme and decide, within limits, the size and timing of contributions; as their own trustees, they keep full control of the investments. They are required to have a pensioner trustee who is independent of the company and who is responsible for ensuring that investments are made in accordance with HMRC regulations. The powers open to the trustees mean that the pension fund's fortunes may be tightly bound to those of the company. For this reason they are usually suitable only for the directors and their families.

The schemes are approved by HMRC which means that they are **tax-exempt**. The contributions are tax-deductible and there is no tax either on investment income or capital gains.

In a private scheme, the key responsibility that lies with the individual is that the individual chooses the investment fund in a scheme administered by an insurance company or asset manager, or the actual investments in a SIPP. It is then up to the individual to monitor the performance of his investments and assess whether it will be sufficient for his retirement needs.

3.3.6 Stakeholder Pensions

A stakeholder pension is simply a type of personal pension that incurs low charges. Stakeholder pensions are available from a range of financial services companies, such as banks, insurance companies and building societies.

Stakeholder pensions must satisfy a number of minimum government standards to ensure that they offer value for money and flexibility, including:

- **Low charges** – for people who joined a stakeholder pension scheme on or after 6 April 2005, the cap is an annual management charge of 1.5% for the first ten years, which will reduce to 1% from ten years onwards if these members remain in the scheme.
- **Low and flexible contributions** – the minimum contribution cannot be greater than £20, and there cannot be a requirement for regular monthly contribution.
- **Transferability** – there must be no charges for transfer to another scheme.

- **Default option** – pension funds can allocate funds between different kinds of investment. A stakeholder scheme must provide a default for those unwilling to choose their own allocation between, say, UK shares, overseas shares or bond funds.

3.3.7 NEST and Auto-enrolment

Government estimates suggest that around seven million people are not saving enough to give them the retirement income they will want or expect. The Pensions Act 2008 is aimed at tackling this challenge. The Act imposes new duties on employers to provide access to a workplace pension scheme for most workers, which start to be introduced from 2012. Employers will have to enrol some or all of their workers into a pension scheme that meets or exceeds certain legal standards, and may need to make a minimum contribution.

Employers will need to automatically enrol workers aged at least 22 but under state pension age who earn more than £7,475 (in January 2011 terms) in a year. These people are known as eligible jobholders and their employers will have to make a minimum contribution into the pension scheme on their behalf. Workers who are automatically enrolled into a scheme can choose to opt out if they want to.

For those workers they must either pay a minimum contribution into a defined contribution scheme or provide a minimum level of benefits from a defined benefit scheme. The total minimum contribution to a worker's retirement pot will be 8% of their qualifying earnings. Of this 8%, the employer will have to contribute a minimum of 3%. The rest will be made up of tax relief and the jobholder's contribution.

NEST (National Employment Savings Trust) is one of the pension schemes employers can use to meet their new duties and is tasked with providing a simple low-cost pension scheme. It will offer flexibility over contribution levels and up to £4,400 per year can be paid into each member's retirement savings pot.

3.4 Investment Bonds

An investment bond is a single-premium life assurance policy that is taken out for the purposes of investment. It is a common form of investment in the UK as, in common with other 'wrappers', it benefits from favourable tax treatment granted by governments interested in promoting savings and investment.

Investment bonds are issued by insurance companies and may be linked to one or more of the insurance company's unit-linked investment funds. They are structured in various ways in order to provide either capital growth or a regular income to investors. There is a wide range of investment bonds available including:

- with-profits investment bonds;
- distribution bonds;
- guaranteed equity bonds;
- unit-linked bonds.

Within these bonds, the investor will have a choice of investment fund with differing levels of risk, geographic coverage and investment style.

They will usually have a choice of two basic charging structures: an initial charge structure and an establishment charge structure. An initial charge involves all of the costs being taken up front, while the other spreads the costs, usually over the first five years. There may also be exit charges for early encashment.

Investment bonds can be a very useful tool for tax planning purposes. Up to 5% of the original investment can be taken from an investment bond each year for 20 years without incurring an immediate tax liability. Also, if the 5% is not taken at the beginning of the investment bond's life, it can be rolled up on a cumulative basis and taken at a later stage, again without an immediate tax liability.

When investment bonds are encashed, the profits made are taxed as income rather than capital gains. As a result, basic rate taxpayers will not be liable to any tax on the proceeds of the bond, providing that the withdrawal does not push them into the higher-rate tax band. Higher rate taxpayers are currently liable to tax at their higher rate less the basic rate (for example, a 40% taxpayer can deduct the basic rate of 20% to leave a further 20% liability) on policy gains.

The ability to defer any tax liability until encashment makes investment bonds particularly attractive to higher rate taxpayers who know that they will become basic rate taxpayers at some point in the future.

This means that during the lifetime of the bond they can make withdrawals and defer the liability on any tax until the policy is encashed. If at the time of encashment the policyholders have become basic rate taxpayers, then there is a good chance that they will incur no tax liability.

Investment bonds are also issued by life assurance companies based in offshore tax havens such as the Channel Islands. The structure of these bonds is similar to the ones available in the UK but their tax treatment differs. A notable difference is that income tax is charged at the full rates and so a basic rate taxpayer faces a 20% charge and a higher-rate or additional-rate taxpayer will pay tax at a full 40% or 50%.

4. Trusts

4.1 What is a Trust?

A trust is the legal means by which one person gives property to another person to look after on behalf of another individual or a set of individuals.

Starting with the individuals involved, the person who creates the trust is known as the **settlor**. The person he gives the property to, to look after on behalf of others, is called the **trustee**, and the individuals for whom it is intended are known as the **beneficiaries**.

4.2 Uses of Trusts

Trusts are widely used in estate and tax planning for high net worth individuals and some of their main uses include:

- providing funds for a specific purpose, such as the maintenance of young children;
- setting aside funds for disabled or incapacitated children in order to protect and provide for their financial maintenance;
- reducing future inheritance tax liabilities by transferring assets into a trust and so out of the settlor's ownership;
- separating out rights to income and capital so that, for example, the spouse of a second marriage receives the income during their life and the capital passes on that person's death to the settlor's children.

Trusts are also the underlying structure for many major investment vehicles, such as pension funds, charities and unit trusts.

4.3 Types of Trusts

There are a number of different types of trust and some of the main ones are:

- **Bare or absolute trusts** – where a trustee holds assets for one or more persons absolutely.
- **Interest in possession trusts** – where a beneficiary has a right to the income of the trust during his/her life and the capital passes to others on their death.
- **Discretionary trusts** – where the trustees have discretion to whom the capital and income is paid, within certain criteria.

Learning Objectives

Chapter Eleven has covered the following Learning Objectives:

9.1   Tax

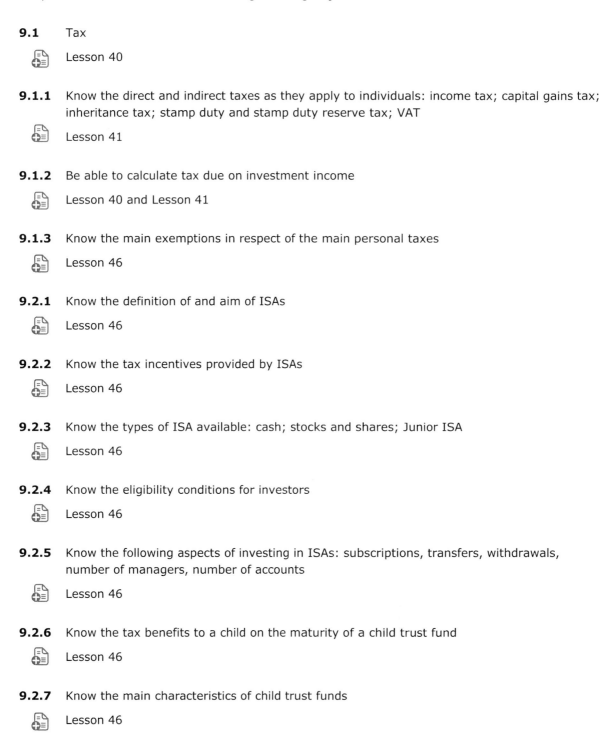 Lesson 40

9.1.1   Know the direct and indirect taxes as they apply to individuals: income tax; capital gains tax; inheritance tax; stamp duty and stamp duty reserve tax; VAT

Lesson 41

9.1.2   Be able to calculate tax due on investment income

Lesson 40 and Lesson 41

9.1.3   Know the main exemptions in respect of the main personal taxes

Lesson 46

9.2.1   Know the definition of and aim of ISAs

Lesson 46

9.2.2   Know the tax incentives provided by ISAs

Lesson 46

9.2.3   Know the types of ISA available: cash; stocks and shares; Junior ISA

Lesson 46

9.2.4   Know the eligibility conditions for investors

Lesson 46

9.2.5   Know the following aspects of investing in ISAs: subscriptions, transfers, withdrawals, number of managers, number of accounts

Lesson 46

9.2.6   Know the tax benefits to a child on the maturity of a child trust fund

Lesson 46

9.2.7   Know the main characteristics of child trust funds

Lesson 46

9.3.1 Know the tax incentives provided by pensions

 Lesson 47

9.3.2 Know the basic characteristics of the following: state pension scheme; occupational pension schemes; personal pensions including self-invested personal pensions (SIPPs)/small self-administered schemes (SSAS); stakeholder pensions; NEST/auto-enrolment

 Lesson 47

9.4.1 Know the tax incentives provided by investment bonds – onshore/offshore

 Lesson 47

9.4.2 Know the main characteristics of investment bonds

 Lesson 47

9.5.1 Know the features of the main trusts: discretionary; interest in possession; bare

 Lesson 48

9.5.2 Know the definition of the following terms: trustee; settlor; beneficiary

 Lesson 48

9.5.3 Know the main reasons for creating trusts

 Lesson 48

Based on what you have learned in Chapter Eleven, try to answer the following end of chapter questions.

📑 End of Chapter Questions

Think of an answer for each question and refer to the appropriate section for confirmation.

1. What are the various rates of income tax?

    Answer Reference: Section 1.2

    ....

    ....

2. What is the personal allowance?

    Answer Reference: Section 2.1

    ....

    ....

3. Is savings income typically paid net or gross?

    Answer Reference: Section 2.1.1

    ....

    ....

4. How is the gross dividend calculated?

    Answer Reference: Section 3.1.2

    ....

    ....

5. What assets are exempt from Capital Gains Tax?

    Answer Reference: Section 2.2

    ....

    ....

6. What is the rate of Inheritance Tax?

    Answer Reference: Section 2.3

    ....

    ....

7. How does Stamp Duty differ from Stamp Duty Reserve Tax (SDRT)?

    Answer Reference: Section 2.4

    ....

    ....

8. What are the two components that make up an ISA?

    Answer Reference: Section 3.1

    ....

    ....

9. How much can be invested in an ISA each year?

    Answer Reference: Section 3.1.4

    ....

    ....

10. What is the difference between defined benefit and defined contribution pension schemes?

    Answer Reference: Section 3.3

    ....

    ....

11. What is an investment bond?

Answer Reference: Section 3.4

....

....

12. Who are the three parties that are typically involved in a trust?

Answer Reference: Section 4

....

....

Multiple Choice Questions

📃 Multiple Choice Questions

1. In which one of the following ways is a professional customer most likely to differ from a retail customer?

    a. The professional will trade in smaller volumes

    b. The professional will be less sophisticated

    c. The professional can be assumed to know what he is doing

    d. The professional will be given a more generous cooling off period

2. The GBP/EUR rate for a retail customer is quoted as:

	Bank buys	Bank sells
GBP/EUR	1.18	1.14

    How many euros can the customer expect to receive for £1,000?

    a. €1,180.00

    b. €1,140.00

    c. €847.46

    d. €877.19

3. A retail customer is about to visit Japan for the first time. She spends £1,500 buying Japanese yen from a bank when the bank is quoting the following:

	Bank buys	Bank sells
GBP/JPY	140	115

    How many Yen will she receive?

    a. 10.71

    b. 13.04

    c. 172,500

    d. 210,000

4. Carlos Jenkinson has £300 on deposit at a bank. He earns interest at a gross rate of 4% for the year, paid at the end of the year. Assuming the bank deducts tax at source and Carlos is a higher rate tax payer, how much will be deducted?

    a. £0

    b. £2.40

    c. £4.80

    d. £12.00

5. Which one of the following best describes a mortgage?

    a. A secured overdraft

    b. An unsecured overdraft

    c. A secured loan

    d. An unsecured loan

6. A credit card has a quoted rate of 12% pa, charged monthly. What is the effective annual rate?

    a. 12%

    b. 12.36%

    c. 12.55%

    d. 12.68%

7. Colin is thinking of establishing a company and wants to confirm the need for a Memorandum of Association. Which of the following is true?

    a. It gives details of the company's name, business objectives and is required by all companies

    b. It gives details of the company's name, business objectives and is required by public companies only

    c. It gives details of the relationship between the shareholders and the company

    d. It gives details of the relationship between the shareholders and the company and is required by all companies

8. Kiwi Stars plc is holding its AGM and a director's reappointment is put to the shareholders as an ordinary resolution. What proportion of votes is required to pass the resolution?

    a. Greater than 50% of those voting

    b. Greater than 50% of all Kiwi shareholders

    c. At least 75% of those voting

    d. At least 75% of all Kiwi shareholders

9. ADC plc has shares in issue that are non-voting, pay a dividend of 3% pa and have the right to convert into ordinary shares after five years. Which of the following best describes these shares?

    a. Non-voting ordinary shares

    b. Convertible ordinary shares

    c. Non-voting preference shares

    d. Convertible preference shares

10. JZ plc has 100,000 shares in issue. It is proposing a 1 for 1 bonus issue when its shares are trading at £8 each. Assuming the bonus issue goes ahead, how much money is raised and what is the share price likely to be after the bonus issue?

    a. £800,000 raised, £4 after the issue

    b. £800,000 raised, £8 after the issue

    c. £nil raised, £4 after the issue

    d. £nil raised, £8 after the issue

11. Emma Ringtone purchases shares in JZ plc ex dividend, just prior to JZ paying a dividend of 3 pence per share. How much will Emma receive in dividends per share?

    a. Zero

    b. A small proportion of the 3p per share

    c. A large proportion of the 3p per share

    d. 3p per share

12. ABC plc has launched a takeover bid for XYZ plc and the directors of XYZ are not recommending acceptance to their shareholders. Which of the following best describes the situation?

    a. A hostile bid

    b. An illegal approach

    c. A friendly bid

    d. A merger

13. Which one of the following exchanges operates an open outcry system of trading?

    a. London Stock Exchange

    b. NASDAQ

    c. Tokyo Stock Exchange

    d. New York Stock Exchange

14. How are shares selected for inclusion in the FTSE 100?

    a. By market capitalisation

    b. By revenue growth

    c. By profit level

    d. By number of shareholders

15. How many stocks make up the Xetra Dax?

    a. 30

    b. 40

    c. 100

    d. 225

16. On the LSE's SETS trading system, how is priority given to the individual orders?

    a. Price and then time

    b. Time and then price

    c. Quantity and then time

    d. Quantity and then price

17. In the UK's CREST system, a company's register of shareholders consists of which of the following?

    a. An uncertificated register only

    b. An operating register and an issuer register

    c. An operator register only

    d. An issuer register only

18. All of the following are alternative terms for the face value of a bond, EXCEPT:

    a. Par value

    b. Nominal value

    c. Principal

    d. Price

19. An index-linked bond is typically indexed in which one of the following ways?

    a. Coupons are uplifted by a stock market index

    b. Coupons and principal are uplifted by a stock market index

    c. Coupons are uplifted by an inflation index

    d. Coupons and principal are uplifted by an inflation index

20. David holds a portfolio of conventional bonds and is worried that interest rates are set to change. If interest rates go up, what is the likely impact on the portfolio?

    a. No impact

    b. Decrease in value

    c. Increase in value

    d. The impact is unpredictable

21. A bond with a 4% coupon is currently trading at 95. What is the flat yield?

    a. 4%

    b. 4.21%

    c. 9%

    d. 38%

22. What is the highest non-investment grade rating provided by Moody's?

    a. Ba1

    b. BB+

    c. Baa3

    d. BBB–

23. All of the following are money market instruments, EXCEPT:

    a. Junk bonds

    b. Treasury bills

    c. Commercial paper

    d. Certificate of deposit

24. A mortgage with an applicable interest rate that cannot exceed a set level for a period, and where the principal is repaid at the end of the mortgage term is typically described as:

    a. Capped repayment mortgage

    b. Capped interest-only mortgage

    c. Tracker repayment mortgage

    d. Tracker interest-only mortgage

25. Which one of the following provides a summary of transactions between one country and the rest of the world?

    a. Balance of payments

    b. Gross domestic product

    c. RPI

    d. PSNCR

26. What is the responsibility of the Monetary Policy Committee of the Bank of England?

    a. To set interest rates

    b. To set the level of government borrowing

    c. To manipulate GDP levels

    d. To issue government debt

27. Which one of the following is traded on exchange and obliges the buyer to pay a pre-agreed sum?

    a. Forward

    b. Option

    c. Future

    d. Swap

28. Prices of all of the following funds are based on net asset value, EXCEPT:

    a. Actively managed OEICs

    b. Passively managed OEICs

    c. Unit trusts

    d. Investment trusts

29. An authorised fund is established as an open ended company and will select stocks based on tracking a stock market index. Which of the following best describes the fund?

    a. Actively managed ETF

    b. Passively managed unit trust

    c. Actively managed investment trust

    d. Passively managed OEIC

30. All of the following are stages of a money laundering operation, EXCEPT:

    a. Origination

    b. Placement

    c. Layering

    d. Integration

Answers to Multiple Choice Questions

1. Answer: C   Reference: Chapter 1

    The professional customer tends to deal in greater volumes, and is more sophisticated than the retail customer. The professional will be given little or no cooling off period because they are more sophisticated and can be assumed to know what he is doing.

2. Answer: B   Reference: Chapter 1

    The customer is buying euros and the bank is selling those Euros. So the rate is €1.14 for each £1 - £1000 x €1.14 = €1,140.00.

3. Answer: C   Reference: Chapter 1

    The customer is buying Yen and the bank is selling the Yen. So the rate is 115 Yen for each £. JPY115 x £1,500 = JPY172,500.

4. Answer: B   Reference: Chapter 2

    Despite being a higher rate taxpayer, Carlos will only be deducted 20% at source. He will pay a further 20% when he submits his tax return.

5. Answer: C   Reference: Chapter 3

    A mortgage is secured on the property that the loan is taken out to purchase.

6. Answer: D   Reference: Chapter 2

    $1.01^{12} – 1 = 12.6825\%$

7. Answer: A   Reference: Chapter 3

    It is the memorandum that gives details of the name, business objectives, etc, and it is required for both public and private companies.

8. Answer: A   Reference: Chapter 3

    An ordinary resolution requires a simple majority of those voting in order to be passed.

9. Answer: D   Reference: Chapter 3

    As preference shares are typically non-voting, describing them simply as convertible preference shares would be sufficient.

10. Answer: C   Reference: Chapter 3

    As a 1 for 1 bonus issue, the number of shares will double and no money will be raised. The doubling of the number of shares will mean that the share price will half in price to around £4.

11. Answer: A   Reference: Chapter 3

    If the shares are purchased ex-dividend, the shareholder will receive nothing from the impending dividend – it will be paid to the seller of the shares instead.

12. Answer: A   Reference: Chapter 3

    The bid will be described as hostile if the directors of the target company recommend that shareholders reject the bid.

13. Answer: D   Reference: Chapter 4

    The NYSE still has a trading floor on Wall Street.

14. Answer: A   Reference: Chapter 4

    Like most stock market indices, the FTSE 100 stocks are selected by market capitalisation.

15. Answer: A   Reference: Chapter 4

    There are just 30 stocks in the Xetra DAX index of the German market.

16. Answer: A   Reference: Chapter 4

    The best buy order is the order with the highest price, and the best sell order is the order with the lowest price. If orders have the same price, the earlier order takes priority.

17. Answer: B   Reference: Chapter 4

    Within CREST, company registers are made up of the uncertificated operator register and the certificated issuer register.

18. Answer: D   Reference: Chapter 5

    The price of a bond is not necessarily equal to the face value.

19. Answer: D   Reference: Chapter 5

    Index-linked bonds are typically linked to an inflation index. Both the coupons and the principal are uplifted to reflect inflation.

20. Answer: C   Reference: Chapter 5

    The standard impact on bonds when interest rates increase is that the bonds will fall in value.

21. Answer: B   Reference: Chapter 5

    $(4 \div 95) \times 100 = 4.21\%$.

22. Answer: A   Reference: Chapter 5

    Moody's ratings uses the lower case 'a' – and Baa3 is the lowest Moody's investment grade rating.

23.   Answer: A   Reference: Chapter 6

     Junk bonds are not money market instruments.

24.   Answer: B   Reference: Chapter 6

     The mortgage is capped and, since the repayment only happens at the end, it is described as interest-only.

25.   Answer: A   Reference: Chapter 7

     The balance of payments provides a summary of transactions with the rest of the world – a surplus means exports exceed imports, whilst a deficit means imports exceed exports.

26.   Answer: A   Reference: Chapter 7

     The Monetary Policy Committee has interest rate setting responsibility to keep inflation within the government's target range.

27.   Answer: C   Reference: Chapter 8

     Forwards and swaps are traded OTC. Options give the buyer a choice, not an obligation.

28.   Answer: D   Reference: Chapter 9

     Investment trusts prices are based on supply and demand and do not necessarily equal net asset value.

29.   Answer: D   Reference: Chapter 9

     An OEIC is an open ended company and tracking a stock market index is passive investment management.

30.   Answer: A   Reference: Chapter 10

     Origination is a term used when banks win business – it has nothing to do with the stages of a successful money laundering operation that consists of placement, layering and integration.

ⓘ Glossary

Acquisition

A term used to describe the takeover or buying of a company by another.

Active Management

A type of investment approach employed to generate returns in excess of the market.

Additional Rate (of Income Tax)

Tax on top band of income, currently 50%.

Alternative Investment Market (AIM)

Established by the London Stock Exchange. It is the junior market for smaller company shares.

Annual Equivalent Rate (AER)

The annualised compound rate of interest applied to a cash deposit or to a loan. Also known as the Annual Effective Rate.

Annual General Meeting (AGM)

Yearly meeting of shareholders. Mainly used to vote on dividends, appoint directors and approve financial statements.

Approved Persons

Employees in controlled functions, who must be approved by the FSA.

Articles of Association

The legal document which sets out the internal constitution of a company. Included within the Articles will be details of shareholder voting rights and company borrowing powers.

Asset

Any item of economic or financial value owned by someone or a company.

Auction

Sales system used by the Debt Management Office (DMO) when it issues gilts. Successful applicants pay the price they bid.

Authorisation

Required status under FSMA 2000 for firms that want to provide financial services.

Authorised Corporate Director (ACD)

Fund manager for an OEIC.

Authorised Unit Trust (AUT)

Unit trust which is freely marketable. Authorised by the FSA.

Balance Sheet

A summary of a company's assets (what it owns), liabilities (what it owes), and owner's equity at the end of a financial year.

Balance of Payments

A summary of all the transactions between a country and the rest of the world. The difference between a country's imports and exports.

Bank of England

The UK's central bank. Implements economic policy decided by the Treasury and determines interest rates.

Basic Rate (of Income Tax)

Rate of tax charged on income that is below the higher-rate tax threshold.

Bear

An investor who believes a stock or the overall market will decline so he/she sells hoping to buy them back at a lower price at a later date.

Bearer Securities

Those whose ownership is evidenced by the mere possession of a certificate. Ownership can therefore pass from hand to hand without any formalities.

Beneficiaries

The beneficial owners of trust property, or those who inherit under a will.

Bid Price

Price at which dealers buy stock. It is also the price quoted by unit trusts that are dual-priced for sales of units.

Bonds

Interest bearing securities which entitle holders to annual interest and repayment at maturity. Commonly issued by both companies and governments.

Bonus Issue

A free issue of shares to existing shareholders. No money is paid. The share price falls pro rata. Also known as a Capitalisation or Scrip Issue.

Broker

An individual who handles orders to buy and sell from its investors or clients. Brokers often charge a commission for the work they perform. A broker who specialises in stocks, bonds or options acts as an agent and must be registered with the exchange where the securities are traded.

Bull

The opposite of a bear. An investor who believes the market or a security will rise and makes investment decisions accordingly (buys shares in the hope of selling them at a higher price later).

CAC 40

Index of the prices of major French company shares.

Call Option

Option giving its buyer the right to buy an asset at an agreed price.

Capital

Cash and assets used to generate income or make an investment.

Capital Appreciation

An increase in the market value of a security (ie, the value of the asset is greater than the price they were bought for).

Capital Gains Tax (CGT)

Tax payable by individuals on profit made on the disposal of certain assets.

Capitalisation Issue

See Bonus Issue.

Central Bank

Central banks typically have responsibility for setting a nation's or a region's short-term interest rate, controlling the money supply, acting as banker and lender of last resort to the banking system and managing the national debt.

Certificated

Ownership designated by certificate.

Certificates of Deposit (CDs)

Certificates issued by a bank as evidence that interest-bearing funds have been deposited with it. CDs are traded within the money market.

City Code (on Takeovers and Mergers)

Rulebook developed by the Panel on Takeovers and Mergers to regulate conduct during a takeover.

Clean Price

The quoted price of a gilt. The price quoted for a gilt excludes any interest that has accrued from the last interest payment date and is known as the 'clean' price. Accrued interest is added on afterwards and the price is then known as the 'dirty' price.

Closed-Ended

Organisations such as companies which are a fixed size as determined by their share capital. Commonly used to distinguish investment trusts (closed-ended) from unit trusts and OEICs (open-ended).

Closing

Reversing an original position by, for example, selling what you have previously bought.

Commercial Paper (CP)

Money market instrument issued by large corporates.

Commission

Charges for acting as agent or broker.

Committee of European Securities Regulators (CESR)

Represented regulatory bodies from across the EU. Now replaced by the European Securities and Markets Authority (ESMA).

Commodity

Items including sugar, wheat, oil and copper. Derivatives of commodities are traded on exchanges (eg, oil futures on ICE Futures).

Competition Commission (CC)

Government agency that decides whether or not a proposed takeover should be allowed on competition grounds.

Consortium

A group of people, companies or banking institutions participating in a joint venture for mutual benefit. A consortium allows the companies to conduct operations that they would not be able to do individually. However, a consortium is not a merger as the companies remain independent.

Contract

A standard unit of trading in derivatives.

Controlled Functions

Job roles which require the employee to be approved by the FSA. There are five groups of controlled functions, four of which are significant influence functions.

Convertible Bond

Bond convertible, at investor's choice, into the same company's shares.

Correction

A quick reverse movement in the price of a stock, share, bond, commodity or index. Market corrections often happens when prices are too low or too high, and they are usually short-term and necessary for the stability of the security.

Coupon

Amount of interest paid on a bond.

Credit Creation

Expansion of loans which increases the money supply.

CREST

Electronic settlement system used to hold stock and settle transactions for UK shares.

Currency

Any form of money that circulates in an economy as an accepted means of exchange for goods and services.

Data Protection Act 1998

Legislation regulating the use of client data.

Dealer

An individual or firm acting in order to buy or sell a security for its own account and risk.

Debt Management Office (DMO)

The agency responsible for issuing gilts on behalf of the Treasury.

Dematerialised (Form)

System where securities are held electronically without certificates.

Deposit

A deposit is a sum of money held at a financial institution on behalf of an account holder for safekeeping.

Derivatives

Options and futures. Their price is derived from an underlying asset.

Dilution Levy

An additional charge levied on investors buying or selling units in a single-priced fund to offset any potential effect that large purchases or sales can have on the value of the fund.

Dirty Price

The price quoted for a gilt excludes any interest that has accrued from the last interest payment date and is known as the 'clean' price. Accrued interest is added on afterwards and the price is then known as the 'dirty' price.

Diversification

Investment strategy of spreading risk by investing in a range of investments.

Dividend

Distribution of profits by a company.

Dividend Yield

Most recent dividend expressed as a percentage of current share price.

Dow Jones Index

Major share index in the USA, based on the prices of 30 major company shares.

Dual Pricing

Involves using the market's bid and offer prices of the underlying assets to produce separate prices for buying and selling of shares/units in the fund.

Economic and Monetary Union (EMU)

System adopted by most members of the European Union where their individual currencies were abolished and replaced by the euro.

Economic Cycle

The course an economy conventionally takes as economic growth fluctuates over time. Also known as the Business Cycle.

Economic Growth

The growth of GDP or GNP expressed in real terms, usually over the course of a calendar year. Often used as a barometer of an economy's health.

Effective Control

Under the City Code on Takeovers and Mergers, effective control arises at 30%.

Effective Rate

The annualised compound rate of interest applied to a cash deposit or loan. Also known as the Annual Equivalent Rate (AER).

Equity

Another name for shares. It can also be used to refer to the amount by which the value of a house exceeds any mortgage or borrowings secured on it.

Eurobond

An interest-bearing security issued internationally.

European Securities and Markets Authority (ESMA)

Replaced the CESR and responsible for drafting, implementing and monitoring EU Financial Regulation.

Exchange

Marketplace for trading investments.

Exchange Rate

Rate at which one currency can be exchanged for another.

Exchange-Traded Fund (ETF)

Type of collective investment scheme that is open-ended but traded on an investment exchange, rather than directly with the fund's managers.

Ex-Dividend (xd)

The period during which the purchase of shares or bonds (on which a dividend or coupon payment has been declared) does not entitle the new holder to this next dividend or interest payment.

Exercise an Option

Take up the right to buy or sell the underlying asset in an option.

Exercise Price

The price at which the right conferred by an option can be exercised by the holder against the writer.

Extraordinary General Meeting (EGM)

A company meeting, other than an AGM, at which matters that urgently require a special resolution are put to the company's shareholders.

Financial Services Authority (FSA)

The UK regulator of the financial services sector created by FSMA 2000.

Financial Services and Markets Act 2000 (FSMA 2000)

Legislation which provides the framework for regulating financial services.

Financial Services and Markets Tribunal

Judicial body to which firms and individuals can appeal concerning FSA regulatory decisions.

Fiscal Policy

The use of government spending, taxation and borrowing policies to either boost or restrain domestic demand in the economy so as to maintain full employment and price stability.

Fiscal Years

Fiscal years run from 6 April to 5 April. They are the periods of assessment for income tax and capital gains tax.

Fit and Proper

FSMA 2000 requires that every firm conducting financial services business must be 'fit and proper'.

Fixed-Interest Security

A tradeable negotiable instrument, issued by a borrower for a fixed term, during which a regular and predetermined fixed rate of interest, based upon a nominal value, is paid to the holder until it is redeemed and the principal is repaid.

Fixed-Rate Borrowing

Borrowing where a set interest rate is paid.

Floating Rate Notes (FRNs)

Debt securities issued with a coupon periodically referenced to a benchmark interest rate, such as LIBOR.

Forex

Abbreviation for foreign exchange trading.

Foreign Equity

Stocks and shares of foreign companies being traded in London.

Foreign Exchange Market (Forex)

A market for the trading of foreign currencies.

Forward

A derivatives contract that creates a legally binding obligation between two parties for one to buy and the other to sell a prespecified amount of an asset at a prespecified price on a prespecified future date. As individually negotiated contracts, forwards are not traded on a derivatives exchange.

Forward Exchange Rate

An exchange rate set today, embodied in a forward contract, that will apply to a foreign exchange transaction at some prespecified point in the future.

FTSE 100

Main UK share index of 100 leading shares ('Footsie').

FTSE 250

UK share index based on the 250 shares immediately below the top 100.

FTSE 350

Index combining the FTSE 100 and FTSE 250 indices.

FTSE All Share Index

Index comprising around 98% of UK-listed shares by value.

Full Listing

Those public limited companies (plcs) admitted to the London Stock Exchange's (LSE) official list. Companies seeking a full listing on the LSE must satisfy the UK Listing Authority's (UKLA) stringent listing requirements and continuing obligations once listed.

Fund

A collective investment scheme where money is combined and invested in a portfolio of shares with a common investment purpose.

Fund Manager

Firm that invests money on behalf of customers.

Fund Supermarket

An internet-based service that provides a convenient way of investing in collective investment funds by allowing a variety of funds to be purchased from a number of different management groups in one place.

Future

An agreement to buy or sell an item at a future date, at a price agreed today. Differs from a forward in that it is a standardised amount and therefore the contract can be traded on an exchange.

Futures and Options Fund (FOF)

Type of authorised unit trust which invests partially in derivatives.

Gilt-Edged Market Maker (GEMM)

A firm that is a market maker in gilts.

Gilt-Edged Security (Gilt)

UK government bond.

Gross

Total amount before deductions (ie, taxes).

Gross Domestic Product (GDP)

A measure of a country's output.

Gross Redemption Yield (GRY)

The annual compound return from holding a bond to maturity, taking into account both interest payments and any capital gain or loss at maturity.

Harmonised Index of Consumer Prices (HICP)

Standard measurement of inflation throughout the European Union.

Hedge Fund

A high-risk investment vehicle which uses advanced and aggressive investment financial techniques in order to make maximum gains.

Hedging

A technique employed to reduce the impact of adverse price movements in financial assets held.

Higher Rate (of Income Tax)

Tax on the band of income above the basic rate and below the additional rate, currently 40%.

HM Treasury

Her Majesty's Treasury. The UK government department responsible for the country's taxes, finance and economy.

Holder

Investor who buys put or call options.

Independent Financial Adviser (IFA)

A financial adviser who is not tied to the products of any one product provider and is duty-bound to give clients best advice and offer them the option of paying for advice. IFAs must establish the financial planning needs of their clients through a personal fact-find, and satisfy these needs with the most appropriate products offered in the marketplace.

Index

A statistical measure of the changes in a selection of stocks representing a portion of the overall market.

Individual Savings Account (ISA)

Savings scheme introduced in 1999 which provides a wrapper in which cash, stocks and shares can be held and benefit from tax concessions.

Inflation

An increase in the general level of prices.

Inheritance Tax (IHT)

Tax on the value of an estate when a person dies.

Initial Public Offering (IPO)

A new issue of ordinary shares, whether made by an offer for sale, an offer for subscription or a placing. Also known as a new issue.

Insider Dealing

Criminal offence by people with unpublished price-sensitive information who deal, advise others to deal or pass the information on.

Integration

Third stage of money laundering.

IntercontinentalExchange (ICE)

ICE operates regulated global futures exchanges and over-the-counter (OTC) markets for agricultural, energy, equity index and currency contracts, as well as credit derivatives. ICE conducts its energy futures markets through ICE Futures Europe, which is based in London.

Interest

The price paid for borrowing money. Generally, interest is expressed as a percentage rate over a period of time, such as 5% per annum.

In-the-Money

Call option where the exercise price is below current market price (or put option where exercise price is above).

Investment Bank

Business that specialises in raising debt and equity for companies.

Investment Company with Variable Capital (ICVC)

Alternative term for an OEIC.

Investment Trust (Company)

A company, not a trust, which invests in a diversified range of investments.

Irredeemable Gilt

A gilt with no redemption date. Investors receive interest in perpetuity.

Layering

Second stage in money laundering.

Liability

An obligation that legally binds an individual or company to settle a debt or a payment.

LIFFE CONNECT

Order-driven trading system on NYSE Liffe.

Limited Company

A privately owned company with limited liability amongst its owners.

Limited Liability

When the liability of the shareholders is limited to the nominal value of their shares. It is therefore a limitation of loss to what has already been invested.

Liquidity

Ease with which an item can be traded on the market. Liquid markets are described as deep.

Liquidity Risk

The risk that shares may be difficult to sell at a reasonable price.

Listing

Companies whose securities are listed on the London Stock Exchange and available to be traded.

Lloyd's of London

World's largest insurance market.

Loan Stock

A corporate bond issued in the domestic bond market without any underlying collateral, or security.

London InterBank Offered Rate (LIBOR)

A benchmark money market interest rate.

London Metal Exchange (LME)

Market for trading in derivatives of certain metals, such as copper, zinc and aluminium.

London Stock Exchange (LSE)

Main UK market for securities.

Long Position

The position following the purchase of a security or buying a derivative.

Market

All exchanges are markets – electronic or physical meeting place where assets are bought or sold.

Market Capitalisation

Total market value of a company's shares. The share price multiplied by the number of shares in issue.

Market Maker

An LSE member firm which is obliged to offer to buy and sell securities in which it is registered throughout the mandatory quote period. In return for providing this liquidity to the market, it can make its profits through the differences at which it buys and sells.

Market Price

Price of a share as quoted on the exchange.

Maturity

Date when the capital on a bond is repaid.

Memorandum of Association

The legal document that principally defines a company's powers, or objects, and its relationship with the outside world. The Memorandum also details the number and nominal value of shares the company is authorised to issue and has issued.

Merger

The combining of two or more companies into one new entity.

Mixed Economy

Economy which works through a combination of market forces and government involvement.

Monetary Policy

The setting of short-term interest rates by a central bank in order to manage domestic demand and achieve price stability in the economy.

Monetary Policy Committee (MPC)

Committee run by the Bank of England which sets interest rates.

Mortgages

A mortgage, or more precisely a mortgage loan, is a long-term loan used to finance the purchase of real estate (eg, a house). Under the Mortgage Agreement, the borrower agrees to make a series of payments back to the lender. The money lent by the bank (or building society) is secured against the value of the property: if the payments are not made by the borrower, the lender can take back the property.

Mutual Fund

A type of collective investment scheme found in the US.

Names

Participants at Lloyd's of London who form syndicates to write insurance business. Both individuals and companies can be names.

NASDAQ

National Association of Securities Dealers Automated Quotations. US market specialising in the shares of technology companies.

NASDAQ Composite

NASDAQ stock index.

National Debt

A government's total outstanding borrowing resulting from financing successive budget deficits, mainly through the issue of government-backed securities.

National Savings and Investments (NS&I)

Government agency that provides investment products for the retail market.

Nikkei 225

Main Japanese share index.

Nominal Value

The amount of a bond that will be repaid on maturity. Also known as face or par value.

Nominated Adviser (NOMAD)

Firm which advises AIM companies on their regulatory responsibilities.

NYSE Euronext (NYX)

European stock exchange network formed by the merger of the Paris, Brussels, Amsterdam and (later) Lisbon exchanges; has since merged with the New York Stock Exchange.

NYSE Liffe

The UK's principal derivatives exchange for trading financial and soft commodity derivatives products. Owned by Euronext.

Offer Price

Price at which dealers sell stock. It is also the price quoted by unit trusts that are dual-priced for purchases of units.

Office of Fair Trading (OFT)

Government agency that refers proposed takeovers to the Competition Commission.

Open

Initiate a transaction, eg, an opening purchase or sale of a future. Normally reversed by a closing transaction.

Open Economy

Country with no restrictions on trading with other countries.

Open-Ended

Type of investment such as OEICs or unit trusts which can expand without limit.

Open-Ended Investment Company (OEIC)

Collective investment vehicle similar to a unit trust. Alternatively described as an ICVC (Investment Company with Variable Capital).

Open Outcry

Trading system used by some derivatives exchanges. Participants stand on the floor of the exchange and call out transactions they would like to undertake.

Opening

Undertaking a transaction which creates a long or short position.

Option

A derivative giving the buyer the right, but not the obligation, to buy or sell an asset.

Ordinary Shares

Most common form of share. Holders may receive dividends if the company is profitable.

Out-of-the-Money

Call option where the exercise or strike price is above the market price or a put option where it is below.

Over-the-Counter (OTC) Derivatives

Derivatives that are not traded on a derivatives exchange, owing to their non-standardised contract specifications.

Panel on Takeovers and Mergers (POTAM or PTM)

A self-regulatory body that produces the City Code regulating takeovers.

Passive Management

An investment approach that aims to track the performance of a stock market index. Employed in those securities markets that are believed to be price-efficient.

Pension Fund

A fund set up by a company or government to invest the pension contributions of members and employees to be paid out at retirement age.

Personal Allowance

Amount of income that each person can earn each year tax-free.

Personal Equity Plan (PEP)

Investment scheme in which investors bought shares through a PEP manager. Income and gains are tax-free. New PEPs have not been allowed since April 1999 and existing ones became ISAs from 6 April 2008.

Placement

First stage of money laundering.

Platform

Platforms are online services such as fund supermarkets and wraps that are used by intermediaries to view and administer their investment clients' portfolios.

PLUS Markets

PLUS is a stock market based in London and is a competitor to the London Stock Exchange. It has two markets, PLUS traded where securities from across Europe can be traded, and PLUS quoted, which is a market for small cap shares and is a competitor to AIM.

Portfolio

A selection of investments.

Pre-Emption Rights

The rights accorded to ordinary shareholders under company law to subscribe for new ordinary shares issued by the company in which they have the shareholding, for cash, before the shares are offered to outside investors.

Preference Share

Shares which pay fixed dividends. Do not have voting rights, but do have priority over ordinary shares in default situations.

Premium

The amount of cash paid by the holder of an option to the writer in exchange for conferring a right.

Premium Bond

National Savings & Investments bonds that pay prizes each month. Winnings are tax-free.

Primary Market

The function of a stock exchange in bringing new securities to the market and raising funds.

Protectionism

The economic policy of restraining trade between countries by imposing methods such as tariffs and quotas on imported goods

Proxy

Appointee who votes on a shareholder's behalf at company meetings.

Public Limited Company (PLC)

A company whose shares can be owned by the general public and are usually bought and sold, through a regulated stock exchange (eg, London Stock Exchange).

Prudential Regulation Authority (PRA)

The new body that will be responsible for prudential regulation of all deposit-taking institutions, insurers and investment banks.

Public Sector Net Cash Requirement (PSNCR)

Shortfall of government revenue compared to government expenditure.

Put Option

Option where buyer has the right to sell an asset.

Quote-Driven

Dealing system driven by securities firms who quote buying and selling prices.

Real Estate Investment Trust (REIT)

An investment trust that specialises in investing in commercial property.

Redeemable Security

A security issued with a known maturity, or redemption, date.

Redemption

The repayment of principal to the holder of a redeemable security.

Redemption Yield

See Gross Redemption Yield.

Registrar

An official of a company who maintains the share register.

Repo

The sale and repurchase of bonds between two parties: the repurchase being made at a price and date fixed in advance.

Resolution

Proposal on which shareholders vote.

Retail Bank

Organisation that provides banking facilities to individuals and small/medium businesses.

Retail Prices Index (RPI)

Index that measures the movement of prices.

Rights Issue

The issue of new ordinary shares to a company's shareholders in proportion to each shareholder's existing shareholding, usually at a price deeply discounted to that prevailing in the market.

RPIX

Index that shows the underlying rate of inflation, excluding the impact of mortgage payments.

Scrip Issue

See Bonus Issue.

Secondary Market

Market place for trading in existing securities.

Securities

Bonds and equities.

Settlor

The creator of a trust.

Shareholders

Those who own the shares of the company. Essentially, they are the owners of the company.

Share Capital

The nominal value of a company's equity or ordinary shares. A company's authorised share capital is the nominal value of equity the company may issue while issued share capital is that which the company has issued. The term share capital is often extended to include a company's preference shares.

Short Position

The position following the sale of a security not owned, or selling a derivative.

SICAV

Type of European collective investment scheme that is open-ended.

Single Pricing

Refers to the use of the mid-market prices of the underlying assets to produce a single price.

Special Resolution

Proposal put to shareholders requiring 75% of the votes cast.

Spread

Difference between a buying (bid) and selling (ask or offer) price.

Stamp Duty

Tax at ½% on the purchase of certain assets including certificated securities.

Stamp Duty Land Tax (SDLT)

Tax charged on the purchase of properties and land above a certain value.

Stamp Duty Reserve Tax (SDRT)

Stamp duty levied at ½% on purchase of dematerialised equities.

State-Controlled Economy

Country where all economic activity is controlled by the state.

Stock Exchange Automated Quotations (SEAQ)

LSE screen display system where market makers display the prices at which they are willing to deal. Used mainly for fixed-income stocks and small cap shares.

Stock Exchange Electronic Trading Service (SETS)

LSE's electronic order-driven trading system.

Stock Exchange Electronic Trading Service – quotes and crosses (SETSqx)

A trading platform for securities less liquid than those traded on SETS. It combines a periodic electronic auction book with stand-alone quote-driven market making.

STRIPS

The principal and interest payments of those designated gilts that can be separately traded as zero coupon bonds (ZCBs). STRIPS is the acronym for Separate Trading of Registered Interest and Principal of Securities.

Swap

An over-the-counter (OTC) derivative whereby two parties exchange a series of periodic payments based on a notional principal amount over an agreed term. Swaps can take the form of interest rate swaps, currency swaps and equity swaps.

Swinging Price

Where a single-priced investment fund moves its pricing as a result of a large number of buy or sell orders.

Syndicate

Lloyd's names joining together to write insurance.

T+3

The three-day rolling settlement period over which all deals executed on the London Stock Exchange's (LSE) SETS are settled.

Takeover

When one company buys more than 50% of the shares of another.

Third Party Administrator (TPA)

A firm that specialises in undertaking investment administration for other firms.

Tracker Fund

A fund that tries to mirror the performance of a chosen share index.

Treasury

Government department ultimately responsible for the regulation of the financial services industry.

Treasury Bills

Short-term (usually 90-day) borrowings of the UK government. Issued at a discount to the nominal value at which they will mature. Traded in the money market.

Trustees

The legal owners of trust property who owe a duty of skill and care to the trust's beneficiaries.

Two-Way Price

Prices quoted by a market maker at which they are willing to buy (bid) and sell (offer).

Underlying

Asset from which a derivative is derived.

Unit Trust

A system whereby money from investors is pooled together and invested collectively on their behalf into an open-ended trust.

Wraps

A type of fund platform that enables advisers to take a holistic view of the various assets that a client has in a variety of accounts.

Writer

Party selling an option. The writers receive premiums in exchange for taking the risk of being exercised against.

Xetra Dax

German shares index, comprising 30 shares.

Yellow Strip

Section on each SEAQ display showing the most favourable prices.

Yield

Income from an investment as a percentage of the current price.

Zero Coupon Bonds (ZCBs)

Bonds issued at a discount to their nominal value that do not pay a coupon but which are redeemed at par on a prespecified future date.

ℹ️ Abbreviations

ABSs	Asset-Backed Securities		**ETF**	Exchange-Traded Fund
ACD	Authorised Corporate Director		**EU**	European Union
AGM	Annual General Meeting		**FATF**	Financial Action Task Force
AIC	Association of Investment Companies		**FCA**	Financial Conduct Authority
AIM	Alternative Investment Market		**FOF**	Futures and Options Fund
APR	Annual Percentage Rate		**FED**	Federal Reserve
AUT	Authorised Unit Trust		**FOS**	Financial Ombudsman Service
CBOE	Chicago Board Options Exchange		**FPC**	Financial Policy Committee
CD	Certificate of Deposit		**FSA**	Financial Services Authority
CDD	Customer Due Diligence		**FSAP**	Financial Securities Action Plan
CESR	Committee of European Securities Regulators		**FSCS**	Financial Services Compensation Scheme
CGT	Capital Gains Tax		**FRN**	Floating Rate Note
CMA	Cash Memorandum Account		**FSMA**	Financial Services and Markets Act (2000)
CP	Commercial Paper		**GDP**	Gross Domestic Product
CPI	Consumer Prices Index		**HICP**	Harmonised Index of Consumer Prices
CTF	Child Trust Fund		**HMRC**	Her Majesty's Revenue & Customs
DMO	Debt Management Office		**ICVC**	Investment Companies with Variable Capital
DJIA	Dow Jones Industrial Average		**IHT**	Inheritance Tax
ECB	European Central Bank		**ICE**	IntercontinentalExchange
ECX	European Climate Exchange		**ICMA**	International Capital Markets Association
EGM	Extraordinary General Meeting		**IFA**	Independent Financial Adviser
ESMA	European Securities and Markets Authority		**IMA**	Investment Management Association
ETD	Exchange-Traded Derivative			

IOU	I Owe You	**S2P**	State Second Pension
IPO	Initial Public Offer	**SDD**	Simplified Due Diligence
ISA	Individual Savings Account	**SSAS**	Small Self-Administered Scheme
JISA	Junior Individual Savings Account	**SDLT**	Stamp Duty Land Tax
JMLSG	Joint Money Laundering Steering Group	**SDRT**	Stamp Duty Reserve Tax
LIBOR	London InterBank Offered Rate	**SEAQ**	Stock Exchange Automated Quotation system
LME	London Metal Exchange	**SETS**	Stock Exchange Electronic Trading Service
LSE	London Stock Exchange		
MiFID	Markets in Financial Instruments Directive	**SETSqx**	Stock Exchange Electronic Trading Service – Quotes and Crosses
MLRO	Money Laundering Reporting Officer	**SICAV**	Société D'Investissement à Capital Variable
MPC	Monetary Policy Committee	**SIPP**	Self-Invested Personal Pension
MTS	An electronic exchange for trading European government bonds	**SOCA**	Serious Organised Crime Agency
		STRIPS	Separate Trading of Registered Interest and Principal of Securities
NAV	Net Asset Value		
NYSE	New York Stock Exchange	**SWIFT**	Society of Worldwide Interbank Financial Telecommunication
NYX	NYSE Euronext		
OEIC	Open-Ended Investment Company	**TSE**	Tokyo Stock Exchange
OTC	Over-the-Counter	**UCITS**	Undertakings for Collective Investment in Transferable Securities
PIBS	Permanent Interest-Bearing Shares		
PLC	Public Limited Company	**UKLA**	United Kingdom Listing Authority
POCA	Proceeds of Crime Act 2002	**VAT**	Value Added Tax
PRA	Prudential Regulation Authority	**VCT**	Venture Capital Trust
PSNCR	Public Sector Net Cash Requirement	**xd**	Ex-Dividend
REIT	Real Estate Investment Trust	**ZCB**	Zero Coupon Bond
RPI	Retail Price Index	**ZDP**	Zero Dividend Preference Shares
RPIX	Retail Prices Index (excluding mortgages)		

Syllabus Learning Map

Securities & Investment (Schools and Colleges)

⭐ Syllabus Learning Map

Syllabus Unit/ Element		eLearning Lesson	Chapter/ Section
ELEMENT 1	**INTRODUCTION**		
1.1	**The Financial Services Industry** On completion, the candidate should:		
1.1.1	know the role of the following within the financial services industry:	Lesson 02	Chapter 2 Sections 2 and 5
	• retail banks • building societies	Lesson 10	
	• investment banks	Lesson 15	
	• pension funds • insurance companies	Lesson 14	
	• fund managers • stockbrokers • custodians	Lesson 23	
	• third party administrators (TPAs)	Lesson 44	
	• industry trade and professional bodies	Lesson 45	
1.1.2	know the function of and differences between retail and professional business and who the main customers are in each case: • retail clients and professional clients	Lesson 02	Chapter 2 Section 5.10
1.1.3	know the role of the following investment distribution channels: • independent financial adviser • tied adviser • platforms • execution only	Lesson 44	Chapter 2 Section 6
ELEMENT 2	**ECONOMIC ENVIRONMENT**		
2.1	**Economic Environment** On completion, the candidate should:	Lesson 07	
2.1.1	know the factors which determine the level of economic activity: • state-controlled economies • market economies • mixed economies • open economies	Lesson 11	Chapter 7 Section 2

Syllabus Unit/ Element		eLearning Lesson	Chapter/ Section
2.1.2	know the functions of central banks: • the Bank of England • the Federal Reserve • the European Central Bank	Lesson 09	Chapter 7 Section 3
2.1.3	know the functions of the Monetary Policy Committee		
2.1.4	know how goods and services are paid for and how credit is created	Lesson 09	Chapter 7 Section 4.1
2.1.5	understand the impact of inflation on economic behaviour		Chapter 7 Section 4.2
2.1.6	know the meaning of the following measures of inflation: • Retail Prices Index • Consumer Prices Index	Lesson 08	Chapter 7 Section 5.1
2.1.7	understand the impact of the following economic data: • gross domestic product (GDP) • balance of payments • Public Sector Net Cash Requirement (PSNCR) • level of unemployment • exchange rates • surplus/deficit	Lesson 12	Chapter 7 Section 5.2

ELEMENT 3	FINANCIAL ASSETS AND MARKETS		
3.1	**Cash deposits** On completion, the candidate should:	Lesson 03	
3.1.1	know the characteristics of fixed term and instant access deposit accounts	Lesson 03 and 16	
3.1.2	understand the distinction between gross and net interest payments	Lesson 40	Chapter 2 Section 3
3.1.3	be able to calculate the net interest due given the gross interest rate, the deposited sum, the period and tax rate	Lesson 03 and 40	
3.1.4	know the advantages and disadvantages of investing in cash	Lesson 03	
3.2	**Money Market Instruments** On completion, the candidate should:		
3.2.1	know the difference between a capital market instrument and a money market instrument	Lesson 17	
3.2.2	know the definition and features of the following:		Chapter 6 Section 2
	• Treasury bill	Lesson 13 and 17	
	• Commercial paper	Lesson 17 and 31	
	• Certificate of deposit	Lesson 16 and 17	
	• money market funds	Lesson 17	
3.2.3	know the advantages and disadvantages of investing in money market instruments	Lesson 17	

Syllabus Unit/ Element		eLearning Lesson	Chapter/ Section
3.3	**Property** On completion, the candidate should:		
3.3.1	know the characteristics of property investment: • commercial/residential property • direct/indirect investment	Lesson 39	Chapter 6 Section 4
3.3.2	know the advantages and disadvantages of investing in property		
3.4	**Foreign Exchange Market** On completion, the candidate should:		
3.4.1	know the basic structure of the foreign exchange market including: • currency quotes • settlement	Lesson 38	Chapter 6 Section 3

ELEMENT 4	EQUITIES		
4.1	**Equities** On completion, the candidate should:	Lesson 06	
4.1.1	know how a company is formed and the differences between private and public companies	Lesson 06 and 18	Chapter 3 Sections 2.1 and 2.2
4.1.2	know the features and benefits of ordinary and preference shares:	Lesson 06	
	• dividend • capital gain • share benefits	Lesson 19	Chapter 3 Sections 4 and 5
	• right to subscribe for new shares	Lesson 22	Chapter 3 Section 5.4
	• right to vote	Lesson 20	
4.1.3	understand the advantages, disadvantages and risks associated with owning shares: • price risk • liquidity risk • issuer risk	Lesson 06 and 21	Chapter 3 Section 6
4.1.4	know the definition of a corporate action and the difference between mandatory, voluntary and mandatory with options	Lesson 22	Chapter 3 Section 7
4.1.5	understand the following terms:	Lesson 19	
	• bonus/scrip/capitalisation issues	Lesson 22	Chapter 3 Section 7
	• rights issues	Lesson 19	
	• dividend payments • takeover/merger	Lesson 22	
4.1.6	know the purpose and format of Annual General Meetings/Extraordinary General Meetings	Lesson 20	Chapter 3 Section 2.3
4.1.7	know the difference between the primary market and secondary market	Lesson 24	Chapter 3 Section 3.1

Syllabus Unit/ Element		eLearning Lesson	Chapter/ Section
4.1.8	know the characteristics of the following exchanges: • London Stock Exchange • New York Stock Exchange • NASDAQ • Euronext • Tokyo Stock Exchange • Deutsche Börse	Lesson 26	Chapter 4 Section 2
4.1.9	know the types and uses of a stock exchange index	Lesson 29	Chapter 4 Section 3
4.1.10	know the advantages and disadvantages of a company obtaining a listing of its shares	Lesson 24	Chapter 3 Section 3.2
4.1.11	know how shares are traded on the London Stock Exchange: • electronic trading platforms • quote-driven • order-driven • SETS/SEAQ/SETSqx	Lesson 27	Chapter 4 Section 4
4.1.12	know to which markets the following indices relate: • FTSE • Dow Jones Industrial Average • S&P 500 • Nikkei 225 • CAC40 • XETRA Dax • NASDAQ Composite	Lesson 29	Chapter 4 Sections 3.1 and 3.2
4.1.13	know the method of holding title – registered/ bearer /immobilised/dematerialised		Chapter 4 Sections 6.1 and 6.2
4.1.14	understand the role of the central counterparty in clearing and settlement	Lesson 28	Chapter 4 Section 5
4.1.15	understand the role played by Euroclear UK & Ireland in the clearing and settlement of equity trades: • uncertificated transfers • participants (members, payment banks, registrars)		Chapter 4 Section 6.3

ELEMENT 5	BONDS		
5.1	**Government Bonds** On completion, the candidate should:	Lesson 13	
5.1.1	know the definition and features of government bonds:		Chapter 5 Section 3
	• DMO maturity classifications	Lesson 13	
	• how they are issued	Lesson 15	

Syllabus Unit/ Element		eLearning Lesson	Chapter/ Section
5.2	**Corporate Bonds** On completion, the candidate should:		
5.2.1	know the definitions and features of the following types of bond: • domestic • foreign • Eurobond • asset-backed securities including covered bonds	Lesson 32	Chapter 5 Section 4
	• zero coupon • convertible	Lesson 33	
5.3	**Bonds** On completion, the candidate should:	Lesson 07	
5.3.1	know the advantages and disadvantages of investing in different types of bonds	Lesson 31	Chapter 5 Section 5.1
5.3.2	be able to calculate the flat yield of a bond	Lesson 30	Chapter 5 Section 5.2
5.3.3	understand the role of credit rating agencies and the differences between investment and non-investment grades	Lesson 31	Chapter 5 Section 5.3

ELEMENT 6	DERIVATIVES		
6.1	**Derivatives Uses** On completion, the candidate should:		Chapter 8 Sections 1 and 2.1
6.1.1	understand the uses and application of derivatives	Lesson 34	
6.2	**Futures** On completion, the candidate should:		Chapter 8 Section 2.2
6.2.1	know the definition and function of a future		
6.3	**Options** On completion, the candidate should:		
6.3.1	know the definition and function of an option	Lesson 36	Chapter 8 Section 3.2
6.3.2	understand the following terms: • calls • puts		Chapter 8 Section 3.3

Syllabus Unit/ Element		eLearning Lesson	Chapter/ Section
6.4	**Terminology** On completion a candidate should:		
6.4.1	• understand the following terms:		Chapter 8 Sections 1, 2.3 and 3.3
	• long • short	Lesson 34	Chapter 8 Section 2.3
	• open • close		Chapter 8 Section 3.3
	• holder • writing • premium • covered • naked		Chapter 8 Sections 2.3 and 3.3
	• OTC • Exchange-Traded	Lesson 36	Chapter 8 Sections 1 and 3.3
6.5	**Derivatives/Commodity Markets** On completion, the candidate should:		
6.5.1	know the characteristics of the derivatives and commodity markets: • trading (metals, energy)	Lesson 35	Chapter 8 Section 4
6.5.2	know the advantages and disadvantages of investing in the derivatives and commodity markets		
6.6	**SWAPS** On completion a candidate should:	Lesson 37	Chapter 8 Section 5
6.6.1	know the definition and function of an interest rate swap		

ELEMENT 7	**INVESTMENT FUNDS**		
7.1	**Introduction** On completion, the candidate should:		
7.1.1	understand the benefits of collective investment	Lesson 42	Chapter 9 Section 1.1
7.1.2	understand the range of investment strategies – active v passive	Lesson 42	Chapter 9 Section 1.2
7.1.3	know the differences between authorised and unauthorised funds		Chapter 9 Section 1.4.1
7.1.4	know the purpose and principal features of UCITS	Lesson 43	Chapter 9 Section 1.4.2
7.1.5	know the differences between onshore and offshore funds		Chapter 9 Section 1.5

Syllabus Unit/ Element		eLearning Lesson	Chapter/ Section
7.2	**Unit Trusts** On completion, the candidate should:		
7.2.1	know the definition of a unit trust		Chapter 9 Section 2
7.2.2	know the types of funds and how they are classified	Lesson 49	Chapter 9 Section 1.3
7.2.3	know the roles of the manager and the trustee		Chapter 9 Section 2
7.3	**Open Ended Investment Companies (OEICs)** On completion, the candidate should:		
7.3.1	know the definition and legal structure of an OEIC		
7.3.2	know the roles of the Authorised Corporate Director and the Depositary	Lesson 49	Chapter 9 Section 3
7.3.3	know the terms ICVC, SICAV and the context in which they are used		
7.4	**Pricing, Dealing and Settling** On completion, the candidate should:		
7.4.1	know how unit trusts and OEIC shares are priced		Chapter 9 Section 4.1
7.4.2	know the ways in which charges can be made by the fund manager	Lesson 49	
7.4.3	know how shares and units are bought and sold		Chapter 9 Section 4.2
7.4.4	know how collectives are settled		
7.5	**Investment Trusts** On completion, the candidate should:		
7.5.1	know the characteristics of an investment trust: • share classes • gearing		
7.5.2	understand the factors that affect the price of an investment trust	Lesson 50	Chapter 9 Section 5
7.5.3	know the meaning of the discounts and premiums in relation to investment trusts		
7.5.4	know how investment trust shares are traded		
7.6	**Real Estate Investment Trusts (REITs)** On completion, the candidate should:		
7.6.1	know the basic characteristics of REITs: • tax efficient • property diversification • liquidity • risk	Lesson 50	Chapter 9 Section 6
7.7	**Exchange-Traded Funds (ETFs)** On completion, the candidate should:		
7.7.1	know the main characteristics of exchange-traded funds	Lesson 45	Chapter 9 Section 7
7.7.2	know how exchange-traded funds are traded		

Syllabus Unit/ Element		eLearning Lesson	Chapter/ Section
7.8	**Hedge Funds** On completion, the candidate should:		
7.8.1	know the basic characteristics of hedge funds: • risk and risk types • cost and liquidity • investment strategies	Lesson 60	Chapter 9 Section 9
ELEMENT 8	**FINANCIAL SERVICES REGULATION**		
8.1	**Financial Services Regulation** On completion, the candidate should:		
8.1.1	understand the need for regulation		Chapter 10 Section 1.1
8.1.2	know the function of UK and European regulators in the financial services industry		Chapter 10 Sections 1.2 and 1.3
8.1.3	understand the reasons for authorisation of firms and approved persons	Lesson 53	Chapter 10 Section 1.3.1
8.1.4	know the five groups of activity (controlled functions) requiring approved person status		Chapter 10 Section 1.3.2
8.2	**Financial Crime** On completion, the candidate should:		
8.2.1	know what money laundering is, the stages involved and the related criminal offences	Lesson 55	Chapter 10 Section 2.1
8.2.2	know the purpose and the main provisions of the Proceeds of Crime Act 2002 and the Money Laundering Regulations 2007		Chapter 10 Section 2.2
8.2.3	understand the three main stages of money laundering		Chapter 10 Section 2.1
8.2.3	know the action to be taken by those employed in financial services if money laundering activity is suspected and what constitutes satisfactory evidence of identity	Lesson 56	
8.2.4	know the purpose of the Bribery Act		Chapter 10 Section 2
8.2.5	know how firms can be exploited as a vehicle for financial crime: theft of customer data to facilitate identity fraud		
8.3	**Insider Dealing and Market Abuse** On completion, the candidate should:		
8.3.1	know the offences that constitute insider dealing and the instruments covered	Lesson 57	Chapter 10 Section 3
8.3.2	know the offences that constitute market abuse and the instruments covered		Chapter 10 Section 4

Syllabus Unit/ Element		eLearning Lesson	Chapter/ Section
8.4	**Data Protection Act 1998** On completion, the candidate should:		
8.4.1	understand the impact of the Data Protection Act 1998 on firms' activities	Lesson 58	Chapter 10 Section 5
8.5	**Breaches, Complaints and Compensation** On completion, the candidate should:		
8.5.1	know the difference between a breach and a complaint		Chapter 10 Section 6
8.5.2	know the responsibilities of the industry for handling customer complaints and dealing with breaches		Chapter 10 Section 6
8.5.3	know the role of the Financial Ombudsman Service	Lesson 59	Chapter 10 Section 6.3
8.5.4	know the circumstances under which the Financial Services Compensation Scheme pays compensation and the compensation payable for investment claims		Chapter 10 Section 6.4
ELEMENT 9	**TAXATION, INVESTMENT WRAPPERS AND TRUSTS**		
9.1	**Tax** On completion, the candidate should:	Lesson 40	
9.1.1	know the direct and indirect taxes as they apply to individuals: • income tax • capital gains tax • inheritance tax • stamp duty and stamp duty reserve tax • VAT	Lesson 41	Chapter 11 Section 2
9.1.2	be able to calculate the tax due on investment income	Lesson 40 and 41	Chapter 11 Section 2
9.1.3	know the main exemptions in respect of the main personal taxes	Lesson 46	Chapter 11 Section 2
9.2	**Investment Wrappers** On completion, the candidate should:		
9.2.1	know the definition of and aim of ISAs		Chapter 11 Sections 3.1 and 3.2
9.2.2	know the tax incentives provided by ISAs		Chapter 11 Sections 3.1 and 3.2
9.2.3	know the types of ISA available • cash • stocks & shares • Junior ISA	Lesson 46	Chapter 11 Sections 3.1 and 3.2
9.2.4	know the eligibility conditions for investors	Lesson 46	Chapter 11 Sections 3.1 and 3.2
9.2.5	know the following aspects of investing in ISAs: • subscriptions • transfers • withdrawals • number of managers • number of accounts		Chapter 11 Sections 3.1 and 3.2

Syllabus Unit/ Element		eLearning Lesson	Chapter/ Section
9.2.6	know the tax benefits to a child on the maturity of a child trust fund	Lesson 46	Chapter 11 Section 3.2
9.2.7	know the main characteristics of child trust funds		
9.3	**Pensions** On completion, the candidate should:		
9.3.1	know the tax incentives provided by pensions	Lesson 47	Chapter 11 Section 3.3
9.3.2	know the basic characteristics of the following: • state pension scheme • occupational pension schemes • personal pensions including self-invested personal pensions (SIPPs)/small self-administered schemes (SSAS) • stakeholder pensions • NEST/auto-enrolment		
9.4	**Investment Bonds** On completion, the candidate should:		
9.4.1	know the tax incentives provided by investment bonds – onshore/offshore	Lesson 47	Chapter 11 Section 3.4
9.4.2	know the main characteristics of investment bonds		
9.5	**Trusts** On completion, the candidate should:		
9.5.1	know the features of the main trusts: • discretionary • interest in possession • bare	Lesson 48	Chapter 11 Section 4
9.5.2	know the definition of the following terms: • trustee • settlor • beneficiary		
9.5.3	know the main reasons for creating trusts		

ELEMENT 10	OTHER RETAIL FINANCIAL PRODUCTS		
10.1	**Loans** On completion, the candidate should:		
10.1.1	know the differences between bank loans, overdrafts and credit card borrowing		Chapter 2 Section 4
10.1.2	know the difference between the quoted interest rate on borrowing and the effective annual rate of borrowing	Lesson 04	Chapter 2 Section 4.4
10.1.3	be able to calculate the effective annual rate of borrowing, given the quoted interest rate and frequency of payment		
10.1.4	know the difference between secured and unsecured borrowing	Lesson 05	Chapter 2 Section 4

Syllabus Unit/ Element		eLearning Lesson	Chapter/ Section
10.2	**Mortgages** On completion, the candidate should:		
10.2.1	understand the characteristics of the mortgage market: interest rates	Lesson 52	Chapter 6 Section 5
10.2.2	know the definition of and types of mortgage: • repayment • interest-only		Chapter 6 Section 5.2
10.3	**Life Assurance** On completion, the candidate should:		
10.3.1	understand the basic principles of life assurance		
10.3.2	know the definition of the following types of life policy: • term assurance • whole-of-life	Lesson 51	Chapter 6 Section 6.1
10.4	**Protection Insurance** On completion, the candidate should:		
10.4.1	understand the main areas in need of protection: • family and personal • mortgage • long-term care • business protection	Lesson 51	Chapter 6 Section 6.2
10.4.2	know the main product features of the following: • critical illness insurance • income protection • mortgage payment protection • accident and sickness cover • household cover • medical insurance • long-term care insurance • business insurance protection	Lesson 51	Chapter 6 Section 6.3

EXAMINATION SPECIFICATION

Each examination paper is constructed from a specification that determines the weightings that will be given to each element. The specification is given below.

It is important to note that the numbers quoted may vary slightly from examination to examination as there is some flexibility to ensure that each examination has a consistent level of difficulty. However, the number of questions tested in each element should not change by more than plus or minus 2.

Element number	Element	Questions
1	Introduction	2
2	Economic Environment	3
3	Financial Assets and Markets	4
4	Equities	5
5	Bonds	3
6	Derivatives	4
7	Investment Funds	9
8	Financial Services Regulation	6
9	Taxation, Investment Wrappers and Trusts	8
10	Other Retail Financial Products	4
	Total	**50**

CISI Membership

Studying for a CISI qualification is hard work and we're sure you're putting in plenty of hours, but don't lose sight of your goal! This is just the first step in your career, there is much more to achieve!

The securities and investments industry attracts ambitious and driven individuals. You're probably one yourself and that's great, but on the other hand you're almost certainly surrounded by lots of other people with similar ambitions. So how can you stay one step ahead during these uncertain times?

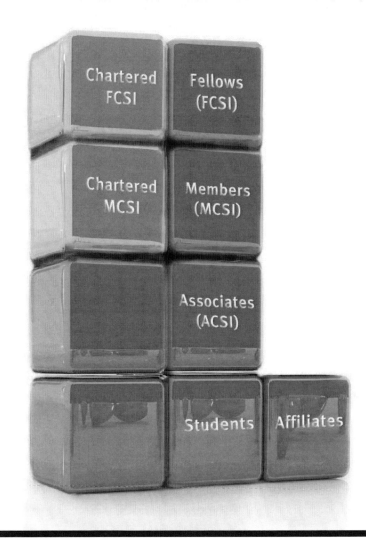

Entry Criteria:	Pass in either: • Investment Operations Certificate (IOC, formerly known as IAQ), IFQ, ICFA, CISI Certificates in, eg, Securities, Derivatives or Investment Management, Advanced Certificates • one or two CISI Diploma/Masters papers
Joining Fee:	£25 or free if applying via prefilled application form
Annual Subscription (pro rata):	£115
International Annual Subscription:	£86.25

Using your new CISI qualification* to become an Associate (ACSI) member of the Chartered Institute for Securities & Investment could well be the next important career move you make this year, and help you maintain your competence.

Join our global network of over 40,000 financial services professionals and start enjoying both the professional and personal benefits that CISI membership offers. Once you become a member you can use the prestigious ACSI designation after your name and even work towards becoming personally chartered.

ie, Investment Operations Certificate (IOC, formerly known as IAQ), IFQ, CISI Certificate Programme

Turn over to find out more about CISI membership

66 *… competence is not just about examinations. It is about skills, knowledge, expertise, ethical behaviour and the application and maintenance of all these*

April 2008
FSA, Retail Distribution Review Interim Report

Becoming an Associate member of CISI offers you...

- ✓ Use of the CISI CPD Scheme
- ✓ Unlimited free CPD seminars
- ✓ Highly recognised designatory letters
- ✓ Free access to online training tools including Professional Refresher and Infolink
- ✓ Free webcasts and podcasts
- ✓ Unlimited free attendance at CISI Professional Interest Forums
- ✓ CISI publications including S&I Review and Regulatory Update
- ✓ 20% discount on all CISI conferences and training courses
- ✓ Invitation to CISI Annual Lecture
- ✓ Select Benefits — our exclusive personal benefits portfolio

Plus many other networking opportunities which could be invaluable for your career.

To upgrade your student membership to Associate,

get in touch...

+44 (0)20 7645 0650
memberservices@cisi.org
cisi.org/membership

CISI
CHARTERED INSTITUTE FOR
SECURITIES & INVESTMENT

CISI Elearning Products

CHARTERED INSTITUTE FOR SECURITIES & INVESTMENT

You've bought the workbook.....
...now test your knowledge before your examination

CISI elearning products are high quality, interactive and engaging learning tools and revision aids which can be used in conjunction with CISI workbooks, or to help you remain up to date with regulatory developments in order to meet compliance requirements.

Features of CISI elearning products include:

- Questions throughout to reaffirm understanding of the subject
- All modules now contain questions that reflect as closely as possible the standard you will experience in your examination*
- Interactive exercises and tutorials

* (please note, however, they are not the CISI examination questions themselves)

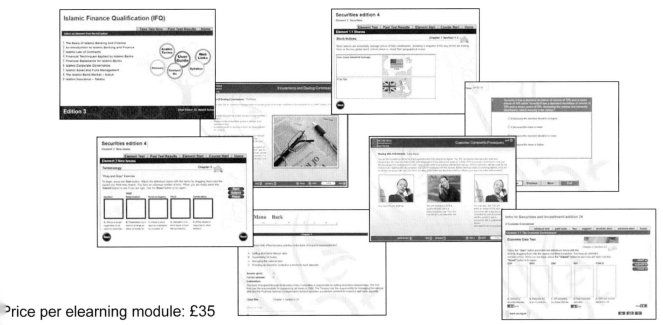

Price per elearning module: £35

Price when purchased with the CISI workbook: £100 (normal price: £110)

For more information on our elearning products call:
+44 20 7645 0756

Or visit our web site at:
cisi.org/elearning

To order call CISI elearning products call Client Services on:
+44 20 7645 0680

Feedback to CISI

Have you found this workbook to be a valuable aid to your studies? We would like your views, so please email us (learningresources@cisi.org) with any thoughts, ideas or comments.

Accredited Training Providers

Support for examination students studying for the Chartered Institute for Securities & Investment (CISI) Qualifications is provided by several Accredited Training Providers (ATPs), including 7City Learning and BPP. The CISI's ATPs offer a range of face-to-face training courses, distance learning programmes, their own learning resources and study packs which have been accredited by the CISI. The CISI works in close collaboration with its accredited training providers to ensure they are kept informed of changes to CISI examinations so they can build them into their own courses and study packs.

CISI Workbook Specialists Wanted

Workbook Authors

Experienced freelance authors with finance experience, and who have published work in their area of specialism, are sought. Responsibilities include:

* Updating workbooks in line with new syllabuses and any industry developments
* Ensuring that the syllabus is fully covered

Workbook Reviewers

Individuals with a high-level knowledge of the subject area are sought. Responsibilities include:

* Highlighting any inconsistencies against the syllabus
* Assessing the author's interpretation of the workbook

Workbook Technical Reviewers

Technical reviewers provide a detailed review of the workbook and bring the review comments to the panel. Responsibilities include:

* Cross-checking the workbook against the syllabus
* Ensuring sufficient coverage of each learning objective

Workbook Proofreaders

Proofreaders are needed to proof workbooks both grammatically and also in terms of the format and layout. Responsibilities include:

* Checking for spelling and grammar mistakes
* Checking for formatting inconsistencies